Program Development, Grantwriting & Implementation

Program Development, Grantwriting & Implementation

From Advocacy to Outcomes

Richard Hoefer and Larry D. Watson

SAN DIEGO

Bassim Hamadeh, CEO and Publisher
Amy Smith, Senior Project Editor
Celeste Paed, Associate Production Editor
Emely Villavicencio, Senior Graphic Designer
Alexa Lucido, Licensing Manager
Ursina Kilburn, Interior Designer
Natalie Piccotti, Director of Marketing
Kassie Graves, Senior Vice President of Editorial
Jamie Giganti, Director of Academic Publishing

Cover and interior image copyright © 2010 iStockphoto LP/kyoshino.

Printed in the United States of America.

3970 Sorrento Valley Blvd., Ste. 500, San Diego, CA 92121

To KG, PH, and SH: You shape my life for the better, every day.

—RH

To Judy—my wife, my love, my best friend, and proofreader extraordinaire.

—LW

Brief Contents

Detailed Contents

Chapter 10 **Program Implementation Planning**   **222**

Preface

The pace of change in the United States human services sector is fast and getting faster. The human services environment is always in a time of transition, but the past 2 years have been especially intense. Civil rights movements have been activated by police violence and other injustices. Important institutions have been called upon to abandon their business-as-usual practices to reach for antiracism instead. At the same time, countervailing forces are attacking the teaching of critical race theory in colleges.

Of course, the COVID-19 pandemic struck in the United States with a vengeance that claimed over 700,000 lives (at the time of this book's publication) and impacted everyone in some way or another. The economic damage has been unevenly spread so that some are being left with little and others have increased their income and wealth considerably.

Into this environment the idea for a new book on program development was birthed. It has been a tough delivery! One of the authors was sickened with COVID-19, which put delivery behind schedule. The other author, though theoretically in retirement, was in demand to assist a nearly overwhelming number of people struggling through the pandemic months, adding turmoil to already difficult issues. In the end, though, with the help of our intrepid and forgiving editor Kassie Graves, who we have worked with on three other books, the manuscript was finished.

We are hopeful that several of the features that are included will be especially helpful to students and faculty members, as well as practitioners who did not have the opportunity to study program design in school. We have provided a road map of the program development process that situates the skills being taught in an accurate, though simplified, way. We like to know where we are going when we go somewhere new, and this figure is in the Prologue and more extensively discussed in Chapter 2.

We also have incorporated a real grant from ACH Child and Family Services in Fort Worth. Wayne Carson, CEO, granted us permission to use the successful grant written by their extraordinarily capable grant writer Katherine Tilley. We incorporate it in many of the exercises we pose for readers as they go through the book.

Each chapter has several elements that are a bit outside the norm for texts like this, but we believe they are valuable. Sometimes they are longer and sometimes shorter, but them being in the chapter helps us process the ideas throughout the book. First, we have a Spotlight on Diversity section, which is a response to the racial and ethnic controversies of these last years. We also have a Difficulties and Joys section in each chapter. Far too often only the difficulties are presented in classes, so we sought to balance the message to learners. Third, we draw lessons from the pandemic for advocacy, grantwriting, program development, and implementation. Others may draw different lessons, but just thinking about the topic is important as we move forward in a time when the pandemic is not yet conquered.

In terms of the chapter topics, we are happy that we begin with a chapter on the larger context and then follow it with a chapter providing an explanation of the program development process and the roles that need to be filled to achieve a program proposal. We also introduce the idea in Chapter 3 that advocacy is the foundation for program planning, particularly programs that rely on government grants. Without dedicated policy entrepreneurs, to use John Kingdon's multiple streams model's term, most grant programs would never have started or would have been ended before now. Readers will see how this application plays out in the context of designing human services programs.

We believe one of the primary directives for human services leaders is the advancement of human rights and social and economic justice. We equip readers to fulfill this directive by helping them develop knowledge, skills, and competencies relating to creating programs that aim to reduce the problems of our society. The competent program designer can then apply these to promote services that seek to end oppression and discrimination and to improve the lives of marginalized populations. As they grow in skill, they ultimately will impact thousands of people individually and collectively.

Human services programs are, ultimately, processes designed to change the behavior and thinking of humans. Program developers should understand theories and conceptual frameworks as they look at improving the world at all levels of intervention. Assessment for, intervention by, and evaluation of programs, interventions, and policies requires the ability to understand, critique, and apply knowledge of designing, implementing, and evaluating programs. All of this takes place in a dynamic social, economic, and political context. This book provides readers with considerable information, coming from many academic disciplines, relating to human behavior in an organizational and social context.

This text combines in one book the essential knowledge needed to be effective in viewing the context of programs before doing any specific planning and to learn how to assess community strengths as well as needs, program evaluation, budgeting, fund development, marketing, advocacy, finding joy in the work, and more—all vital topics of human services program designers and leaders in the 21st century.

AS WE BEGIN ...

Expressing gratitude is conducive to cultivating joy. We wish to express our gratitude especially to the team at Cognella who have been forgiving of delays and turned our manuscript into this beautiful book. Kassie Graves, senior vice president and our editor, has been a steadfast support to whom we owe this book's existence. Family members also deserve our thanks and keep us moving forward in the writing process. Finally, past students inspired us to think we had something valuable to teach them for which we are grateful, too.

Prologue

I t seems likely that you have purchased this book, or you are in this class, because you have an interest in human services management. One of the most challenging and exciting parts of that work is program development and implementation of new program services. In this book, we want to give you the most realistic experience possible in designing a new program within a human services agency. We will start with an overview of the context of human services program development and the process of planning programs. We will add more depth to your understanding of contextual factors by demonstrating how advocacy efforts are needed to ensure resources are available for the services your organization provides or for new ones you want to create. Once you are well grounded in these topics, we will move to a step-by-step process of understanding your community and developing funding opportunities.

Planning a new program is a multitopic body of knowledge, so we have separate chapters relating to the planning process, with a strong bias toward using evidence-based programs. When one is not available just as you need it, you will learn how to adapt one or create a program linked to research to be based on effective conceptualizations. To help in developing a program, you will learn about logic models and program evaluation, in addition to budgeting and financial management, organizational capacity, and implementing a new program within a human services agency. We show you how to create an information sharing plan that provides your stakeholders with important information and can be used to market your successes to funders and policy makers. At the end, we explore the topic of joy and how you can ensure that you have that in your program development work.

That is what is going to be covered in this book. It is a lot, and sometimes might seem unreal. But we have a plan to help you learn as much as possible. It starts with showing you an overall road map of what is coming (see Figure 0.2). While you will see this figure again in Chapter 2 where it will be explained in more detail, it is included here so you can link this information to what you will learn in the next few pages.

The book begins with a chapter on the larger context of human services program development and another on the program planning process and required roles. This is the deep background information you need before moving forward and as such are not represented in Figure 0.2. We then move forward with chapters on the knowledge and skills that make up the bulk of this text. Understanding context (blue rectangle) shows three topics: gathering information, conducting advocacy, and understanding the community. Gathering information is a skill we imagine you come with, but it is covered in detail for the chapters on understanding and conducting advocacy and understanding your community so you can plan appropriate programs. To the right (tan and brown rectangle), two skills are shown: finding funding and program planning. Chapter 5 covers grantwriting and fund development. We introduce how to plan programs in Chapter 6, particularly the use of evidence-based programs (EBPs) and how to create good programs from the ground up, if necessary. Additional chapters are needed to cover other vital topics for planning a program, such as developing logic models and evaluation plans (Chapter 7), budgeting and financial management (Chapter 8), and explaining and expanding organizational capacity (Chapter 9). The receiving program funds oval is mostly unnecessary, but it marks an important event in the program planning universe. It also recognizes that even the best planned programs are not always funded.

Planning for program implementation (Chapter 10) moves us down to the green rectangle, which includes implementing the evaluation plan you have created. The use of a logic model is included not only for planning but also as a monitoring and evaluation tool.

When the evaluation data gathering is complete, or more often if the funder desires, reports need to be written and incorporated into a nonprofit marketing approach to keeping the program going (Chapter 11). Based on what has been learned from the evaluation, program adaptations can be made to improve results, and the one-time process becomes a cycle, where advocacy and understanding the community are needed again.

The final chapter brings us back to a contextual view, but this time the focus is on you. We believe that the human services field needs to prioritize sustainability of programs but also of individuals. Protection against burnout in this field is important, so we turn to the ideas of positive organizational and individual psychology, focusing on how to ensure that joy is part of the daily experience of human services workers, leaders, and program developers (Chapter 12).

We will only feel satisfied with our work when we know you are now prepared to enter the amazing, exciting, frustrating, and rewarding world of program funding, development, implementation, and continuation. It may be that once you have succeeded in this role you will move to new challenges in human services and nonprofit management. We wish you the best of luck and welcome your comments on this and our other books.

Please keep reading on the next page to receive some exciting news!

Richard Hoefer
rhoefer@uta.edu

Larry Watson
larrydwatson@gmail.com

Close your eyes for a moment. Take some deep breaths, and imagine what it would be like to be the executive director of an established nonprofit agency. Try to imagine yourself in this role. You have earned this promotion, but it is still a lot of responsibility, and you are not sure if your "book learning" has been sufficient to meet all the demands you will face. Feel the feelings you have as you imagine this scenario.

This is important because we have a big surprise for you. You have been appointed as the new executive director of Cornerstone Family Services, Inc.! Does that feel a little scary? It should be because it is a big and important job. Go ahead and acknowledge the fear and the magnitude of the tasks ahead, but also be open to the excitement of doing a job you love and making a difference in the lives of others. Isn't that what brought you to human services in the first place?

Below is your appointment letter from the president of the board of Cornerstone Family Services, Inc. We hope you negotiated a good salary because you are going to earn it. Your letter outlines some of the expectations that the board has for you as you start your new position. It is important to understand and agree to these expectations since your evaluation will be based on achieving these tasks. The most important board functions are hiring and firing the executive director. Let's be sure they are happy in their hiring decision!

Look at your appointment letter, the Fact Sheet on Cornerstone Family Services, Inc., and the organizational chart of your new executive team. Congratulations on your appointment. Let's get started!

CORNERSTONE FAMILY SERVICES, Inc.
4582 CADE AVENUE
Anytown, USA

August 1, 20XX
Insert your name here
444 High Hopes Drive
Anytown, USA

Dear _____,

It is my pleasure to offer you the position as executive director/CEO of Cornerstone Family Services, Inc. After an extensive national search, our board of trustees has determined that you are the right person to lead our organization into the future. I will forward an employment contract to you detailing the proposed compensation, benefit package, and relocation reimbursement. We look forward to your acceptance of this offer of employment and the leadership and expertise you will provide for years to come.

I have enclosed a package of material for your review. It includes a history of our agency, an organizational chart, a budget summary, and a history of Cornerstone Family Services, Inc. (CFS). Please let me know if you have questions or need additional information. I look forward to working with you as we lead the organization forward.

Your first board meeting will occur approximately 1 month after you assume office. Since this is your first position as an executive in the nonprofit sector, we request that you be prepared to make a presentation on the state of the nonprofit sector and how you envision your role as the "face" of Cornerstone Family Services in our community.

In addition to overseeing our existing programs, it is our expectation that you will identify a new program area, obtain funding, and fully implement a new program area within the framework of our mission.

Cordially,
Jean Gomez, President
Cornerstone Family Services, Inc.

FACT SHEET

Our Mission: To assist youth in becoming independent self-sufficient adults who contribute to our society.

History: Cornerstone Family Services, Inc. was established in 1895 by Rev. Joseph P. Wilson, a protestant minister. At the turn of the century, Rev. Wilson became very concerned about the number of orphan boys who were unsupervised and becoming juvenile delinquents. In response to this, he worked with other ministers and established the Cornerstone Home and Training School for Boys. Rev. Wilson became the first superintendent of the school and served faithfully for over 25 years. The Home for Boys started in a small frame house near downtown. The Boys Home continued to grow, and in 1962, a beautiful 30-acre location was donated to the institution for a new campus. In 1968, a major fund-raising campaign was conducted to build most of the buildings as they exist today. Through the years the need for "orphanages" decreased and the CFS Board of Trustees developed new programs to meet the changing needs of society. The orphanage model was changed to include therapeutic foster care and independent living for youth with physical disabilities.

Today: Today, CFS has evolved into a multiservice organization with two major programs, including adoption/foster care services and independent living services for youth with physical disabilities. Both residential and community-based services are provided. Our adoption program has dramatically decreased over the years, and we have been notified that our rehabilitation funding for youth with disabilities is being cut by 65% in the next fiscal year.

Budget and Funding: CFS has a $2.5 million annual budget and 45 employees. Our funding sources include fees for service, church contributions, individual contributions, foundation grants, wills and estates (unrestricted), and grants and contracts from the State Rehabilitation Commission and the Department of Protective Services. We have a small amount of income from renting one of our buildings to another agency, and we have investment income from our $2 million endowment fund.

Board: The board of trustees has 25 members, and we meet monthly for a 1-hour lunch meeting. The agenda is developed by the executive director and the president of the board of trustees.

FIGURE 0.1   Executive Team—Cornerstone Family Services, Inc.

Program Planning and Implementation Process

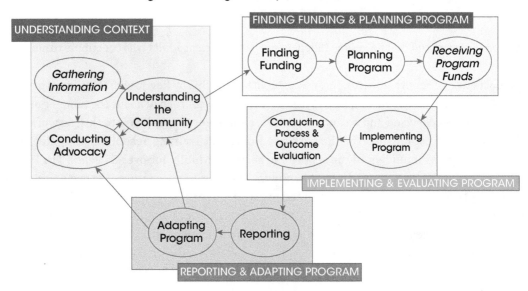

FIGURE 0.2   Program Planning and Implementation Process

CHAPTER ONE

The Larger Context of Human Services Program Development

AN INTRODUCTORY NOTE FROM COAUTHOR DR. RICHARD HOEFER

As a master's student (in social work), I took a course on program development. It was called something like "program development and grantwriting." This makes a great deal of sense because most grant applications call for developing a program. I'm sure I learned a lot—in fact, I used the information from that course to put together a program proposal for the Lawrence Police Department! (More about that in a later chapter.)

After a number of years, I began teaching classes on grantwriting, administration, budgeting, and other human-services and administration-related topics. I was dissatisfied with the usual approaches to program design and development and the textbooks that were in use. It's not that there was anything incorrect about what was being taught, but I began to feel that the usual approach was less than complete. Too often, developing programs was presented as something that happens all on its own.

When Dr. Larry Watson and I worked together as colleagues, we talked about the need to understand the program development process, which begins long before you are ready to envision a new program. First, you have to have a good and deep understanding of the context of the community, agency, and program. This is often not taught well in program design and grantwriting courses. Sure, there is the week or two on developing a "needs statement" or "statement of the problem" so that you can write a grant to address the issue, but that really is not enough. Program development, in our view, is at least as much about advocacy, community organization, and organizational leadership as it is about grantwriting. Yet these topics are seldom featured.

This book embeds program design and development into the larger currents of organizational practice in the human services field, no matter what discipline you are in: social work, public administration, public health, nonprofit administration, and so on. This chapter sets the stage for that exploration.

OVERVIEW

In this chapter we explore the larger context of program development in human services. To understand the role of program planning in human services, we believe it is necessary to understand the wider context that shapes program development decisions. We begin with an exploration of the macroeconomic and political realms, describing the tri-sector model and changes that are occurring. With this under our belt, we highlight five different issues that you must grasp as you examine your organization and potential programs. These issues are (a) the ongoing impact of the COVID-19 pandemic; (b) the increasing importance of organizational and program planning; (c) unsteady funding; (d) increasing diversity in the workplace; and (e) political challenges to human services programs.

STARTING WITH THE BIG PICTURE

The larger context of program planning must be considered before reading chapters on any other topic in this book. When you think about program design, planning, or development, your thinking must extend beyond the limits of your program or organization. Just as individuals are affected by their environment, so too are agencies and the individual programs within them. By understanding the big picture, you will be able to fit your individual knowledge and competencies into a larger framework so that their importance is clearer. Human services agencies (both government and private), where most programs are created, operate as part of society, and the natures of the broader culture and trends have considerable impact on what individual nonprofit managers, leaders, and planners can accomplish and how they go about their work. They are considered as part of the human services field, which is defined as an area that

> has the objective of meeting human needs through an interdisciplinary knowledge base, focusing on prevention as well as remediation of problems, and maintaining a commitment to improving the overall quality of life of service populations. (American Public Human Services Association, n.d., para. 1)

Understanding what is happening in the environment and the context for practice allows nonprofit workers of all types to understand how to do their work better. Organizational program planners will be especially able to use their knowledge and understanding to work at a broader level, but everything that influences the organization and community has ramifications for individuals, families, and groups in the community.

Change in human service organizations' context is a constant. Two decades ago, the literature focused on how managers and program developers needed to be aware of, and deal with, changes in their agencies' worlds. Important issues at that time included managed care (Jones, 2006; McBeath & Meezan, 2006), an uncertain political and economic climate (Golensky & Mulder, 2006; Hopkins & Hyde, 2002; Schmid, 2004), policy reform (Regehr et al., 2002; Reisch & Sommerfeld, 2003), and the introduction of performance measurement systems (Zimmermann & Stevens, 2006). Most of these topics are still relevant today.

Human services leaders and program developers are expected to have more competencies at higher skill levels than in the recent past. Challenges and the range of skills are greater now for human services agencies than ever before (Hopkins et al., 2019). Increasingly, cross-sector partnerships involving the government, business, and nonprofit sectors are used to achieve progress on social issues (Almog-Bar & Schmid, 2018; Clark & Crane, 2018; Vestergaard et al., 2021), which shows the need for staying abreast of new topics and skills. Another example of increasingly broad skillsets needed is the expansion in use of the term **social enterprise**, which has arisen to incorporate for-profit principles into nonprofit operations (Fernando, 2017; Linton, 2018; see Box 1.1 for more information on social enterprise). Program developers must respect and understand how to collaborate with counterparts in other sectors who have different perspectives. The most important skill of all, given the rapidly evolving landscape of human services, may be the ability to enable and manage change (Cheng & Catallo, 2020). The changes that may be the most important are also those that happen slowly and are not always noticed. Just as tectonic plates move slowly over long periods of time, only to emerge as a crippling earthquake, one of the most important of such changes is the nature of the human services sector within the larger U.S. economic structure.

THE TRI-SECTOR MODEL AND PROGRAM DESIGN

The economy in the United States is frequently described as consisting of three components, or sectors: the public, private, and nonprofit sectors. They have been viewed as distinct entities with clearly defined functions. The private, or business, sector is driven primarily by market forces surrounding the exchange of goods and services. The public, or governmental, sector is built on the foundation of authority, as only government can tax or exercise police powers of enforcement. The nonprofit sector can be viewed as a mechanism for cooperation through which government and business intersect and foster the cooperation of local communities to achieve public purposes (Swanstrom, 1997). Within the framework, the three sectors are depicted as independent but intersecting (Watson, 2007; See Figure 1.1).

We often think of HSOs as being part of the nonprofit sector, and indeed, a significant percentage of charitable nonprofits are human services organizations. The National Center for Charitable Statistics (NCCS, 2020) breaks out the subsectors of charitable organizations in the United States. Of the 318,015 total number of public charities in the United States in 2016, the largest percentage subsector was human services, comprised of such services as food banks, homeless shelters, youth services, sports organizations, and family or legal services (35.2%, 111,797). This category is more than two times larger than the second, education, which includes booster clubs, parent-teacher associations, and financial aid groups, as well as academic institutions, schools, and universities (17.2%, 54,632). The third largest subsector was health (12.2%, 38,853). These three subsectors of organizations cover nearly two thirds of the entire charitable organization sector. All of them design and administer programs of some sort and provided employment to 12.3 million employees in 2016 (Friesenhahn, 2016).

It is important to understand, however, that human services providers are also embedded in the public (government) and the private for-profit sectors as well. Thus, the design and provision of human services can be understood using the tri-sector model (Watson & Hegar, 2013). The **tri-sector model** details

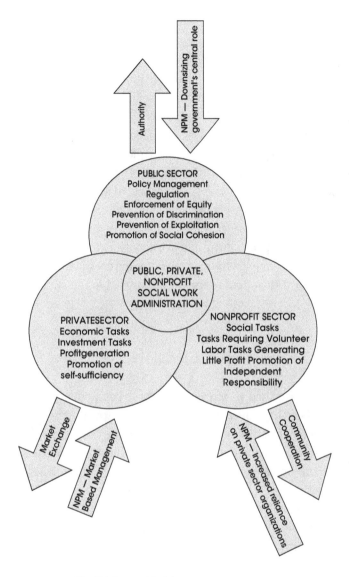

FIGURE 1.1   **The Tri-Sector Model**

the areas of the economy that HSOs operate in the public sector (government), the private sector (business), and the nonprofit sector (nonprofits).

The relationships between the nonprofit, government, and business sectors are complicated, multidimensional, and fluid. Unfortunately, popular stereotypes of the sectors can disguise the complex nature of their interrelationships (Brinkerhoff & Brinkerhoff, 2002). The public often views governments as monolithic, bloated bureaucracies in need of an injection of the types of business practices and market solutions preferred by the for-profit sector. Although many see practices such as downsizing as the most effective ways to allocate resources and provide cost-effective solutions, the business sector may simultaneously be viewed as uncaring or more concerned with enriching private interests than with promoting societal good. According to Brinkerhoff and Brinkerhoff (2002), the public image of nonprofits involves being value driven, softer, kindhearted, and able to mobilize voluntary efforts. A more balanced assessment reveals the many connections and linkages among the sectors and examines both their differences and interrelationships.

An important question for human services professionals and program developers is what is the "best" auspice for a new program, or in what sector of the economy it might best fit. Young (1998) uses exchange as the basis for exploring the relationship between government and nonprofits (and, implicitly, between them and for-profits). He observes that these relations in the United States are not one dimensional, but complex, and that they must be viewed on multiple levels. In his view, economic theories support three views of government-nonprofit relationships: supplementary, complementary, and adversarial.

In the **supplementary model**, nonprofits are seen as fulfilling a demand for public goods left unsatisfied by the government, and potentially not available or too expensive from the business sector for many potential recipients who desire the service. Using Young's (1998) ideas, we might say that nonprofits should design and operate human services programs when government is not providing those services and when for-profits are unable to make a profit in providing them. In these situations, nonprofits gather private resources to offer the services. Unfortunately, the supply rarely equals the demand, and many still go without the services desired.

In the **complementary approach**, nonprofits are partners to government, helping to deliver public goods largely financed by the government. This is supposed to use the beneficial elements of governmental revenue generation, policy control, and accountability for use of tax dollars while preserving the more philanthropic aspects of nonprofit organizations. In some cases, nonprofits pioneer new service strategies and approaches that for-profits can adapt to provide the same (or similar) services at a profit. Evidence suggests that for-profit nursing homes, for example, overcharge Medicare significantly more often than do nonprofit nursing homes and are more likely to engage in fraud than nonprofits (Pintas & Mullins Injury Lawyers, 2020). Other research indicates that "the nation's largest for-profit nursing home chains deliver significantly lower quality care because they typically have fewer staff nurses than non-profit and government-owned nursing homes" (Fernandez, 2011, para. 1).

In Young's (1998) **adversarial relationship view**, nonprofits prod government into making changes in public policy and into maintaining accountability to the public. Reciprocally, government attempts to influence the behavior of nonprofit organizations by regulating their services and responding to their advocacy initiatives (Young, 1998, p. 33). Much of the literature on government-nonprofit relationships takes its perspective from either the governmental or nonprofit standpoint. Young (1998) is one of few who looks at both sides of the equation and acknowledges that relationships are reciprocal and are based on decisions made by both governmental and nonprofit administrators (Najam, 2000). The for-profit sector is seen as wanting access to governmental resources and subsidies to provide human services while arguing for the least restrictive contract provisions possible for themselves. For-profits sometimes argue that nonprofits have an unfair advantage in being able to bid lower on contracts (because nonprofits do not pay taxes at the same rates as businesses do).

The takeaway in this discussion is that the location of any human service program within one or more of the sectors is not a simple decision. As a program designer, this type of question may have an impact on you and your ability to successfully propose your solution. Decisions of this nature are set during high-level policy discussions (which is why we believe advocacy is part of the program development process—but more on that later in this chapter and in Chapter 2).

CHANGES IN THE TRI-SECTOR MODEL

Although the description of a hard and fast division between the three sectors was never entirely true, the general idea had a great deal of merit until the expansion of the role of the federal government into social programs in the mid-1960s. As the role of the government increased, so did the need to better understand changes occurring within the division of labor and tasks assigned to each sector.

Two important adaptations and changes have developed: new public management and the growth of hybrid organizations. These continue to impact program designers today.

New Public Management

The role of government has changed over the past 30 years, and a cluster of reform initiatives known collectively as **new public management (NPM)** has been a force driving many of the changes. As a part of these reform initiatives, numerous traditional government functions have shifted to the private and nonprofit sectors (Kettl, 2000). Frederickson and Smith (2003) identify common elements in the various forms of this movement as "1) adoption of market-based management and resource allocation techniques, 2) increased reliance on private sector organizations to deliver public services, and 3) a deliberate and sustained effort to downsize the decentralized government's role as the central policy actor in society" (p. 208).

The advent of market-based management brings the values and techniques of the private sector into the public and nonprofit sectors by introducing competition into the marketplace for social services. The NPM goal of downsizing and decentralizing the government's role has been accomplished by shifting many functions to either the private or the nonprofit sectors. This trend has been highly controversial, both in the United States and in Europe, where observers in countries such as Sweden characterize NPM as an undesirable turning away from universal public-sector responsibility for social welfare (e.g., Blomberg & Jan, 2010; Höjer & Forkby, 2011).

Hybrid Organizations

In some human services fields—such as foster care of children—nonprofits, for-profits, and government institutions all provide similar services. Handy (1997) contends that each sector attracts a share of the market because consumers (or funders) are willing to trade perceived quality in one sector for anticipated efficiency and lower costs in another. Handy suggests this tradeoff is the reason that organizations from each of the three sectors can coexist in the same industry, a reality that has led many agencies to seek alternative organizational structures.

Traditionally, private organizations in the United States are divided into for-profit and nonprofit groups. In seeking new organizational forms, program developers operating between the two categories have used creative partnerships, subsidiaries, or joint ventures to accomplish their goals (Gottesman, 2007). The desire to function across or between the for-profit and nonprofit sectors has also led to a new organizational form: hybrid organizations. **Hybrid organizations** are not classified as subsidiaries or partnerships but instead represent new organizational types that function at the intersection of the traditional nonprofit and for-profit sectors (Gottesman, 2007). Hybrid organizations are particularly relevant for social enterprises that may combine governmental incentives to create programs aimed to solve social problems with market-based approaches, often being administered by a nonprofit. An example could be a program to train people with mental health issues or mobility challenges to work in a subsidized coffee house or other retail situation. Once trained, it would be hoped the service recipients could later use their upgraded skills in a purely market-based setting.

Hasenfeld and Gidron (2005) list several fields of service that have developed hybrid organizations. These include some racial-, ethnic-, and gender-based organizations (Minkoff, 1995); religious charitable organizations (Allahyari, 2000); women's nonprofit organizations (Bordt, 1998); and peace and conflict resolution organizations (Gidron et al., 2002).

Organizational leaders and program designers of every stripe will discover that the traditional for-profit–nonprofit dichotomy has less relevance in today's environment than it did in the past. The need for creative problem solving and program design across sectors continues to expand and grow. Program designers and human services leaders may well switch employment from one sector to another, depending on the opportunities that present themselves. Sector swapping already occurs (mostly people in the for-profit sector being hired for nonprofit leadership positions) but may become more common in the future. Skills and experience will be seen as the ticket for a successful career in organizational leadership and program design, not a particular degree (MBA, MPA, MPH, MSW, etc.) or having longevity in a sector.

BOX 1.1	**What Is Social Enterprise?**

Definitions of social enterprise "differ professionally, legally, and by country" (Linton, 2013, p. 458). Even in 2017, Defourny and Nyssens argued that "the SE [social enterprise] field will benefit much more in the future from linking conceptualization efforts to the huge diversity of social enterprises and forms of social entrepreneurship than from an additional and ambitious attempt at providing an encompassing definition" (p. 2469).

Still, within the human services arena, there is a definition that is generally agreed upon: "Social enterprise is a management practice that integrates principles of private enterprise with social-sector goals and objectives. [It] includes a variety of sustainable economic activities designed to yield social impact for individuals, families, and communities" (Fernando, 2017, Summary section). While many authors believe social enterprise is beneficial for human services organizations as a potential source of additional funds and greater legitimacy, critics of social enterprise argue that it injects a damaging neoliberal perspective into human services; supporters argue it is necessary to bolster lagging public and governmental financial support.

ISSUES AFFECTING HUMAN SERVICES PROGRAMS

In this chapter, we touch on five current issues that are having a significant impact on human services leaders and program developers. After reading about these factors, you will better understand why specific preparation and continued education for being a program planner is important. You will also begin to comprehend the value of looking at the entire context of programs and program planning before jumping into the nitty-gritty of program development.

Issue 1: The Ongoing Impact of the COVID-19 Pandemic and Recovery

The global pandemic caused by COVID-19 is one of the most impactful issues of the 21st century and will impact human service organization for the foreseeable future. Reaching every part of the globe, this virus has caused untold misery along with millions of deaths. Organizations of all types, including human service organizations and governments, have had to adapt rapidly to continue operating. Even as vaccines become more available, new and old variants continue killing people. While the decline in cases in the United States is to be celebrated, the resulting "return to normalcy" is creating the conditions for continued change in the running of human services.

One of the concerns of human service planners is how to position programs to be safe for clients and staff. While vaccines are a wonderful preventative measure, a sizeable percentage of the population in the United States continues to express hesitancy toward becoming inoculated. For some people of color, this is rooted in historic discrimination and racist practices in medical situations. Others say they think COVID-19 is not a threat to them, either because it is not a serious illness or they have already had it and recovered. Some assert that regulatory approval has been rushed, the vaccines may have unknown side effects, and it is still experimental. Some people

The COVID-19 pandemic has impacted all aspects of society and altered how human service organizations operate.

subscribe to debunked ideas. In addition, it has become a partisan issue, with Republicans of all ages much more likely to say they will not get a vaccine (Thompson, 2021). This issue means that the safety of clients and staff is not simple. While employers may be able to mandate workers receive the vaccinations, it is less likely that clients can be forced to do so. Still, the threat of new variants spreading among both the unvaccinated and vaccinated is real.

Another issue that is going to be ongoing is how to deal with staff members who now prefer working from home rather than coming in to an office. Fairness in policy creation as well as retention of employees are two areas where employers must be careful. Some human resources experts predict a large number of people quitting their jobs as society seeks to "normalize." This prediction is being called "The Great Resignation" (Hsu, 2021). In short, many workers are no longer satisfied with working the prepandemic norm of 40 or more hours per week in an office setting, combined with commuting and other stresses that once seemed unavoidable. How human service organizations address this issue has a large impact on having sufficient staff to cover the needs of new programs. Clients' and volunteers' needs must also be considered. Safety for all must be the watchword.

Issue 2: Increasing Importance of Organizational and Program Planning

Given the current level of unpredictability in the world of human service organizations, you may wonder if program planning makes much sense. When political leaders make decisions that change human services funding on a whim rather than according to thoughtful analysis, what can program developers count on? Or when the amount of available philanthropic funding swings wildly, depending on how many natural disasters have occurred recently, how can development plans last more than a month or two? In other words, some might ask, "Why bother planning, when nothing is stable or predictable anymore?" As Allison and Kaye (2015) state, "Defining the direction and activities of an organization in an ever-changing environment is daunting and can almost seem futile" (p. 2).

Perhaps counterintuitively, the rapid changes we see in the human services world indicate that careful planning is more important than ever. The key words here are "careful planning." Careful strategic planning, for example, focuses on big questions and big issues that are often stable over longer periods, such as 5–10 years. In fact, some of the big questions have been the same for decades, if not hundreds of years. Examples include, "How do we define social justice?" and "What are the societal problems we most want to work to eliminate?" These questions can never be ultimately answered, but the struggle to seek answers within the current environment is what propels organizations to continue striving.

Most organizations keep the same mission (or something closely aligned) for many years. The American Red Cross's (n.d.) mission statement, for example, is that it "prevents and alleviates human suffering in the face of emergencies by mobilizing the power of volunteers and the generosity of donors" (Mission Statement). The purpose of strategic planning is not always to change the mission and vision but to get better at achieving them. If organizations seek to tackle big problems, they need to put in time and energy to plan their responses. They do this by creating strategic goals and operationalizing them with program planning to achieve measurable desired outcomes. Planning includes creating sets of action steps that translate resources (e.g., funds, staff and volunteer time, physical space, etc.) into concrete actions that achieve outcomes. Procedures to measure achievements are needed to show how well the agency is doing. Only by doing the work of planning can organizations continue to meet the increasing demands for accountability, the difficulties of sustaining operations, and attacks from political figures.

Program planning is also more important than ever because it is the only way to overcome the seeming chaos of the world and the desire to achieve more. When organizations plan, they craft options (Allison & Kaye, 2015). They may seek to do more of the same things they are currently doing to have a larger impact. Given the constant financial constraints facing human service organizations, simply "doing more by growing bigger" may not be possible. Fortunately, Allison and Kaye (2015) provide three alternative ways to have a greater impact:

- *Improve processes*: Do the same work more efficiently, thus achieving more at the same cost.
- *Improve design*: Do the same work with a novel approach to achieve more.
- *Improve strategically*: Do different things to get better results. (p. 3)

In addition, the pandemic required quick shifts in program procedures and practices. Program planners now see the importance of contingency planning for any number of potential disasters or changes in the way their organization must operate. Program planning must now prepare how to deal with interruptions in access to the office environment and to be able to pivot with enhanced technology. For example, in Arizona, 74% of nonprofits closed their physical location for at least 1 month in 2020, and 54% were considering using a hybrid remote/in-person plan when the survey was conducted in early 2021 (Merrifield, 2021, p. 2). Building in flexibility is now a requirement.

Issue 3: Unsteady Funding

Put simply, human services leaders and program developers operate in an environment of unsteady resources and increased competition (including heightened accountability requirements) for those resources. Funding from government at local, state, and federal levels is strained due to political pressure to lower tax rates (or at least keep them steady, despite inflation). Many states and localities have delayed contracted payments to nonprofit organizations for months, causing those nonprofits to face cash-flow problems and undermining the service providers' fiscal health (Crain's New York, 2021). Some nonprofits have found that getting a government contract causes more harm than benefit because the amount they are paid is lower than the cost of providing the services required to fulfill the terms of the contract.

In 2020 and early 2021, the COVID-19 pandemic put intense strain on many organizations and individuals, including human services organizations and their employees. One report indicates that the top challenge facing nonprofit leaders for 2021 is the difficulty in "predicting future funding"; meanwhile, their top goal in 2021 was to "obtain new funding sources/obtain more funding from current sources" (Bebes et al., 2021, p. 3). In Arizona, over half of responding nonprofits saw decreases in revenue from individuals, 67% fewer donations from corporations, and about 45% less revenue from foundations and government grants. The average Arizona health and human services nonprofit lost almost $600,000 in revenue in 2020 (Merrifield, 2021, p. 4), and 54% of them saw a decrease in year-end giving from previous years of 11%–25% in 2020 (Merrifield, 2021, p. 5).

While numbers fluctuate depending on the source chosen and years of comparison, there is no dispute that the number of nonprofits has grown. According to McKeever (2019), approximately 1.56 million nonprofits existed in the United States in 2015. This number of nonprofits grew by over 10% between 2005 and 2015. Additionally, a greater number of nonprofits are turning to foundations and government grants for support, even though funding from those sources is unsteady. Successfully competing for a contract or grant is more difficult than ever.

Charitable giving did increase overall in 2020 (compared to 2019) reaching $471.44 billion. Three areas together (religion, education, and human services) received over half of the total giving (Giving USA, 2021). Still, a smaller percentage of households are giving funds or time to nonprofits at all, particularly among lower income individuals (Jones, 2020). Some researchers believe a giving gap is following the wealth gap (Callahan, 2018; Johnson Center at Grand Valley University, 2019). Nonprofits are thus relying more on wealthy people who are able to give large amounts of funding which can skew nonprofit priorities (Jones, 2020).

The ability of middle-class, middle-aged donors to give has been impacted by uncertainty over home values, long-term employment situations, and volatility in the value of retirement nest eggs. Increasingly, these families have had increased financial responsibilities toward young adult children and parents with medical and other issues. This "sandwich generation" has been hard-pressed to keep their giving to charity at the same level as in prior years.

Concentration in donations can lead to problems, as a more limited set of well-to-do donors, sometimes with clear ideological and policy intentions, control which organizations receive and which do not (Levine, 2019). An increasing number of major donors put their donations into donor-advised funds in which they personally influence which entities receive funding rather than leaving it to a more transparent process (Rooney, 2018). Observers anticipate that the growth in donor-advised funds will continue (Rolland, 2020).

A final drag on individual giving is the Tax Cuts and Jobs Act of 2018, which decreased taxes and changed the ability of taxpayers to deduct donations to charities. One estimate is that 21 million families will no longer be able to deduct their giving to nonprofits. Economists on both the Right and the Left believe the change in the tax code will decrease the amount of giving that will occur, although disagreement exists as to the level of decrease that should be expected (Bicoy, 2018). The impact of the CARES Act funding, however, was seen as very or somewhat positive by 75% of nonprofits in the *Plante Moran Nonprofit Outlook Survey Report* (Bebes, 2021, p. 4).

Another important aspect of the difficulties in sustainability is that evidence-based practice and research/program evaluation are becoming more important to funders and other stakeholders. As the need to compete for resources intensifies, human service agencies must become more effective in serving clients and in presenting their positive accomplishments. One way to accomplish this is to use service technologies that have the research to support their claims of helping solve client problems. The movement toward evidence-based practice, while compelling theoretically, may require culture change within agencies (Johnson & Austin, 2006). As difficult as this is to accomplish, some grant-providing agencies, such as the federal Substance Abuse and Mental Health Services Administration (SAMHSA), provide strong incentives and greater funding opportunities for agencies willing to use program models that have been tested empirically and have evidence of effectiveness. Interventions that have received research validation are listed by the Evidence-based Practices Resource Center (available online at https://www.samhsa.gov/ebp-resource-center). Additional reviews of evidence-based programs are located on the website for the Campbell Collaboration (https://www.campbellcollaboration.org/) and elsewhere.

Similarly, program evaluation within agencies is usually required as a condition of receiving a grant. Agencies struggle with how to cope with such demands, having neither the staff time nor the knowledge base to analyze the data they collect. The Council on Foundations (2021) offers 35 keys to effective evaluation due to "the need for scarce grant dollars" and the "need to make certain those dollars are spent as effectively as possible" (para. 1). Performance measurement, within the context of program evaluation and accountability, is a salient example of the need for additional research skills for nonprofit managers and program planners (Zimmermann & Stevens, 2006). Salipante and Aram (2003) argue that nonprofit managers must move beyond being *users* of knowledge to becoming *generators* of knowledge. Program planners need to ensure that this is part of program development.

Issue 4: Increasing Diversity in the Workplace

Considerable attention has been given to the decreasing percentage of people in the United States who are of European ancestry and the increasing percentage of people from Hispanic, African American, and Asian backgrounds. According to the United States Census Bureau (2019), non-Hispanic White people account for 60.1% of the population, with Hispanic people being 18.5%. Black people are 13.4%. Asian people account for 5.9% of the population, with 1.3% coming from American Indian and Alaska Native populations. Two or more races are 2.8%. Native Hawaiian and other Pacific Islander people contribute an additional 0.2%.

This type of diversity, racial and ethnic, is extremely important for the running of nonprofits, particularly in terms of program planning needs and leadership style. But other types of diversity exist as well and need to be included when we think about the topic (Kozan, 2019). Women are more likely than men to have attended 4 years of college or more since 2014, with the highest difference in 2020 (38.3% of women compared to 36.7% of men; Statista, 2021).

Women should thus be expected to occupy more top leadership positions in the human services sector (and

Image 1.2

Increasing racial and ethnic diversity (as well as other types of diversity) in the United States must be incorporated into program operations and planning to increase equity, inclusion, and effectiveness.

elsewhere), including planning programs. Unfortunately, not only are women seriously underrepresented in the leadership of nonprofits (particularly large ones) but also when they are promoted, they are paid less than men, by about 8.9& or more when there is room for negotiations over salary (Drexel Now, 2021).

Human service organization leaders are also challenged to be able to relate to differences between younger workers and their older counterparts. Maintaining relationships is important not only within the organization, in terms of supervision and leadership styles, but also among donors. For example, gay, lesbian, bisexual, and transgender persons have distinct viewpoints about many human services issues, and their communities often are strongly engaged stakeholders and donors to certain types of nonprofits (Dale, 2018).

This type of discussion can often make it seem as if diversity were a problem when, in fact, it is definitely a positive aspect of today's nonprofit workforce! The range of ideas and experiences in the workplace may now be broader than at any other time in history. Still, having a larger variety of people in the workplace is an issue that must be addressed and sometimes "managed" so that various stakeholder groups, with their unique perspectives, see value in the differences that can sometimes cause misunderstandings or even conflict. One way to remove at least some of the unconscious bias in the hiring process may be to use artificial intelligence to screen applications, though this process is not without pitfalls of its own (Biswas, 2018). Another approach is to ensure that the leadership within human services nonprofits is reflective of the larger society, especially the stakeholders of an agency, including the local community, staff, clients, and other supporters.

Issue 5: Political Challenges

Social service organizations tend to want to avoid becoming deeply involved in partisan battles. They instead wish to build bridges to government officials and other stakeholders regardless of their political affiliation. Organization leaders may privately agree with the policy direction of Democrats and disagree with those of Republicans, but they, like all nonprofit workers, must start where the client is. Given that the political party of the moment may be out as soon as the next election, wisdom dictates avoiding making enemies of the "other" party. Program planners working in government agencies are required to adapt to current elected officials' positions as a part of our laws and traditions. This standard advice is generally good, but what happens when one party becomes antagonistic to the very core of what human services strive for?

Political polarization now seems to be a fact of life in the United States, with less overlap in policy positions between Republicans and Democrats, making compromise less achievable (DellaPosta, 2020). Some elements of the Republican party are hostile to human services programs that vulnerable populations depend on for their life and livelihoods. Programs such as Social Security, Medicare, food stamps, housing assistance, and direct cash payments have been targeted for decreases in support (Stein, 2017). Legal asylum seekers have been vilified as a group by the most recent former Republican president who is supported by large numbers of elected officials. On the other hand, Democrats tend to support the position of keeping abortion rights legal, a position at odds with the religious views of many people, including some nonprofit workers. Some agencies end up on different sides of the political spectrum, depending on the issue being discussed. Catholic Charities (n.d.), for example, provides considerable assistance to refugees but is also against abortion. Secular agencies can face similar conflicts. How do nonprofit leaders operate ethically in such environments, balancing their sense of ethical behavior and policy with the demands to promote the interests of their organizations? How do they design and implement programs that may anger one side of the political spectrum or the other?

 SPOTLIGHT ON DIVERSITY

Related to the information noted in Issue 4, above, we have written a Spotlight on Diversity section in each chapter. It is impossible to understand the context of program planning without referring to the Black Lives Matter movement, the murder of Georgy Floyd by a White police officer sentenced to over 20 years in prison, the killing of many other Black citizens by police officers, and disputes over teaching the history of racism in America from its beginnings.

It is impossible to ignore this larger context while planning programs. Any organization that is not seriously looking inward to examine its own programs and attitudes is behind the times. We are not able to dive into this topic deeply, but we hope to help readers see how diversity, equity, and inclusion initiatives are needed in every program and organization. We have listed resources in the Additional Resources section at the end of the chapter.

DIFFICULTIES AND JOYS

It is easy to say that program developers will have a challenging job ahead of them. The issues mentioned above are important for understanding current conditions, and the context for program development must be carefully monitored, as well as other topics that also impact human services. Instructors and textbook authors are sometimes prone to wanting to "tell the truth" about the work so that students are not naïve about what may await them. The problem with this approach, we find, is that the job of program planner, developer, or creator has a lot of wonderful moments that are often left out of descriptions. We want to give hope and recognize the truth that a well-designed and expertly run program offers a way to help people live better lives. If you prepare yourself to do that, there is much joy every day, along with any difficulties that also exist on the job.

We believe it is important for human service leaders (including program designers) to embrace the teachings of positive organizational behavior to assist in overcoming the difficulties in our work (Celestine, 2021). Diener et al. (2020), for example, indicate that positive emotions such as joy help create "favorable worker and workplace outcomes," including self-efficacy, creativity, work engagement, coping, and health at the individual level (p. 458). Social outcomes derived from positive emotions include teamwork and cooperation, good relationships, customer/client satisfaction, and higher performance. In addition, charismatic, transformational, and authentic leadership styles are also linked to positive emotions (Diener et al., 2020). Research indicates that people who are happy become better in all areas of their life. This is the reverse of what we frequently hear, which is if you become better in your job, you will be happier (Achor, 2012). We encourage you to read and watch the resources provided in the Additional Resources section to explore this topic further.

LESSONS FROM THE PANDEMIC

The COVID-19 pandemic has been devastating for millions of individuals. Organizations of all types have tried to cope in many ways. The fallout continues, not only in the United States but across the world. With the ability of the virus to mutate with new variants, COVID-19 may never be eradicated, only managed, much like influenza. Protecting clients, workers, and volunteers is top priority. As new variants become widespread, past practices may need to be maintained or reinstituted, such as wearing masks, closing or reducing hours in offices, maintaining social distancing, and meeting with colleagues and clients virtually.

The tri-sector economic system described in this chapter may be forever changed or it may return in much the same manner as it was. What we have learned, however, is that when a disaster of such magnitude occurs, the situation requires rapid change and resiliency. We hope that organizations and those who work within them are able to stay or become even more resilient as human service organizations always need to be. According to the Occupational Safety and Health Administration (2020), this includes developing an infectious disease preparedness and response plan and staying on top of guidance from national, state, local, territorial, and tribal health agencies.

CONCLUSION

This chapter highlights five trends that are shaping the world of human services. Program planners, administrators, and leaders need to be aware of these, as well as others that are more local in nature. Each of these trends is a challenge to handle on its own, but in combination, they can become overwhelming without careful attention to how they affect your clients, your organization, and your community.

Of course, these trends are evolving and will never be truly "over with" in a permanent way. We believe that only skilled practitioners, armed with knowledge and experience, have a chance to deal with their repercussions successfully. This book is our effort to bring insight and experiential learning to the classroom by focusing on the wider context of developing human services programs.

The trends identified in this chapter (the ongoing impact of the COVID-19 pandemic and recovery; the increasing importance of planning; unsteady funding; diversity in the workplace; and political challenges) must not be examined in isolation, because human service planners do not face these trends sequentially; rather, they come forward simultaneously, with varying strength, each day. Just as individuals face intersectional challenges (such as discrimination based on both gender and race) simultaneously, organizations need to prepare for confronting multiple interacting trends. Think of the situation for a planner wanting to create a program for refugees who may or may not be documented and only speak Spanish (when only one person on staff speaks that language) in a state where the governor (who has presidential ambitions) wants to build his own wall on the border to keep "such people" out of the country. Despite a strong need, can this project come to fruition and be sustainable?

As difficult as the job of a human service program developer may be, it is also extremely rewarding. Prepared with commitment to clients, appropriate job competencies, practical experience, and the will to move forward, you can make an important difference in your organization and communities every day. We invite you to overcome the daily difficulties and to experience the many joys of this vital professional career.

Understanding the larger context of program planning and development is a vital task because it will affect all aspects of the process. The context includes the basic economic system of the United States, with a shifting balance of nonprofit, government, and for-profit human services organizations. Other issues are enumerated, as they also impact the human services ecosystem and must be incorporated into planning processes in order to increase the odds of success. The challenges in the field are large, but the rewards are also. We believe this book will be a significant aid for understanding, entering, and thriving in your program design career.

 ## SUMMARY/KEY POINTS

- Change in the context of human services is a constant. Being aware of the larger economic and social forces will help you become a better human service program developer and planner.

- The tri-sector model helps explain macroeconomic situations for human services. It shows how nonprofits, for-profits, and government organizations all contribute to the overall system of service production.
- In the past, the three sectors were largely separate. Over the past several decades, however, their roles have become more blurred and overlapping. Leaders in all three sectors must now be aware of and able to work with each other on common goals.
- Hybrid organizational forms, such as social enterprises, demand more and different knowledge and skills to be successful compared to being knowledgeable about only one sector.
- Adapting to the COVID-19 pandemic has been stressful, causing many changes for clients, workers, volunteers, and organizations. These types of changes will continue, perhaps in new forms, as variants emerge and prevent a total return to past practices.
- Organizational and program planning, despite the seemingly constant chaos of change, has become more important than ever. So has the ability to shift plans rapidly.
- Funding for human services remains unsteady despite increases from some types of donors and funders. Giving is becoming more concentrated as a smaller percentage of Americans are giving to charities.
- Evidence-based practice and higher demands for accountability have emerged in the human service world.
- The increasing diversity in the United States brings fresh ideas and viewpoints to the workplace. Without significant effort to promote diversity, equity, and inclusion (DEI), however, organizations will tend to perpetrate "business as usual" for clients, staff, and volunteers. Black Lives Matters and other movements show the need to acknowledge and act on past racist policies and practices.
- Increasing polarization in political matters presents dangers in working for human service programs. Some office seekers and elected officials promote an agenda that seeks to cut funding for services and even to eliminate the Affordable Care Act, which has provided lower cost care to untold numbers of people in the United States. Government and nonprofit organization workers find advocating for clients can feel risky, if its services are funded by government bodies or tax allocations.
- Positive organizational behavior studies can provide evidence-based ways to improve the human services workplace and increase service effectiveness.

KEY TERMS

Adversarial relationship view: In an adversarial relationship view, nonprofits prod government into making changes in public policy and into maintaining accountability to the public. Reciprocally, government attempts to influence the behavior of nonprofit organizations by regulating their services and responding to their advocacy initiatives (Young, 1998, p. 33).

Complementary approach: In this approach, nonprofits are partners to government, helping to deliver public goods largely financed by the government. This is supposed to use the beneficial elements of governmental revenue generation, policy control, and accountability for use of tax dollars while preserving the more philanthropic aspects of nonprofit organizations.

Hybrid organizations: Human service organizations that function at the intersection of the traditional nonprofit and for-profit sectors (Gottesman, 2007).

New public management: "A movement with various definitions but common elements are that 1) adoption of market-based management and resource allocation techniques, 2) increased reliance on private sector organizations to deliver public services, and 3) a deliberate and sustained effort to downsize the decentralized government's role as the central policy actor in society" (Frederickson & Smith, 2003, p. 208).

Social enterprise: "… a management practice that integrates principles of private enterprise with social-sector goals and objectives. [It] includes a variety of sustainable economic activities designed to yield social impact for individuals, families, and communities" (Fernando, 2017).

Supplementary model: Nonprofits are seen as fulfilling a demand for public goods left unsatisfied by the government, and potentially not available or too expensive from the business sector for many potential recipients who desire the service. They thus supplement or add to what government and for-profit organizations provide.

Tri-Sector Model: A conceptualization of the economy and structure of society that has three components: government, for-profit, and nonprofit. Some scholars see the emergence of hybrid organizations combining two of the three approaches.

ADDITIONAL RESOURCES

COVID-19 Issues

Council of Nonprofits. (2021, April 9). *What nonprofits need to know as staff and volunteers return from remote work to in-person operations* [Video]. YouTube. https://www.youtube.com/watch?v=L0e6RthrkEs

Council of Nonprofits. (2021, April 9). *How every nonprofit can help the communities we serve get vaccinated* [Video]. YouTube. https://www.youtube.com/watch?v=asy6fWpx6NU

Diversity, Equity, Inclusion, and Antiracism Frameworks

Matrix360. (2020). *Anti-racism roadmap for everyday action: Macro-level overview*. Matrix360. https://cdn.ymaws. com/www.bomatoronto.org/resource/resmgr/2020/diversity/matrix360_-_anti-racism_road.pdf

National Museum of African American History and Culture. (n.d.). Talking about race: Being antiracist. https://nmaahc.si.edu/learn/talking-about-race/topics/being-antiracist

Positive Organizational Psychology

Achor, S. (2012). *The happy secret to better work* [Video]. YouTube. https://www.youtube.com/watch?v=fLJsdqxnZb0&t=316s

Dutton, J., & Spreitzer, G. (Eds.). (2014). *How to be a positive leader: Small actions, big impact*. Berrett-Koehler Publishers.

Linley, P. A., Harrington, S., & Garcea, N. (2013). *The Oxford handbook of positive psychology and work*. Oxford University Press.

Wrzesniewski, A. (2014). *Job Crafting—On creating meaning in your own work* [Video]. YouTube. https://www. youtube.com/watch?v=C_igfnctYjA&t=305s

DISCUSSION QUESTIONS

1. In what ways is it helpful to understand the tri-sector model as a program creator (developer/ designer)? How will this help you envision your future career in the field of human services?
2. How are you working on incorporating the information regarding diversity, equity, inclusion, and antiracism into your professional and personal life (of course, these can never be fully separated)? Is your college or university providing skills and information that is helpful to you? What else might they do?
3. Which of the five issues discussed in this chapter seems most likely to pose the greatest challenges for you?
4. In what ways can you see benefits from developing skills in positive organizational psychology?

 YOUR TURN

Read through the description of the agency you are now the leader of (see Prologue). Looking over the issues listed in this chapter, write a 3–4 page analysis of how one of them would affect your organization and programs you would want to have developed in your community in the next 5 years, if you could find funding for them.

REFERENCES

Achor, S. (2012). *The happy secret to better work* [Video]. YouTube. https://www.youtube.com/watch?v= fLJsdqxnZb0&t=316s

Allahyari, R. A. (2000). *Visions of charity: Volunteer workers and moral community.* University of California Press.

Allison, M., & Kaye, J. (2015). *Strategic planning for nonprofit organizations: A practical guide for dynamic times.* John Wiley & Sons.

Almog-Bar, M., & Schmid, H. (2018). Cross-sector partnerships in human services: Insights and organizational dilemmas. *Nonprofit and Voluntary Sector Quarterly, 47*(4), 119-S-138S. https://doi.org/10.1177/0899764018771218

American Public Human Services Association. (n.d.). *What is human services?* https://www.nationalhumanservices.org/what-is-human-services#:~:text=The%20field%20of%20Human%20Services,of%20life%20of%20 service%20populations

American Red Cross. (n.d.). *Mission statement.* https://www.redcross.org/about-us/who we are/mission-and-values.html

Bebes, J., Ray, K., & Meacham, L. (2021). *2021 Plante Moran Nonprofit outlook survey report.* https://go.plantemoran. com/rs/946-CTY-601/images/Nonprofit%20Outlook%20Report%202021.pdf

Bicoy, B. (2018). Commentary: The impending decline of charitable giving. *Peninsula Pulse.* https://doorcounty-pulse.com/commentary-the-impending-decline-in-charitable-giving/

Biswas, S. (2018). Can artificial intelligence eliminate bias in hiring? *HR Technologist.* https://www.hrtechnologist.com/articles/recruitment-onboarding/can-artificial-intelligence-eliminate-bias-in-hiring/

Blomberg, S., & Jan, P. (2010). The increasing importance of administrative practices in the shaping of the welfare state. *Social Work & Society, 8*(1). https://socwork.net/sws/article/view/24/67

Bordt, R. L. (1998). *The structure of women's non-profit organizations.* Indiana University Press.

Brinkerhoff, J. M., & Brinkerhoff, D. W. (2002). Government–nonprofit relations in comparative perspective: Evolution, themes and new directions. *Public Administration & Development, 22*(1), 3–18. https://doi.org/10.1002/pad.202

Callahan, D. (2018). Philanthropy forecast 2018: Trends and issues to watch. *Inside Philanthropy.* https://www.insidephilanthropy.com/home/2018/1/7/philanthropy-forecast

Celestine, N. (2021). *What is positive organizational psychology?* PositivePsychology.com. https://positivepsychology.com/positive-organizational-psychology/

Cheng, S., & Catallo, C. (2020). Conceptual framework: Factors enabling collaborative healthcare and social services integration. *Journal of Integrated Care, 28*(3), 215–229. https://www.emerald.com/insight/content/doi/10.1108/JICA-11-2019-0048/full/html

Clark, A., & Crane, A. (2018). Cross-sector partnerships for systemic change: Systematized literature review and agenda for further research. *Journal of Business Ethics, 150*, 303–313. https://doi.org/10.1007/s10551-018-3922-2

Council on Foundations. (2021). *35 keys to effective evaluation.* https://www.cof.org/content/35-keys-effective-evaluation

Catholic Charities. (n.d.). *Catholic Charities is committed to helping immigrants & refugees.* https://www.catholic-charitiesusa.org/our-ministry/immigration-refugee-services/

Crain's New York. (2021). *Report: Nonprofits lost $9M in revenue in 2020.* https://www.crainsnewyork.com/health-pulse/report-nonprofits-lost-9m-revenue-2020-situation-worsened-government-delays

DellaPosta, D. (2020). Pluralistic collapse: The "oil spill" model of mass opinion polarization. *American Sociological Review, 85*(3), 507–536. https://doi.org/10.1177/0003122420922989

Defourney, J., & Nyssens, M. (2017). Fundamentals for an international typology of social enterprise models. *Voluntas: International Journal of Voluntary and Nonprofit Organizations, 28*, 2469–2497. https://doi.org/10.1007/s11266-017-9884-7

Diener, E., Thapa, S., & Tay, L. (2020). Positive emotions at work. *Annual Review of Organizational Psychology and Organizational Behavior, 7*, 451–477. https://doi.org/10.1146/annurev-orgpsych-012119-044908

Drexel Now. (2021). *Study: Gender pay gaps in nonprofits are even greater when there is room for salary negotiations.* https://drexel.edu/now/archive/2021/May/Study-on-gender-pay-gaps-at-nonprofits/

Fernandez, E. (2011). *Low staffing and poor quality of care at nation's for-profit nursing homes.* University of California San Francisco. https://www.ucsf.edu/news/2011/11/98499/low-staffing-and-poor-quality-care-nations-profit-nursing-homes

Fernando, R. (2017). Social enterprise. In C. Franklin (Ed.), *Encyclopedia of social work.* https://oxfordre.com/socialwork/view/10.1093/acrefore/9780199975839.001.0001/acrefore-9780199975839-e-1027

Frederickson, H. G., & Smith, K. B. (2003). *The public administration theory primer.* Westview Press.

Friesenhahn, E. (2016). Nonprofits in America: New research data on employment, wages, and establishments. *Monthly Labor Review*, U.S. Bureau of Labor Statistics. https://doi.org/10.21916/mlr.2016.9

Gidron, B., Katz, S. N., & Hasenfeld, Y. (2002). *Mobilizing for peace: Conflict resolution in Northern Ireland, Israel/ Palestine, and South Africa.* Oxford University Press.

Giving USA. (2021). *$471.44 billion* [Infographic]. https://blog.stelter.com/2021/06/15/giving-usa-2021-inside-the-numbers/

Golensky, M., & Mulder, C. A. (2006). Coping in a constrained economy: Survival strategies of nonprofit human service organizations. *Administration in Social Work*, *30*(3), 5–24.

Gottesman, M. D. (2007). From cobblestones to pavement: The legal road forward for the creation of hybrid social organizations. *Yale Law & Policy Review*, *26*(1), 345–358. https://www.jstor.org/stable/40239695

Handy, F. (1997). Coexistence of nonprofit, for-profit and public sector institutions. *Annals of Public & Cooperative Economics*, *68*(2), 201–223.

Hasenfeld, Y., & Gidron, B. (2005). Understanding multi-purpose hybrid voluntary organizations: The contributions of theories on civil society, social movements, and non-profit organizations. *Journal of Civil Society*, *1*(2), 97–112. https://doi.org/10.1080/17448680500337350

Höjer, S., & Forkby, T. (2011). Care for sale: The influence of new public management in child protection in Sweden. *British Journal of Social Work*, *41*(1), 93–110. https://doi.org/10.1093/bjsw/bcq053

Hopkins, K. M., & Hyde, C. (2002). The human service managerial dilemma: New expectations, chronic challenges and old solutions. *Administration in Social Work*, *26*(3), 1–15.

Hopkins, K., Meyer, M., Cohen-Callow, A., Mattocks, N., & Afkinich, J. (2019). Implementation and impact of results-based accountability learning: Successes and challenges with human service professionals of color in urban agencies. *Race and Justice*, *9*(1), 80–94. https://doi.org/10.1177/2153368718809835

Hughes, V., Delva, S., Nkimbeng, M., Spaulding, E., Turkso-Ocran, R., Cudjoe, J., Ford, A., Rushton, C., D'Auost, R., & Han. H.-R. (2020). Not missing the opportunity: Strategies to promote cultural humility among future nursing faculty. *Journal of Professional Nursing*, *36*, 28–33.

Hsu, A. (2021). *As the pandemic recedes, millions of workers are saying 'I quit.'* NPR. https://www.npr.org/2021/06/24/1007914455/as-the-pandemic-recedes-millions-of-workers-are-saying-i-quit

Johnson Center at Grand Valley University. (2019). *11 trends in philanthropy for 2019: Anticipate and embrace what's coming next.* http://johnsoncenter.org/11-trends-for-2019/

Johnson, M., & Austin, M. J. (2006). Evidence-based practice in the social services: Implications for organizational change. *Administration in Social Work*, *30*(3), 75–104.

Jones, J. M. (2006). Understanding environmental influence on human service organizations: A study of the influence of managed care on child caring institutions. *Administration in Social Work*, *30*(4), 63–90.

Jones, J. M., (2020). *Percentage of Americans donating to charity at new low.* Gallup. https://news.gallup.com/poll/310880/percentage-americans-donating-charity-new-low.aspx

Kettl, D. (2000). Public administration at the millennium: The state of the field. *Journal of Public Administration Research and Theory*, *10*(1), 7–34.

Kozan, K. (2019, February 13). *6 best workplace diversity trends for 2019.* https://ideal.com/workplace-diversity-trends/

Linton, K., (2013). Developing a social enterprise as a social worker. *Administration in Social Work*, *37*(5), 458–470. https://doi.rog/10.1080/03643107.2013.828000

McBeath, B., & Meezan, W. (2006). Nonprofit adaptation to performance-based, managed care contracting in Michigan's foster care system. *Administration in Social Work*, *30*(2), 39–70.

Merrifield, K. (2021). *A year later: COVID-19's impact on Arizona's nonprofit sector*. Alliance of Arizona Nonprofits. https://cdn.ymaws.com/arizonanonprofits.org/resource/resmgr/COVID-19-_A_Year_Later_Final.pdf

Minkoff, D. C. (1995). *Organizing for equality: The evolution of women's and racial-ethnic organizations in America, 1955–1985*. Rutgers University Press.

Najam, A. (2000). The four C's of third sector–government relations. *Nonprofit Management & Leadership*, *10*(4), 375–396.

National Center for Charitable Statistics. (2020). *The nonprofit sector in brief in 2019*. https://nccs.urban.org/publication/nonprofit-sector-brief-2019#number

Occupational Safety and Health Administration. (2020). *Guidance on preparing workplaces for COVID-19*. https://www.osha.gov/sites/default/files/publications/OSHA3990.pdf

Pintas & Mullins Injury Lawyers (2020). *For-profit vs. nonprofit nursing homes*. https://www.pintas.com/blog/for-profit-vs-non-profit-nursing-homes/#:~:text=According%20to%20federal%20health%20inspectors,various%20means%20than%20non%2Dprofits

Regehr, C., Chau, S., Leslie, B., & Howe, P. (2002). An exploration of supervisor's and manager's responses to child welfare reform. *Administration in Social Work*, *26*(3), 17–36.

Reisch, M., & Sommerfeld, D. (2003). Welfare reform and the future of nonprofit organizations. *Nonprofit Management & Leadership*, *14*(1), 19–46.

Rolland, A. (2020). *Research and trends in philanthropy: Donor-advised funds*. Lilly Family School of Philanthropy. https://blog.philanthropy.iupui.edu/2020/02/18/research-and-trends-in-philanthropy-donor-advised-funds/

Salipante, P., & Aram, J. D. (2003). Managers as knowledge generators: The nature of practitioner-scholar research in the nonprofit sector. *Nonprofit Management Leadership*, *14*(2), 129–150.

Schmid, H. (2004). Organization-environment relationships: Theory for management practice in human service organizations. *Administration in Social Work*, *28*(1), 97–113.

Shear, M., & Kanno-Youngs, Z. (2021). Biden aims to rebuild and expand legal immigration. *The New York Times*. https://www.nytimes.com/2021/05/31/us/politics/biden-immigration.html

Statista. (2020). *Percentage of the U.S. population who have completed four years of college or more from 1940 to 2020, by gender*. https://www.statista.com/statistics/184272/educational-attainment-of-college-diploma-or-higher-by-gender/

Stein, J. (2017). Republican officials say targeting welfare programs will help spur economic growth. *The Washington Post*. https://www.washingtonpost.com/news/wonk/wp/2017/12/06/house-republicans-welfare-restrictions-are-needed-for-the-economy-to-grow/?utm_term=.95d3349166ec

Swanstrom, T. (1997, April 16–19). *The nonprofitization of housing policy: Slipping between the horns of policy dilemmas* [Paper presentation]. Annual Meeting of the Urban Affairs Association, Toronto, Canada.

Thompson, D. (2021). Millions are saying no to the vaccines. What are they thinking? *The Atlantic*. https://www.theatlantic.com/ideas/archive/2021/05/the-people-who-wont-get-the-vaccine/618765/

United States Census Bureau. (2019). *Quick facts, people*. https://www.census.gov/quickfacts/fact/table/US/PST045219

Vestergaard, A., Langevang, T., Morsing, M., & Murphy, L. (2021). Partnerships for development. Assessing the impact potential of cross-sector partnerships. *World Development*, *143*. https://reader.elsevier.com/reader/sd/

pii/S0305750X21000590?token=8A13ECCAD8DD9F2F6DCE2B564DF2DEB5D01E2D31D3B5372BE24CFEC6AF7 C2E907AE7E608915DD9122CD08CB20CFE5875&originRegion=us-east-1&originCreation=20210624192803

Watson, L. D. (2007). *Factors influencing the relationship between nonprofit child care providers and the Texas Department of Family and Protective Services as a predictor of policy outcomes.* (Unpublished doctoral dissertation). University of Texas at Arlington, Texas.

Watson, L. D., & Hegar, R. (2013). The tri-sector environment of social work administration: Applying theoretical orientations. *Administration in Social Work*, *37*(3), 215–226.

Young, D. R. (1998). Complementary, supplementary, or adversarial? A theoretical and historical examination of nonprofit-government relations in the United States. In E. T. Boris & C. E. Steuerle (Eds.), *Nonprofits and government: Collaboration and conflict* (pp. 31–67). The Urban Institute Press.

Zimmermann, J. M., & Stevens, B. W. (2006). The use of performance measurement in South Carolina nonprofits. *Nonprofit Management & Leadership*, *16*(3), 315–327.

Figure Credits

CHAPTER TWO

The Program Planning Process and Required Roles

OVERVIEW

In this chapter we describe what programs are, why we have them, and what program design/development is. We provide a road map for the program creation and implementation process cycle. This turn-by-turn overview will enable you to know the steps you will be going through from beginning to understand the community, through one entire cycle in the life of a program. All the aspects are covered so you can run a program and then continue with an improved program in the next cycle.

We also provide a detailed account of the roles that are needed to develop a program. This does not mean that each role needs a different person to perform those tasks, but it is helpful to be able to see which role does what. If you need to combine roles or separate them in a different way, that is allowable, of course. You must mix and match according to the human resources you have available.

By the end of the chapter you will understand what the entire program planning process entails and how to put together a program planning team. You will also be able to explain what you expect from each person on the team. In this chapter, as in all the chapters, we have short, focused explorations regarding diversity as it applies to the chapter's material, the difficulties and joys of this part of program design, and lessons that can be learned from the COVID-19 pandemic. (And so much more.)

WHAT ARE PROGRAMS?

People in the human services field toss around the word "program" with little thought of how they would define it. It means many different things in different contexts. Students study and get credits to complete their educational program, going on to graduate so they can work in a human service program. Staff members work for programs, clients go through programs, communities are impacted by programs, funders provide money for programs, evaluators assess programs, and so on. The United States Department of Health and Human Services (HHS, n.d.) "administers more than 100 programs [which] ... protect the health of all Americans and provide essential services, especially for those who are least able to help themselves" (Programs and Services section). But rarely is the term actually given a precise definition.

Martin (2021) describes definitions offered by other authors (Kettner et al., 2017; Lynch et al., 2017; Weinbach & Taylor, 2015), none of which he treats as definitive, although they overlap. Fortunately, Martin provides a clear consensus definition. A **program** is, he writes, "a major ongoing agency activity or service with its own set of goals, objectives, policies, and budgets that produces a defined product or service" (Martin, 2021, p. 9). Martin argues that defining programs is not as easy as looking at a traditional chart, which usually shows organizational units. He prefers a programmatic diagram that deconstructs units into programs, as defined earlier. Further, each program should have a **program manager** who has both programmatic and financial oversight. The program manager may or may not be a full-time job—the same person may oversee more than one program or have responsibilities other than management, such as providing direct client services (Martin, 2021).

WHY DO WE HAVE PROGRAMS?

Imagine you are experiencing some sort of problem in your personal life. Here are some possibilities:

- You need acute medical care because you have cancer.
- You have trouble with an addiction.
- You have parents with deepening memory issues, making it dangerous for them to live on their own.
- Your family doesn't have enough food every month.
- You lost your job when it was moved to another location and you do not have money to pay your rent (again). You and your children are about to be evicted and have nowhere to stay.
- You need day care for your toddler so you can work.
- You had an emergency room visit and now owe the hospital tens of thousands of dollars.

The number of possible problems and associated needed services is nearly endless. The American Public Human Services Association (n.d.) provides a description of the field of human services as one that has "the objective of meeting human needs through an interdisciplinary knowledge base, focusing on prevention as well as remediation of problems, and maintaining a commitment to improving the overall quality of life of service populations" (What Is Human Services? section).

People disagree on the cause of problems. Some believe that many issues are the result of conscious decisions at the individual or family level and should be addressed by those people on their own. In our economic system, if you have enough money you can almost always find someone who, for a price, will provide treatment or help. Private-pay addiction treatment centers exist to assist you, or home assistance agencies can provide someone to stay with your loved one experiencing memory problems. Services purchased from organizations can be quite expensive, however, and not everyone can afford the fees, so many people are in need of help but cannot afford it.

Most people can see that not all life problems are caused by "bad" choices. All types of discrimination impact life chances, due to no fault of the person discriminated against. Natural disasters do not strike in entirely unpredictable ways, often damaging areas that are full of people with low incomes. Homes there are often rental units in poor repair.

In each situation you may reach out for help from an organization that fits into the human services world. This has the generic name of "human service organization" (HSOs). *Human service organizations* work to prevent and also to remediate problems their clients experience. HSOs often conduct advocacy to change laws and policies to improve the life chances of clients and to improve society as well. Although individual helpers working on their own exist, most

Program staff bring solutions to people with needs through program efforts.

human services are provided by people who are employed in organizations. These HSOs are formal collections of people who work together to achieve specified goals for the benefit of their clients and communities. They typically do so by working within specific programs that have been designed to achieve those goals. Where do these programs come from, and how are they created?

WHAT IS PROGRAM DESIGN OR DEVELOPMENT?

A quick note on terminology: In this book we use the terms **program design**, program planning, and **program development** interchangeably. All refer to a process of showing how to achieve desired outcomes through creating or amending a program. You can think of it in terms of planning a trip. You are at Point A and you would like to get to Point B. There is almost always more than one way to do that, so you must consider your preferences and the desires of those you may be driving with as you select your route. Do you like slow scenic routes, even if they take longer, or would you rather travel on boring interstates to get there more quickly? You also most likely have other criteria to think about. Are you sure that your means of transportation is reliable and safe, or must you take into account a breakdown that is likely to occur? How about the cost? Is money no object, or will you need to pinch every penny to ensure you will have enough funding? How much faith do you have that the route will actually get you where you want to go? Is your travel plan based on good information? Are there other items you need or want to take with you, such as snacks, or is stopping to eat what you prefer? Again, if you have passengers, you will need to take their ideas into account as well. Read Box 2.1 to learn about the three **design parameters** and how tradeoffs are inevitable when resources are limited (and they always are!).

BOX 2.1	**The Three Design Parameters and Their Tradeoffs**

A general rule of thumb in designing almost anything is that three parameters exist in most situations: speed, cost, and quality, and if you try maximizing one of them, it will have an impact on the other two. Doing something quickly will entail higher costs and possibly lower quality. Keeping costs low will impact quality and speed of accomplishment. And finally, requiring only high-quality results will cost more and generally take more time.

Keep this in mind as you design your programs. You may be able to design the best program imaginable but not have the finances to implement it with highly qualified staff members. Or you may hire the best workers at fair wages but not have the resources for recruiting clients. Tradeoffs must be made because it is unlikely you will ever have enough funding to have the best of everything and have it done quickly.

The same sorts of tradeoffs will face you as you design a program. You must first know what you want to accomplish. How will future clients be different or change as a result of the program? Will they know more or behave differently? You also need to know quite a bit about the current situation. How many people are affected, and in what ways? What are the best guesses for why people have the problem you see? Is it possible that where you see an issue, the potential clients are not troubled in the same way? Is the program you want to design attractive to the people you want to be in it? Assuming you can recruit people to participate in your program, do you have a set of research-based ideas for how to guide them successfully to achieve the goals of the program?

The program design process takes into account all of these issues and more. For example, as you design a new program, you must estimate how much it will cost to conduct all the hiring and training of staff, acquire sufficient materials, have an appropriate amount of space for offices and meeting rooms, and so on. Even as you put together the initial funding requests, you also need to plan for long-term program sustainability—if your evaluation shows the program works. Figure 2.1 is an overview of all the steps that are typically completed as you design a program.

THE PROGRAM DESIGN/DEVELOPMENT PROCESS

When doing something for the first time, you likely prefer to have a goal in mind and a set of procedures to follow to arrive there. Figure 2.1 shows an overview of the steps of program development so you see the entire process in one view. As with any single picture, however, we acknowledge that there is usually more to the process in "the real world" than is captured in a diagram. In practice, some steps are inevitably omitted or truncated along the way given tight deadlines or other issues that arise, such as a higher level decision being made to move in one direction or another. In addition, delays may occur and cause a time line to become untenable, and the design effort is abandoned. While our process map indicates several iterative processes or times when steps are revised, not all have been included. We offer it is as an overview more than as the definitive Google Maps version of creating a program. The book will in general follow the steps so that when you finish, you will have done the work of program design and have a product that you can use to showcase your new skills.

COMPONENTS OF THE PROGRAM DEVELOPMENT PROCESS

The process of developing a program is comprised of four stages broken into steps. Stage 1 is Understanding Context. Within this are the discrete steps of Conducting Advocacy (Chapter 3) and Understanding the Community (Chapter 4), with Gathering Information integral to both (no separate chapter). Stage 2 is Finding Funding and Planning Program where we discuss two steps: Grantwriting and Fund Development: Finding and Applying for Funding (Chapter 5) and Planning Programs for Your Organization (Chapter 6). The planning program step has several distinct pieces in addition, which we break into separate chapters (Chapter 7, Logic Models and Program Evaluation Planning; Chapter 8, Budgeting and Finance; and Chapter 9, Organizational Capacity). Assuming all has gone well, you will be Receiving Funds (which we will assume, so there is no chapter on that). Stage 3 is Implementing and Evaluating Program, with two steps: Implementing Program (Chapter 10, Program Implementation Planning) and Evaluation (putting into effect your evaluation plan, covered in Chapter 7). Stage 4, Reporting and Adapting Program, is comprised of the steps Reporting (Chapter 11, Developing an Information Sharing Plan) and Adapting Program as a result of lessons learned from evaluation and other sources (no specific chapter). These stages and steps are shown in Figure 2.1.

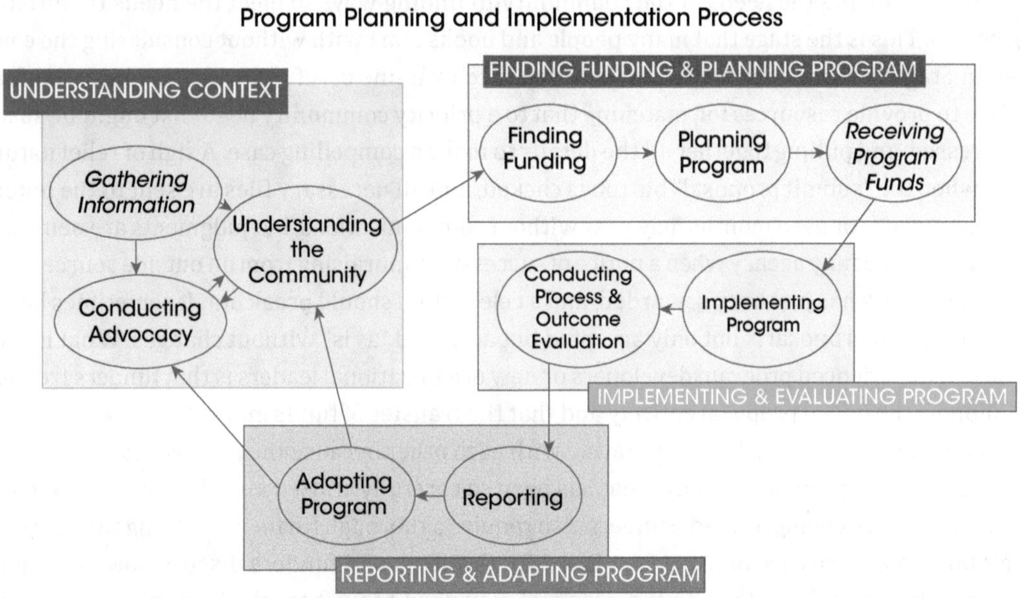

Program Planning and Implementation Process

FIGURE 2.1   **Program Development Process**

Stage 1: Understanding Context

Looking at Figure 2.1 on the upper left side we see the stage labeled "Understanding Context." This acknowledges that we must spend time assessing a situation before we can try to improve it. Some possible questions we need to address in this stage are:

- Who lives in the community now, and how might this have changed over time?
- How has the history altered or added to community problems in recent years?
- What are the strengths of the organization and community as a whole to provide appropriate services?
- What advocacy for the community and its needs has been planned and/or completed?
- Do local leaders have opinions about the highest priority aspects of the community?
- Are elected officials supportive of community services that are needed?

In all, the understanding context stage of program development requires more than a shallow understanding of the community's strengths and weaknesses. The program development effort gathers information about advocacy efforts by and for the community to support a new or modified program. It is the best time to begin reaching out to community stakeholders to gather information and to build a stakeholder group to support an information campaign to grow support for local resources (governmental bodies, charitable foundations, and private donors).

Stage 2: Developing Program and Receiving Funds

We next shift to the upper right corner, with Stage 2, "Finding Funding and Planning Programs." This takes us from knowing the needs of the community to finding ways to meet the needs to initiate the new program. This is the stage that many people and books start with without considering the context covered in Stage 1 of our approach. The first step is to examine carefully what the potential funder would like to provide resources for, matching that to a priority community need that might be successfully addressed, and pulling together all the details to make a compelling case. A sigh of relief naturally emerges when the "submit proposal" button is clicked, and all necessary files are sent to the potential funder. Many weeks or even months may pass without communications, but judgments are being made.

It is a happy day at any agency when a notice of successful fundraising from an outside source arrives! A great deal of work has just been rewarded, and a celebration should break out. It sometimes happens that the submitted proposal is not only accepted but accepted "as is" without changes. What is often a surprise to inexperienced program developers or new organizational leaders is that funders frequently do not support the initial proposal entirely and that the transfer of funds may take months. This leads to the funder and the organization negotiating with each other because the proposal is not going to be fully funded. The scope of the proposal that has been so carefully crafted must be downsized to fit the new level of resources being offered. Funders also require a thorough financial auditing to ensure fiscal accountability measures are in place (see Box 2.2). Grantees and funders discuss how much money will be provided and which items in the proposal may need to wait for the future. This is when the program developer will be glad to have amassed sufficient details for why things are listed as costing the amount stated. Discussions happen between the funders and organization, and changes are made to the proposal's original budget and program ideas so a close alignment reemerges. It is essentially a reversion to the planning program step. This does not require its own chapter but is essential to be prepared for. It can feel deflating to have to cut out some of the program ideas, but it is still a victory to have the funding in hand.

BOX 2.2	**The Unprepared Organization**

A number of years ago, the federal government was seeking to support refugee-settling agencies with a close connection to the newer diverse populations that were coming to the United States. This desire came after advocacy efforts by the leaders from these populations lobbying for the shift in policy. They desired agencies that were more closely tied to the populations to get contracts rather than the "old-time" multirefugee population agencies that had come to dominate the receipt of funding efforts.

A professional colleague, who was an excellent grantwriter, worked with such a population-based organization to develop an application. Because it was a very good proposal and the competition was not intense, the federal agency communicated that an award was going to be made, contingent on showing results of a recent successful audit and other fiscal processes being in place. A visit to the agency was scheduled.

The organization consisted of the director and a board of directors who worked with the faith community of this population to provide "just-in-time" services, such as food, furniture, rent assistance, clothing, and other necessities that refugees needed immediately upon locating in their new homes. The grant was going to provide the opportunity to do a great deal of good for these refugees.

Unfortunately, financial records and processes were almost entirely nonexistent. When asked how he kept track of the income and expenses, the director pointed to his head and said, "I keep it up here." No one thought he was being dishonest or misusing the funds, but it was decided to pull the offer of federal funding from this group, and the resources were routed to the main refugee-serving agency in the area that did not have contacts or connections with the population in question.

Stage 3: Implementing and Evaluating Program

Moving down in Figure 2.1 brings us to Stage 3, "Implementing and Evaluating Program." It has two steps, though each is really a compilation of separate aspects. The chapters you will find here include important substeps. This is the "real work" of the program where staff members are hired, clients are recruited, and the service plans are put into action. When the services are completed and evaluated, the hope is that the world has been improved by reducing or eliminating the problem it addresses. A great deal of effort is expended in this part of the process, not only to provide services to recipients but to ensure that the services provided are the ones that were described in the proposal.

Programs that are evidence based to achieve desirable outcomes generally have little leeway to be changed without calling into question prior research-supported outcomes. If a program is in the proposal to be delivered as a one-session-per-week 12-week program, for example, but is suddenly switched to be delivered in twice-a-week classes over 6 weeks, potential implementation and evaluation problems arise quickly. Monitoring of accurate program delivery (ensuring program fidelity) is essential because only then can we expect the results to occur as promised. Data on program implementation (process) and outcomes must be collected and examined as the program goes along so that trends and issues can be spotted as soon as possible.

Stage 4: Reporting and Adapting Program

The information will usually be written and disseminated to the key stakeholders (including the funder) no less often than annually, and sometimes as often as quarterly. It takes time to write such data-heavy reports and also to potentially have a lay person's version that hits the highlights and can be used to garner advocates for continued funding.

Almost all grants or donations are for a fixed amount of time, possibly 3–5 years. This time span allows for the ability to ramp up the operations, conduct the program with several groups of clients, analyze data to see where gains were made and where they were not, and learn from the specific program in a particular place. Sometimes evaluations are published in professional journals and lead to support of the program ideas among a wider group of program proponents who can advocate for continued and expanded funding opportunities.

From the first day of implementation, however, organization leaders know the clock is running out on that original grant. Sustaining the program beyond the initial funding is a constant concern, assuming that positive outcomes are being achieved. This may require adapting the program because of what the evaluation discovers, keeping up with current contextual issues in the community, and so on. This is certainly a time to make improvements and possibly seek out different or additional funding sources. The agency does not need to return to the same funder in order to keep a program going.

This section has provided an overview of the entire program development process. A great amount of detail is omitted at this point but is covered in later chapters. Now that we know the basics of what the process of program development is, we turn to the **program development roles and skills** required to make it all happen. At the outset we need to stress that the roles do not refer to individual people. Indeed, it is unlikely that each person involved in a program development effort occupies only one role. At its most intense, the same person is responsible for filling all the roles, having all the skills, and completing all the tasks. This is a situation that is very difficult for that one person.

Having a sense of all the roles and skills needed can bring clarity in the runup to starting to design a program. Knowing what is coming and how to organize your efforts can allay a considerable amount of anxiety, no matter how much effort is required.

THE PROGRAM DEVELOPMENT TEAM: NECESSARY ROLES AND SKILLS

Program development is rarely a one-person effort. Before deciding to start the process, it helps to have an overview of not only the process (as shown in Figure 2.1) but also the roles and skills that are needed to accomplish the process as successfully as possible. Table 2.1 is a helpful look at this element of program design: the people and skills side, not just the "what happens" aspects. An important part of team development is to realize that the "team" is often only a small set of people working together on an ad hoc basis and that the design process is only part of their work. Program design comes on top of the other duties they complete in most smaller nonprofits and government agencies. Rarely do such organizations have departments dedicated to program development alone. Grantwriters in a nonprofit may also manage the grants that are awarded, supervising direct care staff or middle managers. Research supporting program development efforts may come after hours or on weekends so that the "real job" is completed. Many roles can be subsumed by one person, while others need more specialized training or skills to accomplish well. A few roles are linked to people in certain organizational positions (approvals come from the top levels), although other roles are shifted according to who is available on short notice or for a limited time. Even though every case is different, common elements exist, as shown in Table 2.1.

TABLE 2.1   The Program Development Team: Necessary Roles, Skills, and Attributes

Role	Skills and Attributes
Final decision maker	• Positional authority to authorize plans • Strong proponent for organizational vision and mission • Clear sense of organizational needs, abilities, and capacities • Ability to grasp strategic implications of program development decisions • Ability to advocate for new projects in line with community needs, both outside the organization and within
Team leader (TL)	• Connected with both strategic- and program-level decision makers in the organization • Connected with current academic and professional thinking about the substantive topic, including successful programs in other locations • Experience with substantive program topic area • Active listening to all members of team • Task management skills (keeping everything moving along in a timely way) while also having people skills to ensure commitment to the effort • Delegation and coordination skills
Researcher (R)	• Helps everyone on team with collecting required information • Understands needs of other team members and can locate what they need to have • Knowledge of the research process • Experience with specific substantive area and program development in general • Can translate information needs into to written support of development efforts
Fundraiser (F) or Grantwriter (G)	• Familiar with all aspects of raising funds to support programs • Strong technical writing ability • Excellent oral communication skills • Up to date on newest and most successful program ideas in the field
Program developer (PD)	• Well-versed in design thinking and organizational dynamics • Connects community needs to appropriate program ideas, particularly evidence-based ones • Can adapt program ideas to the community's needs and situation • Works with fundraiser and top decision makers to gain support for ideas to assist future clients • Excellent written and oral communication abilities • Skillful use of logic models and other visual products to assist understanding of program plans • Comfortable promoting and using community stakeholders in program planning efforts

(Continued)

TABLE 2.1   (Continued)

Program evaluator (PE)	• Understands essential elements of all types of program evaluations (e.g., process, outcome, etc.), research design, and measures • Able to translate academic language and processes into information that others understand and support • Strong and analytic writing skills, including the best way to present results
Outside stakeholder (OS)	• Community members (including potential clients) willing to assist in developing and supporting program ideas • Advocates for the substantive area, client population, organization, and staff

Final Decision Maker (FDM)

For every program development effort, someone has to be authorized to approve the project. Without a clear end point of revisions and "'how-about-this?' discussion," the process can continue (seemingly) indefinitely. The final-decision-maker role is needed so that the ideas are set in stone (for the initial or subsequent submissions). Time passes, deadlines loom, and crises emerge. Putting the task into a designated person's (or possibly a committee's) hands ensures completion and moving in one direction or another. Having a clear FDM is also important for more minor decisions encountered during the development process. This role may shift from one decision to another, depending on necessary competences and knowledge, or it may be the same person in every case.

Between the time the program planning process begins and the end of developing the ideas, the final decision maker will be required to be a strong proponent for the organization's vision and mission. No matter how clever or otherwise well done a program design is, if it is not aligned with preexisting program values and statements, the process should be ended or drastically altered. Because of the FDM's strong identification with the organization, its mission and values and client service ethos, the person in this role should also have skills to reach outside the walls to communicate and advocate on behalf of the agency and client populations.

Team Leader (TL)

Just as there is a final decision maker at the end of the process, a team leader role is necessary to ensure that the work gets done to be able to be judged by the FDM. The TL must be well-versed in the overall organization's strategic-level thinking and how the program being developed will fit into the strategies previously chosen. As befits a person with such knowledge, the team leader must be aware of advances in evidence-based programs and ideas emerging from academic and professional circles. A successful new approach to the problem being addressed may have been spotted since the previous deep review. If so, this should be highlighted and showcased in the program development process.

A good amount of experience in the substantive area is important so that everyone on the team respects the TL's knowledge, practice wisdom, and honesty about why decisions are made. Some ideas may be floated by staff or board members that hard-won experience and/or organizational values contradict. The TL needs to be able to separate ideas that are better from those that are worse based on a wide knowledge base.

The person in the team leader role will ideally have been through the process of program development before and thus be able to guide other team members in their tasks through judicious delegation and coordination skills. Using active listening (and other skills), team members need to feel valued so they will commit to achieving the tasks set before them. (The TL will find it is helpful to be able to engage in appropriate self-talk and listening, too.)

Image 2.2

Team leaders ensure work is completed in a timely and competent manner.

Researcher

The person in the researcher role is one of the most important figures for creating a program that is based on facts, theory, practice experience, and acceptance by outside funders and stakeholders. The researcher needs to be included in every discussion of program ideas, funding, and how to ensure potential clients want to be involved once the program is running.

Far from this role being given to a newly hired staff member in the office, the researcher needs to be known to other team members and supported as being vital to the effort. This is due to the necessity of everyone feeling comfortable reaching out for both general and specific bits of information, as needed. By having previous experience on a program development team, the researcher better understands the needs of the team members. Having prior knowledge of the substantive area allows them to understand ideas and input more quickly and thoroughly than someone new to the process, topic, and larger context. Oral and written communication skills should be high, especially when translating information to actionable steps that program staff can complete when the program is implemented.

Fundraiser or Grantwriter

Being a fundraiser or grantwriter is one of the more clearly understood roles in nonprofit organizations. It does not apply as much in government agencies as it does in nonprofit organizations, because funding for government agencies is allocated through a legislative process. In this case, the grantwriter role may shift to a role of supporting the education and influencing of legislators or members of the agency's executive cadre. Within nonprofit organizations, grantwriters who can consistently develop proposals that are funded are prized for the good they achieve for their organization's clients.

The skills of fundraising (as opposed to grantwriting) may turn more to individual donors to support programs than to writing grants, but individual donors can frequently donate large sums to initiate a program. This role is perhaps the most easily separated in concept (bring in money), but the tasks to do so overlap with other roles. The major reason for this is because money comes to the organization to create programs and accomplish changes in the world, not just to come to the agency and be held. Even the most isolated grantwriter, working away in a basement office, needs to leave the agency's boundaries to understand, feel, see, and be comfortable in the community being served.

Program Developer (PD)

Before reading about all the different roles described in this section of the chapter, you might have thought there was only one role: program developer (or planner). As you can see, however, much more goes on (in terms of roles and skills) that sets up a successful program design outcome.

The PD's roles and skills range widely. This role is responsible for connecting community needs to appropriate program ideas, particularly ideas that have a solid evidence base for efficacy with the population in question. As part of that skill, the PDs must understand human behavior in a social environment, applying theory and knowledge derived from psychology, sociology, social work, political science, public administration, and many other fields. Using the discipline of design thinking (see Box 2.3) and understanding organization dynamics help in thinking of client flow from intake to program completion. Whenever possible, the program should assist the transition from client to former client and successful graduate who is part of the larger community, so the program developer must be able to walk in the potential program services recipients' shoes.

BOX 2.3	**What Is Design Thinking?**

In recent years, people studying innovation have come to see that having a clear process in mind can lead to better solutions even while reducing risks of innovation failure or disappointment. Dubbed "design thinking," the tenets are relatively few and easy to comprehend, even if practice is required to use them well. Perhaps the most important element is to ask more interesting questions to get to superior solutions (Liedtka, 2018). The key word is "interesting." By "interesting," we mean that the question should lead to an answer that was not known before or is not the result of a quick internet search. When designing a program, for example, a less interesting question might be "How do we reduce teen pregnancy?" This question all too often devolves into a policy debate over different varieties of sex education and delayed sexual onset. A more interesting question would get beyond this, to the point of focusing on the lives we want for the teens and they want for themselves. This approach incorporates two vital aspects of design thinking: employing user-driven criteria and incorporating diverse voices.

Antionette Carrol has partially rejected traditional design thinking as being too exclusionary and siloed. She prefers the term "creative problem solving" to "design thinking." After adapting her ideas and applying them within the city of St. Louis after the shooting death of Michael Brown by police, two principles emerged in her work as a social justice advocate and director of Creative Reaction Lab: "act fast—then keep iterating" and "approaches, not solutions" (Miller, 2017).

As your knowledge of program design increases, you may find a deeper dive into the processes of design thinking leads to more successful programs with these elements in place.

Program Evaluator

Habit 2 from Steven Covey's (1989) book *The 7 Habits of Highly Effective People* is "Begin with the end in mind." This advice directs the reader to have a goal, a purpose, or a destination in mind before starting out. The use of a program evaluator at the beginning of the program design process keeps the team focused on what the purpose of the program is at least as much as what the activities of the program are. Evaluators called in after a program is designed to create an evaluation plan frequently find many problems that may jeopardize the ability of the program to either work at all in assisting clients or hamper effective outcome achievement.

Program designers usually look at clients' initiation into the program and work toward their successful exit. Evaluators often are excellent at looking at the goals achieved (the program exit) and working their way back to the clients' start. These two roles may come up with the same plan in the end, but the processes are different enough as to frequently show potential gaps, misunderstandings, and problems that can be ironed out before submission.

Evaluation plans for the new program must be created before the program begins.

While many program evaluation consultants can be found in academic institutions, a host of private consulting firms offer similar services. For a program design team, however, it may be best to have someone in-house with sufficient skills to get the basic plan written and approved. A person like this is more likely to understand the context of the evaluation and the other people on the team than a person from the outside, regardless of academic qualifications. Sometimes, though, for complex programs, only a true expert will do.

Outside Stakeholder (OS)

An outside stakeholder is anyone not employed by the organization but who is nonetheless interested in working toward the same goals and mission. These range from the people who might be most interested in being clients of the program itself to those who are community leaders willing to commit to the ideas being developed. These stakeholders are essential for employing design thinking strategies (see Box 2.3) of asking better questions by incorporating user-driven criteria and ensuring diverse voices.

Organization leaders must cultivate appropriate outside stakeholders on a continuing basis in order to make the relationship mutually beneficial. Staff and community members are all busy, and trying to get information and support for a program development effort after having had no contact for a substantial time is not going to work well in the long run.

 ## SPOTLIGHT ON DIVERSITY

Planning programs can at times seem to be an intellectual exercise, bringing together best practices, evidence-based programs, and a great number of details that fit into the organization's and funder's ideas of what is needed to address particular issues. All of this is true, but it misses the most basic aspect of the process. Programs are embedded in communities and organizations for the purpose of solving problems. As noted at the start of this chapter, the reason we develop programs is that people are in need: Physical, mental, and social aspects of their being are not being addressed sufficiently. To be able to plan how to alleviate these individual and community ills is a noble calling, even in the midst of all the details that must be kept straight!

The old data analysis admonition of GIGO (garbage in, garbage out) applies here. If your data have been poorly conceptualized, inadequately collected, and improperly coded, whatever results you arrive at are not going to be useful for accomplishing what you hoped to achieve. Applying this to program planning and diversity, we cannot emphasize enough the vital nature of having a variety of voices in the process.

Far too often the racial, ethnic, and cultural aspects of the eventual client population are not well known to the people doing the planning. This means that a mismatch between what is proposed and what will be successful is almost inevitable or will depend on the ability of front-line program staff to bridge the divide. An example is the teaching of sex education in schools. In some areas of the United States, a strong cultural aspect is a Christian faith that equates teen sex with moral failure. These communities frequently do not want their children learning in school anything other than to practice abstinence from sex. Research shows that abstinence-only sex education is not as effective as more comprehensive approaches. No matter whether the approach is better from an evidence-based perspective, a program that does not have parental approval will lead to many children not attending classes where more effective techniques are taught. This is one type of diversity that cannot be ignored. Similar sorts of mismatches can occur due to racial and ethnic groups' ideas about proper behavior and relationships between program staff and program participants. This is the sort of information that comes best from outside stakeholders. Hiring staff members from the potential client population also helps, but this may come too late if staff are not hired until funding is in hand.

Program planners can run into problems with diversity by clustering groups of nonhomogenous people into one category. Black people have many different viewpoints; Latinx populations are from different countries and heritages and have different preferences from each other. Asian Americans and Pacific Islanders are also considerably different culturally. Yet these differences are often invisible to people from other groups. When program planners are from the majority culture, the problems may be exacerbated—not intentionally but from a lack of education and cultural humility. Not understanding one's own possible ageism, ableism, prejudice against some sexual identities, and a host of other characteristics are also problems when designing programs for members of the public or specific subgroups. It is impossible to become culturally competent in all these ways, but to not attempt to do so can lead to failures in addressing important issues. An alternative that has been developed is to focus on increasing one's cultural humility.

Writing in the *Journal of Professional Nursing*, Hughes et al. (2020) promote the idea that nurses should seek to increase their level of cultural humility. We believe that the same goal should be adopted by those involved in program planning and design, no matter the field of practice. Arguing that **cultural humility** is "a lifelong process of self-reflection" that "allows an individual to be open to other people's identities" (p. 28), Hughes et al. (2020) propose several suggestions for nurses to increase their cultural humility. These ideas have wide applicability for program planners as well, whatever their professional background (Hughes et al., 2020, p. 31):

- Professional education (formal and post-degree) should include material regarding what cultural humility is and why it is important. Practical exercises and role-plays to increase learner understanding should be incorporated into the educational efforts.
- Learners should increase their cultural fluidity (the ease of movement in the space between their own culture and others' cultures). Fluidity should exist at intrapersonal, interpersonal, and systemic levels.
- System-level cultural humility requires critical assessment of the institution's current practices and culture; mission and vision statements, training curriculum, and continuous evaluation of efforts and progress are aspects of the development of cultural humility into the organization.

Is Your Organization Ready to Go Further to Ensure Equity in Developing Programs? An Antiracist Intersectional Approach

Inspired by contemporary debates and movements, such as Black Lives Matters, many agencies have adopted a larger vision for their program efforts and, indeed, their entire organization. One approach is to conduct a deep self-assessment of the ways they and their staff engage in racist practices. Given the prevalence of institutional racism in the United States, it is safe to say that no organization, even those in human services, is immune to contributing to current problems. Using an antiracism intersectional framework, for example, is an approach that requires considerable effort but yields significant results. If done well, the commitment will change all aspects of organizational life.

An example of an organization that has embarked on the journey to improve is the Center for the Study of Social Policy (CSSP, 2020):

> CSSP uses an anti-racist intersectional frame to ensure that all our work grapples with oppression and power. The frame is a conceptual tool that we use to examine the power held by institutions and systems as well as the oppression that Black, Indigenous, and people of color (BIPOC) face. The frame also provides a guiding approach for working with and in communities to create a more just and equitable society. (p. 1)

Scholars are exploring what an **antiracist intersectional approach** would look like even in extremely large government and nonprofit agencies, such as child welfare systems (Dettlaff & Boyd, 2021). This topic is only briefly touched upon here, but we hope it will open up conversations for readers wanting to make significant modifications within their practice and their organizations.

DIFFICULTIES AND JOYS

This chapter—an overview of what program planning and design is, what the process is, and what the roles and skills needed on the team are—provides strong clues as to what the difficulties and joys of working in the field are.

The first difficulty is simply that program design is not easy: The tasks associated with developing a program that has a reasonable chance of positively changing the world are many, the details daunting, and the effort intense.

Another difficulty, as shown by all the necessary roles shown in Table 2.1, is that working with others is necessary but not always enjoyable. With any important project (and designing a program is an important project!), opinions may be strong and discussions may become heated over appropriate strategies and ideas. We have learned that such conflict often leads to better proposals and encourages working through disagreements. If that is not possible, turn to the person in the final-decision-maker role to resolve things and then move forward.

The final difficulty to touch on is the fact that your program proposals will frequently be turned down, either by higher-ups in your own organization or by funders. Rejection hurts. As you receive the rejection notice, you may want to crumple the letter and burn it (or do the email equivalent). This would be a mistake—perfectly natural, but still a mistake. Many potential funders provide a useful critique of what they see as the plusses and minuses of what they read. If you have access to this feedback, be sure to study it carefully for information regarding how to improve. With effort and practice the percent of rejections will decrease and the joys of being successful will become more apparent and emerge more often.

The joys of program development can be so strong as to make the foregoing difficulties seem unimportant, over the long term.

The ultimate joy is in the creation and implementation processes—bringing together strong ideas in a persuasive document that is implemented and results in life-changing programs for the service recipients is priceless.

Working with likeminded others within and outside of your organization brings a special joy as well—the joy of engaging in an effort larger than oneself for a worthwhile purpose. Becoming more culturally humble lets you experience more authentic relationships with people you might not otherwise have the opportunity to learn from.

Finally, an often-overlooked joy of program planning is that you become better at it yourself and can speed the growth and knowledge of those you work with. You are probably not directly working with service recipients later in your career, but you certainly can become a mentor to staff people you work with. In this way your wisdom and skills are passed on to those working far into the future.

LESSONS FROM THE PANDEMIC

The mad scramble to react to the vicious COVID-19 virus left the world of program design searching for new approaches. One of the most pressing issues was how to continue designing and providing programs to assist client populations. Many service recipients were among the hardest hit in terms of job loss, possible evictions from rental units, and contracting the illness.

Workers in both nonprofit and government positions had to switch to working from home. Access to files and other important information had to come quickly and securely even when not being at the office.

Flexibility becomes key in crisis situations.

Technical solutions are not necessarily possible in the short run. Some barriers included:

- Security of client and program records was spotty in many cases.
- Employees do not always have a full array of hardware with appropriate software they can take home, nor is internet access always assured.
- Working from home, particularly if children are present, poses extra burdens on caretakers, who more often than not are women. This makes a tough situation even more difficult.

An important lesson from the pandemic is that, when creating "disaster" plans, greater attention to disruptive events, even very unlikely ones, should be prioritized and updated regularly in every human services organization. Many agencies and organizations had very limited ideas regarding how to have a massive shift from the office to home.

Program designers should keep two principles in mind as they continue their work, according to Bennett et al. (2020): Keep equity at the forefront, and remain flexible and open to change. These two principles lead to other design considerations.

Think Critically About the Use of Technology

Technology knowledge and use is not equitably spread throughout society. While designers may be able to work on laptops at home with good internet connections, service recipients may be relying on spotty connections or using a cell phone to access information they need to participate. People in rural areas may have no internet access at all. Thus, technology must be relied on for services access only to the extent it is equitable to do so.

Adopt Flexible Programming Models

Participation at required attendance times may be impossible to enforce when uncertainty and job loss by service participants is widespread. Service providers should adopt asynchronous teaching models when possible to allow for the most flexibility to consume required materials. Short videos with key information edited from a longer session are preferable to one or two longer (and nonedited) videos. Transcripts and video captions should be provided for everyone, not only persons with hearing issues, for example.

Support Program Staff

In the same way that program recipients need flexibility and support to learn new ways of learning, program staff are under a great deal of pressure to relearn their work duties and also take care of pressing issues in their own lives. They need to have the proper resources and tools to do their work.

While the COVID vaccine distribution has brought a sense of relief to many program designers and organizational leaders, the changes experienced in 2020–2021 will not quickly disappear. Remote work and the need to remain flexible in the pursuit of social equity and justice remain.

CONCLUSION

We have covered a lot of territory in this chapter. The main point is to provide a clear map of the process of developing a program. It may still feel quite abstract, but that is natural at this point. The rest of the book brings forth greater detail, and the exercises in each chapter provide the opportunity to explore in a more real way what the chapter includes. We invite you to work on your own, with your colleagues, and with your instructor to flesh out the necessarily limited amount of information that we share. Your efforts will deepen and speed your learning.

 ## SUMMARY/KEY POINTS

- Human service organizations, where many programs designers work, are distributed across the three sectors of the economy: public (government), nonprofit, and for-profit. The clear demarcations between these sectors have become blurry, and increased efforts across sector lines is occurring.
- The entire process can be conceptualized as having four stages with a number of steps in each stage. It begins with Stage 1, understanding context, and has information on conducting advocacy and knowing the community.
- It continues to Stage 2, finding funding and planning program, and has three steps: finding funding, planning program and receiving program funds.
- Stage 3, implementing and evaluating program, is where the heart of the process is—providing services to the intended recipients.
- Two steps are in Stage 3: implementing the program and conducing process and outcome evaluation.
- Stage 4 is reporting and adapting program. The funder will want to know how well you have done with the funding and what you have achieved. This is true whether the resources come from within or outside of your organization. Thus, you must write and disseminate reports. While there is an accountability portion to this step, information can also be used to inform other stakeholders about the program's impact and other aspects of your agency. Information compiled with marketing in mind can be used in advocacy and other efforts to influence future funding opportunities.
- Based on evaluation results, the steps in Stage 4 include adapting the program as needed.
- A considerable amount of effort goes into every program design effort. Many roles must be filled to be successful, even if many roles are played by one person. Being familiar with the full gamut of roles and skills needed helps in the planning process.
- Efforts to reduce structural inequities within any program-design effort should be encouraged. Cultural humility and the use of an antiracist intersectional framework are suggested as potential steps in that direction.

KEY TERMS

Antiracist intersectional approach: While many different approaches exist and all are complex and layered, one approach is described by the Center for Social Policy Research (2020) as being a critique of "society's structure and its treatment of people and communities while providing a guiding approach for how to work towards a more just and equitable society" (p. 2).

Cultural humility: "A lifelong process of self-reflection" that "allows an individual to be open to other people's identities" (Hughes et al., 2020, p. 28).

Design parameters: Attributes of the design process that have a large impact on the finished product (program design). Three traditional ones are speed, cost, and quality.

Program: A program is "a major ongoing agency activity or service with its own set of goals, objectives, policies, and budgets that produces a defined product or service" (Martin, 2021, p. 9).

Program design: A process of showing how to achieve desired outcomes through creating or amending a program.

Program development: A process of showing how to achieve desired outcomes through creating or amending a program.

Program development roles and skills: A set of skills required to perform the tasks of design or development.

Program manager: In Martin's (2021) view, someone who spends at least some work time formally managing both the programmatic and the financial aspects of a program.

ADDITIONAL RESOURCES

Gathering Information (Research)

Faulkner, S., & Faulkner, C. (2019). *Research methods for social workers: A practice-based approach*. Oxford University Press.

Sustainability

Charity Navigator. (2020, November 20). *The future of giving and nonprofit sustainability: The role of impact and data*. [Video]. YouTube. https://www.youtube.com/watch?v=e4fK7kbS_ks

Nonprofit Quarterly. (2014, November 25). *The sustainability mindset* [Video]. YouTube. https://www.youtube.com/watch?v=cG_ya7xvQO4

DISCUSSION QUESTIONS

1. Looking over the steps of the program design process (Figure 2.1), where do you envision you will have the most joy as you design a program? Where might you find yourself struggling some?
2. Knowing all the roles of the process (review Table 2.1), where do you feel your current talents would be best suited? How do you envision that you could improve on your current skills for that type of work?
3. Having the overview as shown in this chapter regarding both the steps in the process and the required roles, are you feeling more drawn to the topic? Why, or why not?

 YOUR TURN

1. Review the material regarding your appointment as the executive director/CEO of Cornerstone Family Services, particularly the fact sheet and the organization chart. Using what you have learned in this chapter, who would you put onto a program planning team and in what roles? Who is missing from the organizational chart that you would want to include? NOTE: You do not need to use everyone on the executive team for this exercise, but be sure to have a good reason for including the people you select and your assignment to one or more roles. Discuss with one or more colleagues. Who did they choose, and why?
2. Do a self-assessment of your own skillset. At this point, where do you see your strengths and areas of needed growth for working in the field of program planning? If you were pitching yourself for one or more of the roles shown in Table 2.1, which would they be? What skills are you ready to use at this time? Which role would be the worst one for you to take on now, in your view? Why, and what are the steps you might take to overcome your weaknesses in relationship to the required roles for program design efforts?

REFERENCES

American Public Human Services Association. (n.d.). *What is human services?* https://www.nationalhumanservices.org/what-is-human-services#:~:text=The%20field%20of%20Human%20Services,of%20life%20of%20service%20populations

Bennett, V., McDonnell, R., Lee, S., & Ostrye, M. (2020). *Redesigning training programs for the COVID era and beyond*. JFF. https://jfforg-prod-new.s3.amazonaws.com/media/documents/CTA-Framework.pdf

Center for the Study of Social Policy. (2020). *Using an anti-racist intersectional frame at CSSP*. https://cssp.org/wp-content/uploads/2019/09/Antiracist-Intersectional-Frame.pdf

Covey, S. (1989). *The seven habits of highly effective people*. Free Press.

Hughes, V., Delva, S., Nkimbeng, M., Spaulding, E., Turkso-Ocran, R., Cudjoe, J., Ford, A., Rushton, C., D'Aoust, R., & Han, H.-R. (2020). Not missing the opportunity: Strategies to promote cultural humility among future nursing faculty. *Journal of Professional Nursing*, *36*, 28–33.

Kettner, P., Morony, R., & Martin, L. (2017). *Designing and managing programs: An effectiveness-based approach* (5th ed.). Sage Press.

Liedtka, J. (2018). Why design thinking works: It addresses the biases and behaviors that hamper innovation. *Harvard Business Review*. https://hbr.org/2018/09/why-design-thinking-works

Lynch, T., Sun, J., & Smith, R. (2017). *Public budgeting in America* (6th ed.). Melvin & Leigh.

Martin, L. (2021). *Financial management for human service administrators* (2nd ed.). Waveland Press.

United States Department of Health and Human Services. (n.d.). *Programs and services*. https://www.hhs.gov/programs/index.html

Weinbach, R., & Taylor, L. (2017). *The social worker as manager: A practical guide to success* (7th ed.). Pearson.

Figure Credits

CHAPTER THREE

Advocacy as the Foundation for Program Development

OVERVIEW

In this chapter we look at what advocacy is, why advocacy is important for creating and designing programs, theoretical perspectives that help support an advocacy-informed approach to program development, the three different approaches to advocacy, and the steps you take when conducting advocacy.

By the end of the chapter, you will know the importance of advocacy when engaging in the program design process. You will also know how to conduct effective advocacy to acquire resources to fund programs to help solve community needs.

We start this chapter with a question: Why do some problems get paid attention to, find new funding opportunities, and have programs designed and implemented to fix them while other problems continue to occur unnoted or unchecked? We believe that one of the most important underlying answers to this is that for some issues, some organizational leaders understand how to conduct effective advocacy efforts to draw attention to situations that they believe need changing. These savvy leaders know how to focus the spotlight on a particular social ill in their community and then to build support for funding and other resources that address the problem.

WHAT IS ADVOCACY?

People who understand the importance of policy decisions for the creation of programs, who work to change policy and programs, and who seek to alter decisions about allocations of resources are advocates. The work they do is advocacy. Advocacy can mean many things. Schneider and Lester (2001) catalogued over a dozen separate definitions. In this chapter, we use the word **advocacy** to mean "a process of education, persuasion, and/or negotiation to achieve the goal of acquiring resources (of all kinds) to allow the creation of programs addressing specific social issues." Advocacy can be targeted at legislators and their personal and committee staff members, people working in the executive branch of any level of government, regulators, businesses, nonprofits, other organizations, and even within one's own organization. The key element of correctly choosing an **advocacy target** is that their decisions can impact the distribution of resources to your organization or program ideas.

This chapter explores the world of advocacy with an eye to helping you become better at the processes involved in order to solve problems for your community, state, or country. Issues in our communities need remedies put forward by dedicated and savvy people who understand linking problems with solutions and getting the resources needed to implement change. This chapter will help you become such a person.

Why Include Advocacy in a Book on Program Development?

When it comes to describing the program development process, it is rare that advocacy is mentioned, much less the subject of an entire chapter, so you may wonder why it is included in this book. One of our principle tenets is that programs never exist in a vacuum. Programs are developed in a social context that promotes or dampens thinking about particular social issues and whether these topics are "worth" addressing.

In an ambitious examination of the role of nonprofit organizations in the United States nearly 50 years ago, the Commission on Private Philanthropy and Public Needs (1975; also known as the Filer Commission) stated, "The monitoring and influencing of government may be emerging as one of the single most important and effective functions of the private nonprofit sector" (p. 45).

This statement from decades ago has not come entirely true, partially because nonprofit leaders have not been taught a systematic approach to advocacy that fits in with other skills they have had the opportunity to develop. Program developers, in general, may not have thought these skills were needed in their work. In addition, public support for expanding human services changed over this same time, bringing governmental **load shedding** (i.e., governments declaring they are not responsible for solving certain

Image 3.1

Successful advocacy for new program ideas and funding involves bringing together many stakeholders.

problems), **decentralization of programmatic responsibility** (i.e., if government remains responsible, it should be done at state and local levels), and shifts towards **privatization of service provision** (i.e., human services should be provided by nonprofits and businesses). Somewhat paradoxically, advocacy remains an important function of every entity that wants to develop and provide human service programs *because* governments are trying to abdicate responsibility for them.

Many argue that in order to have programs, funding must be secured. Ruggiano and Taliaferro (2012), for example, argue that lobbying is important for nonprofits to gain the resources they need to serve the public good. This happens both for tangible (e.g., cash and favorable legislative/regulatory interventions) and intangible (e.g., awareness, connections, goodwill) resources.

Hwang and Suarez (2019) note that, in their study of San Francisco–area nonprofits, more than half of their respondent service providers provide both advocacy and services.

Policy Entrepreneurs

Another term for policy or program advocates that is sometimes used is **policy entrepreneur**. This expression is associated with John Kingdon's classic 1984 book *Agendas, Alternatives, and Public Policies*. Kingdon chose these words because policy entrepreneurs, like people who start businesses, have a "willingness to invest their resources—time, energy, reputation, and sometimes money—in the hope of a future return" (Kingdon, 1984/2011, p. 122). Policy entrepreneurs can be considered to be advocates because they are seeking to alter government policy and expenditures through education, persuasion, and negotiation. The reward to the policy entrepreneur is policy adoption and implementation, increased reputation, and possibly higher income. None of these outcomes is assured, however. It is easy to see how the roles of advocate and policy entrepreneur overlap considerably. Looking at Box 3.1, we see the skills of a policy entrepreneur seem to be the same as a policy advocate.

BOX 3.1	**Required Skills of Policy Entrepreneurs**

According to Mintrom (2019), policy entrepreneurs should seek to become skilled in these seven areas:

- Thinking strategically: Policy entrepreneurs need the ability to "choose a particular goal and then determine the set of actions they will need to take and the resources they will require to pursue that goal."
- Building teams: Getting along well with others and being widely connected are associated with greater levels of success because policy entrepreneurs can then better "understand the ideas, motives, and concerns of the people whose support they must garner."
- Collecting Evidence: "The art of evidence collection is to establish a rigorous, defensible base of data to support a given position and to present it and discuss it in ways that most effectively draw others to the cause."
- Making arguments: It is not enough to have evidence. Policy entrepreneurs need to put the information they have together in a way to "both build support for a policy innovation and to diminish opposition to change. When gaps in evidence and data serve to weaken a preferred position, it is incumbent on the policy entrepreneur to consider ways that new evidence or data can be found."
- Engaging multiple audiences: Policy entrepreneurs "need to tell the same story in different ways. Doing so means emphasizing different points to different audiences while maintaining a consistent broader message."
- Negotiating: New ideas disrupt the status quo and upset those who benefit from the way things currently are. For policy entrepreneurs, "the key is to look for ways to make positive impacts salient and find ways to reduce negative impacts or mitigate them by offering additional benefits that tend to compensate for any losses."
- Networking: Due to the need for access to information (substantive and contextual), policy entrepreneurs "seeking to have influence in policymaking must develop excellent awareness of the nature of the policy networks operating around them and determine effective ways to participate in them."

Source: Adapted from Mintrom (2019).

With basic information about advocacy, advocates, and policy entrepreneurs in mind, we now turn to theories that help us understand the larger context of program development and advocacy more clearly. We focus on resource dependence theory, the political economy perspective, and the population ecology model first to explain ideas in how resources from the environment come to support policy innovations. Then we look closely at Kingdon's multiple streams model and the role of policy entrepreneurs in obtaining resources that can be turned into programs to solve issues in the community for their organizations. The question we want to answer is, how do organizations obtain resources to keep going and to create programs for clients?

THEORETICAL PERSPECTIVES ON HOW ORGANIZATIONS OBTAIN RESOURCES

For organizations to create and sustain programs, they must obtain resources. Three theories are particularly useful to understand how skilled advocacy by program planners and other organizational leaders helps achieve organizational and program survival: resource dependence theory, the political economy perspective, and the population ecology model. In addition to these, we examine a theory that explains how policy decisions are made—the multiple streams model. You will also learn about policy entrepreneurs. We make the case that program designers and organizational leaders must take on the role of policy entrepreneur (or advocate) in order to acquire resources to address problems and concerns in their communities.

Resource Dependence Theory

Most organizations are dependent on material resources that are controlled by others in the external environment. **Resource dependence theory** posits that the greater any organization's dependence is on resources controlled by another entity, the more dependent it is on that other body and the stronger is the influence of external interests on processes within the organization (Schmid, 2000). The theory assumes that organizations and their leaders prefer to be more independent than more dependent and so will exert effort to be as independent as possible, knowing that some dependence and interdependence cannot be avoided.

Resource dependence theory also argues that when dependence is noted, an organization may work to decrease reliance on a supplier (particularly a single supplier) of the resource by building up reserves of the resource (a strategy called **buffering**) or adopting various **bridging** strategies, such as finding alternative source(s) of the same resource, using another production approach that reduces the need for that resource, or changing or restructuring to supply the resource itself. Of course, some combination of these approaches may be tried. For example, in order to reduce the reliance on government funding, a human services organization may seek foundation grants (reduce dependence), reduce spending on a program (reduce need for resource), or charge fees to clients when the services were previously free (create self-reliance).

Political Economy Perspective

This perspective shares the idea of the importance of the larger organizational environment for understanding how organizations act, explicitly recognizing the context within which any single human services organization operates. The **political economy perspective** states that for organizations to survive and to produce services, they must secure legitimacy and power, as well as production or economic resources. From this perspective, *political economy* refers to a system of distribution not only of resources but also of status, prestige, power, legitimacy, and related social amenities. The political economy perspective views the organization as a collectivity that has multiple and complex goals, paramount among them being survival and adaptation to the environment (Hasenfeld, 2000). The capacity of the organization to survive and to provide services depends on its ability to mobilize power, legitimacy, and economic resources—for instance, money, personnel, and clients (Wamsley & Zald, 1976).

Thus, leaders must manage the environment of the organization at least as well as the internal impacts of the organization itself to ensure an adequate supply of resources. Managing the environment may be even more important than managing the organization (Aldrich & Pfeffer, 1976). Pfeffer (1992) notes that changes in the external and internal political economies result in changes within the organization. Internal power relations shape internal structure and resource allocation.

We believe skillful use of advocacy techniques is essential in ensuring survival of individual programs and also the organization itself. In the past few decades, the number of nonprofits has grown quickly and the competition for a limited amount of resources has intensified. Resource dependence theory and the political economy perspective provide ideas for how to sustain organizations, especially when combined with the concepts of advocacy and policy entrepreneurs.

Population Ecology Model

Population ecology views the organization within the context of the community of organizations and services. In this view, dynamics of the founding and survival of organizations—that is, the founding and failure of organizations—are explained by population dynamics and density dependence. Population dynamics is seen as a factor in stimulating the founding of new organizations. For example, if there is an identified community need and there is the perception that there are resources to meet this need, then chances are that groups will work to develop a new organization or service to meet this need. Conversely, as new organizations or services are founded, then there is a perception of competition, and therefore, the creation of new programs or organizations is discouraged. The concept of density dependence means that an increase in the density of organizations or services signals legitimacy of the services being provided and that resources are available for such services. In this view, the administrator must employ macro strategies to position the organization within the larger community of organizations and services and recognize that environmental forces set limits on the success of administrative practice (Hasenfeld, 2000).

AGENDA SETTING AND POLICY-PROCESS THEORIES

It is not enough to say that advocacy is necessary for organizations to extract from their environments enough resources to sustain themselves. We must also examine how organizational leaders can use policy-process theory to understand *when* the best times are to advocate for resources and *how* to do so. The multiple streams model provides clues about agenda setting in the policy process. Understanding agenda setting is important for planners and agency leaders when they work to obtain resources from the environment. Advocating at "a bad time" can completely stymie efforts.

Kingdon's Multiple Streams Model (MSM)

Considerable political science literature addresses the topic of agenda setting. In this chapter we build on that research knowledge as well as resource dependence theory to create a case for the value of understanding advocacy as an essential skill for program developers and organizational leaders.

Developed by John Kingdon in 1984 (with a major update in 2010), the multiple streams model (MSM) is a well-respected approach for analyzing policymaking across a variety of policies and countries. Kingdon (2010) argues that many different possible solutions exist to any policy problem. The most important question addressed in the MSM is why one solution is selected over the others.

The MSM makes three important assumptions. The first is that ambiguity in problem definition prevents simple rationality from being useful in understanding policy outcomes. Different actors define the same situation differently, so goal maximization (a vital element of the rational approach to policy selection) is not useful. Let's take homelessness as an example: Is it a problem caused by a lack of affordable housing, a lack of individual morality, or simply an effect of poverty? Each approach has its adherents but choosing one definition over the others prevents finding common ground.

A second assumption of the multiple streams model is that time and other resources are limited. Individual decision makers have only so much time and capacity to tackle problems, whereas the world seems to be full of almost unlimited problems that might be addressed.

According to the MSM, decision makers may have shifting preferences for policy over time. Preferences can change based on current (limited) information that is superseded with new information or because the time frame for deciding changes. Emergencies need to be dealt with immediately with whatever ideas and information are currently available. In addition, decision makers often have little or no information on whether a proposed policy idea will actually help solve the problem at hand. This is called having *unclear technology*. On top of this, fluid participation in the decision-making process means that new ideas or barriers can be introduced as different institutions and people are involved. Thus, a seeming consensus can fall apart or emerge at the last moment before a definitive decision is made.

The final assumption in the MSM is that independent processes occur when policy decisions are made. Thus, **policy problems** (like the one the program planner wants to solve), **policy solutions**, and **political conditions** shift constantly and without clear linkages to the others. These are the streams in the multiple streams framework. Let's look at each of the streams and add a few additional concepts that are also part of the MSM.

Policy Problems Stream

In the MSM, situations are not, in an objective sense, problems. Situations must be defined as problems before political action will be taken. But this is not a sure outcome; in fact, some policy actors may reject that the issue needs to be discussed (put on the agenda) at all—others who want the situation "handled" may look at the same objective situation but define the "problem" quite differently.

Kingdon (2010) indicates that problem definitions are ambiguous and contested. Generally, each view of what the problem is has champions who may be called "problem entrepreneurs." These people want decision makers (often government bodies and officials) to pay attention and do something about the problem as they define it, but they may not necessarily have a particular preferred way to solve the problem in mind.

Problem definitions can result from the slow development of information over time or sudden focusing events, such as a stock market crash, a sudden worsening in the situation, a terrorist attack, or a natural disaster. At this point, the problem is put on the agenda for definition and action. Kingdon (2010) characterizes whatever becomes the accepted definition of the problem as a situation searching for a solution.

Program designers working in agencies may face similar situations in terms of getting a situation defined as a problem that needs to be addressed, so it is vital they understand the importance of problem definition. Program personnel know that negative situations exist, and they want to make life better for people in their community. They must first, however, convince decision makers in their own organization to allow them time to research the problem and to develop information to support the extent of the need in the community and develop a solution that might work, if funded appropriately. Until the topic is placed on the agenda for decisions to be made, no changes should be expected.

BOX 3.2	**Defining the Problem Example: Why Won't People Work for $7.50 Per Hour? Unemployment Benefits Too Generous or Wages Offered Too Low?**

Let us look at just one topic to illustrate the problem stream. Every month a report is issued by the federal government describing the number of people filing for unemployment benefits for the first time. The number of people who are unemployed that month varies; sometimes it is higher and sometimes it is lower.

A large number of people receiving unemployment benefits is not inherently a problem; it is a situation and might be considered a successful policy outcome because when jobs are lost, the number of people receiving this income support is *supposed* to increase. In April 2020, during the initial traumatic experiences of COVID-19 layoffs and shutdowns, unemployment was the worst in the United States since the Great Depression of the 1930s, peaking at 14.8%. Months later, in December 2020, the level of unemployment was much lower but still high, compared to usual figures (Congressional Research Service, 2021). Unemployed people were still eligible to receive benefits for a longer amount of time and at a higher level of benefits due to emergency legislation. The policy seemed to be working well.

In early summer 2021, however, some restaurants and other businesses were having trouble recruiting enough workers to fully staff their operations. The owners claimed unemployment benefits were too generous and people would rather stay home collecting "free money" than work. Workers and their supporters argued that the problem was not with them; rather, it was that the business owners were not willing to pay a living wage. Who is "right" in their definition of the problem, if there is indeed a problem to start with?

The MSM highlights the ambiguous and political nature of defining problems. Whichever side of the argument wins the battle to define the nature of the problem (a process called "framing") will likely be able to see its preferred solution be adopted.

Policy Solutions Stream

Just as problem entrepreneurs push for decision makers to take action on particular definitions of situations as problems, policy solutions entrepreneurs have a solution that they believe is useful in many situations. The ideas of free markets and deregulation are two "solutions" that have been advocated in many arenas from the airline industry to voucher schools. If you think of any situation you define as a problem, it is likely that someone is advocating for the use of the free market as a way to solve that problem. Often, policy entrepreneurs have an ideological focus. Thus, their decision-making process does not need to rely on research or pilot tests of the concepts. Researchers note that not all policy ideas have equal chances of being accepted (Kingdon, 2010). Some are beyond the limits of acceptable policy in any given context, others lack feasibility, and some are just seen as too expensive. For policy proposals that pass the initial filters, though, the MSM characterizes them as solutions looking for a problem to solve.

For some program designers in agencies, we see an analogous dynamic. A person can come back from a conference having heard of a new approach that then "must" be tried out in the next grant proposal. Management fads, such as total quality management, come and go (Madsen, 2020), although some concepts, such as evidence-based practice, become institutionalized (Charleton & Miles, 1998). People in this situation become proselytizers of the ideas and may succeed in getting some efforts adopted by their organization.

Political Stream

The political stream is perhaps the most difficult stream to explain. It is a combination of the mood around the policy arena, the people active in the decision making, and the various groups that have an interest in the policy or program topic. What the term "political stream" refers to is the level of openness to change and willingness to take action that exists within decision makers and other policy actors. When the political stream is "ready," then it is more likely that a problem and a solution will be connected, and an authoritative decision will be made.

At some point, an opportunity for action emerges where a defined problem exists, along with a solution that is acceptable. Political will exists to do something. This short period of time is called a **policy window**. Policy entrepreneurs at this point couple, or join, a problem with a policy and push to get decision makers to support this problem/policy package. If this occurs successfully (and frequently policy windows close without action being taken), then new laws are enacted, policies are adopted, or programs are created. Once the window closes, the system moves on to the next decision.

The main point to remember from this approach to explaining policymaking or program creation is that policymaking is not a rational process where clear goals are achieved through customized solutions. Rather, the process is random and depends on skilled framing and coupling of both problems and general solutions to appeal to a majority of decision makers during a brief time when action is possible.

The practical lesson for social welfare program designers is to become skillful advocates of particular problem definitions and acceptable solutions. While political conditions may be beyond anyone's control, certain situations (such as after changes in leadership, new crises emerge, or other inflection points) are more amenable to becoming windows for policy and program decisions. One must be prepared with considerable work already done. Once a particular window closes, it may be quite a long time before a similar opportunity presents itself.

STYLES OF ADVOCACY

Being prepared with a problem or a solution while waiting for the window to open is conceptually easy. You may be wondering, however, what to do in the meantime! How do policy entrepreneurs or advocates spend their time to get the political stream to come to a willingness to make a decision (hopefully one that is in line with the program ideas you want to see adopted)?

Advocacy can be seen to have three different approaches, or styles. Each style is used to reach agreement between the advocate and the decision maker. None are mutually exclusive, but each has strengths and limitations. These styles are education, persuasion, and negotiation. We cover each in turn.

Education

In clinical psychology or social work, when you want to get a client to think about changing a behavior that is a problem or potential problem, you might use the stages of change model (Prochaska et al., 1994). For example, although everyone knows that smoking is a dangerous habit, that does not necessarily mean that all smokers are thinking about quitting. So someone trying to change that person's behavior must introduce the idea of smoking cessation in a way that assists the smoker to consider stopping. The client is in what is known as the precontemplation stage, and the change agent wants to move the smoker to the next stage, called the contemplation stage, where they are actively considering a shift in thinking pattern or behavior. This requires overcoming the defenses of the client.

How is this relevant to advocacy? There is a direct correspondence to an advocate bringing a new issue to the target. It is often the case that the target you have chosen is not informed about the issue that you are passionate about. The target may not ever have thought about the topic and so is in the precontemplation stage in terms of being willing to act as you desire (such as authorizing a new program for the organization's clients). You will need to overcome the target's defenses to obtain action.

Suppose that you work for a program that matches high school students looking for volunteer opportunities to address community needs. It has become known as a place where teens work with children in grades 3–5. But you have found that fewer littles are available and some of the older students are not finding other opportunities. You have heard about an emerging situation at a local assisted living center where many of the residents are *unbefriended*, meaning they have no family member or friends who visit. You think that this might be a great way to have the teens in your program find a different population to assist, helping the teens and the residents. You think it over and think of possible objections (or defenses) that your agency director might come up with.

- Denial and minimization: "I've never heard of any other assisted living facility having this problem. It's probably the management's fault. And I'm sure it isn't that bad if the residents are still having their bills paid!"
- Rationalization: "Our mission statement says we're a youth-serving organization. Working with the elderly would mean we have to change the mission and vision."
- Projection and displacement: "This is not our problem. That's a for-profit assisted living facility. They can afford to hire people to do that work."

- Internalization: "I'm sure this is a problem for them but I just don't know what to do for them—there are probably big issues in these cases. It sounds like a huge legal minefield, and that's just too much to deal with here."

Before you can get your preferred solution adopted, you need to move your agency director from precontemplation to contemplation. Two empirically supported techniques to use in this process are consciousness-raising and social liberation (Prochaska et al., 1994).

Consciousness-Raising

Before being able to change, the precontemplator needs to realize the damage being done by current behavior or conditions. Sometimes, this is simply a matter of not having accurate information, and all a policy entrepreneur has to do is to present the information collected in earlier steps of the program development process. The information may be so compelling that the target quickly converts to wanting to take action. At other times, you must confront the defenses of denial and minimization, rationalization, projection and displacement, and internalization. If the defenses are not removed, the target may not hear the information you are presenting.

The first step in the consciousness-raising process involves building a relationship with the target. Only then can you get beyond the defensive walls blocking the information from getting through. Sometimes you already have a relationship, and this is not a problem. In some instances, you can make a connection quickly, although developing a relationship may take longer. Important aspects of the advocate role in consciousness-raising include the following:

- Do not push someone into action too soon: They may seem to comply, but they may also push back and refuse to engage in further discussion with you.
- Do not focus exclusively on one thing: Have other concerns to discuss and at least sometimes provide positive feedback on things you and your target agree on.
- Do not give up: Presenting accurate information over time, in different ways, and in different contexts can help get past defenses, as the target learns more and sees your determination.

Social Liberation

Social liberation is a process of "creating more alternatives and choices for individuals, providing more information about problem behaviors, and offering public support for people who want to change" (Prochaska et al., 1994, p. 100). Examples of successful advocacy efforts revolving around social liberation include no-smoking sections in restaurants, wheelchair accessible public facilities, and public awareness campaigns regarding drinking and driving and the dangers of using drugs. Three techniques have been identified as being helpful in using the social liberation approach:

- Ask "Who is on the target's side and who is not?" In other words, who gains and who loses if the target supports the advocacy effort? What benefits accrue to the target?
- Ask "Whose side is the target on?" Is the target on the side of the problem and/or the side that benefits from people having the problem? Or is the target on the side of people wanting to improve the situation and make the world a better place?

- Seek and welcome outside influences who already have the target's ear and who support the advocacy effort's desired outcomes.

The main objectives of education are to get the target knowledgeable about the topic and to develop a relationship if you have not yet done so. You also want to move the target from not even thinking about the topic to wanting to take action. If you are lucky, you may find your target is completely on board with what you are advocating for simply by hearing the facts from you. Other times, you may need to engage in the processes of negotiation and/or persuasion.

Persuasion

Persuasion is another approach to resolving differences between actors. In persuasion, however, one side gets what it wants and so does the other side. How is this possible? It is possible only when one side changes its mind about what it wants. When both parties now want the same thing (because one side changed its view of what it wanted), the result is a very positive outcome for everyone. To put it in personal terms, think about choosing where to eat dinner. In a negotiation, you might start off wanting to eat at a fancy, expensive restaurant, while your partner wants to eat frugally and prepare dinner at home. Perhaps in the end, you "split the difference" and eat at a moderately priced diner. Neither of you got what you wanted, but you reached an acceptable compromise. In persuasion, though, imagine that your partner reminds you that you both want to go on a cruise to the Bahamas. If you both agree to take the money that would have been spent on the expensive dinner and place it in the vacation savings account, you might decide that you did not want the fancy dinner after all. You have been persuaded and feel that you are getting what the two of you both want.

Persuasion has a great deal of scientific study that shows how best to be convincing. Although there is not enough space in this chapter to cover the topic fully, experts agree that persuaders must pay attention to four factors: the context, the message, the message sender, and the message receiver. Each factor plays a vital role in the persuasion effort.

Persuasion is a key skill in advocacy.

Context

Context is the way that the people involved in the persuasion effort (both the person doing the persuasion and the person or people being persuaded) view the situation. One of the key elements of any advocacy issue is the way it is seen. In other aspects of social work practice, practitioners sometimes talk about "reframing" a situation—that is, changing the way the situation is seen. Advocates should make every effort to have their view of the situation (their frame of reference) become adopted by the others involved because this starting point frequently leads to a more easily agreed-on solution. For example, Kingdon (1984/2010) describes the debate about transportation policy for people with disabilities as a struggle over which frame would be adopted. Is it a policy dispute about transportation (in which case the emphasis is on the most efficient and easiest to use method of getting from one place to another), or is it a struggle about civil rights for people with disabilities (in which case the emphasis is on making having a disability irrelevant to being able to move from one place to another without any more hindrances than nondisabled people)?

Different policies may ensue from the different frames used to create policy in this area. For example, in Sweden, people with disabilities were provided with vouchers to use to ride in a taxi for the same price as taking a bus. The emphasis was on quickly and easily providing transportation. Taxi transportation is usually more comfortable, pleasant, and convenient than bus travel, with door-to-door service from your home to your destination. This pragmatic approach, particularly in Sweden, where the winter weather lasts a long time, was also combined with environmental changes, such as curb cuts and crosswalk lights that made faster ticks to indicate how much time was left to cross the street.

In the United States, on the other hand, the view that was adopted aimed to make public transportation easier for people with disabilities to use, such as with wheelchair lifts, and to make curb cuts and other structural changes in the environment. This approach made everyone more equal, in that everyone used the same public transportation system. Although it is expensive to retrofit buses and make other changes, the ongoing costs are relatively low once the initial investment is made. Such environmental changes also assist others in the community who might not be labeled as "disabled" by eliminating transportation barriers for all.

If your advocacy effort does not seem to be gaining ground, you may want to try to reframe the issue to something more beneficial for your side. Popular frames for advocates of a cause include the following:

- It isn't fair (to have things this way or to make this proposed change).
- It won't work.
- It can be done in other ways.
- It costs too much.
- It will hurt the public (or clients, or some other identified group).
- It will help the public (or clients, or some other identified group).
- The benefits outweigh the costs.
- If it saves one life, it will be worth it.
- After what they've been through, they deserve it.

When you are in an advocacy situation, such as wanting to grow support for a new program, be sure to analyze what frame for the issue is best for your position. Also examine the other party's words to uncover how they see the situation. Their frame may be very different and not acceptable to you if you want to have your proposal adopted.

Message

Your message is the information that you intend to communicate to your target. According to research, six elements of the message are important in persuasion: intent, organization, sidedness, repetition and redundancy, rhetorical questions, and fear appeals (Cialdini, 2021).

Announcing your intention to persuade someone is frequently counterproductive, as the target quickly raises walls for defense. This generality is not true in two specific situations: When you merely want to ask for minor changes in a proposal that all parties basically agree on, it is best to be up-front about wanting to make small changes. Your forthrightness should put the target at ease, knowing that you do not want large changes. Also, when the target expects you to be trying to be persuasive (as when you are talking to an elected official), there is no point in acting coy. Admit what you are trying to do (which is what the target will believe you are trying to do whether you admit it or not) and press forward.

It is always better to be more organized than less. Take the time to plan what you are going to say, the order you wish to say it, and how you want to close the discussion. You may not get to deliver your message just the way you have it planned, but being organized and to the point demonstrates respect for your target and never hurts your case.

Sidedness refers to whether you should present only your viewpoint or also discuss the other side's perspective. Research indicates that presenting both sides comes across as being fairer to listeners, but for it to be effective in promoting your cause, you must not only mention the other side but also attack it. Otherwise, you merely give that other position more credence (Cialdini, 2021). Repetition (saying the same thing over and over) and redundancy (sending similar, but not identical, messages) are important in persuasion. When done well, as long as you have sufficient time to engage in both processes, you can be more persuasive. Repetition is important because people often do not tune in to your message on your first effort, and redundancy is important because people quickly grow used to hearing your arguments if they are always phrased the same way. Both principles are clearly used in advertising campaigns.

Rhetorical questions are effective, aren't they? Of course they are because they make a statement that is hidden in the guise of a question. People who are not actively listening will often accept the embedded implied information within a rhetorical question without seriously thinking about it (Cialdini, 2021).

Fear appeals are also effective—if people are scared, they tend to take action to ease their fears. An important point behind using fear appeals, however, is that you must not only scare your target into action but must also provide a feasible solution to calm the fears you have aroused.

Sender

According to communications research, no matter how well-crafted the message is, a great deal of persuasiveness is dependent upon aspects of the sender. The most important element that you should strive to create and maintain is your credibility. You must be believable to be persuasive. Credibility is composed of three aspects: *expertise* (you must know what you are talking about), *trustworthiness* (you must come across as honest and lacking bias), and *likeability* (you won't be believed if you are not liked; Cialdini, 2021). All three aspects also have details that are important, but the basic concepts behind expertise, trustworthiness, and likeability are not difficult to grasp. You must know what you are talking about, be sincere, and do your best to get along, even if you disagree with what your target supports.

Receiver

This is the final piece of the persuasion puzzle. Persuasion takes place within a relationship (even if it is a short-term relationship). You cannot be persuasive if the receiver does not choose to listen to you. So you, as the advocate, must tailor your topic's frame, your message, and even yourself (to some degree) to meet the desires of your target. Bedell (2002) argues that you must fulfill some need of the target (such as the target's need to win, to gain security, or to be accepted). You also must evaluate how much the target seems to care about the issue. Someone who does not care much will not likely pay much attention to your presentation but will probably be easier to persuade to your viewpoint. People who are not much involved with the topic are more likely to be persuaded by emotional presentations. People who are more involved and knowledgeable will only be convinced with strong arguments and a well-researched point of view (Cialdini, 2021).

This section has covered a great deal of material, skimming over a topic that has volumes of research associated with it. If you are curious about those details, you can look for the latest research on the topic by the authors listed in the references. In the end, you will see that advocates can greatly increase their chances of advocacy success with even a bit of knowledge of the best ways to persuade.

Negotiation

The process of negotiation, when done well, can be quite structured. It requires a planning process all its own, particularly involving research about what your target's current stance on the issue is, what they hope to gain from future decisions about the issue, and areas of agreement and disagreement between yourself and the target. The more research you can conduct ahead of time, the more you can build on areas of agreement and the more you can counter probable objections to your plan.

You should have a negotiation plan that includes the best possible outcome you can imagine, the worst possible outcome you can accept (your limit), and various outcomes in between these two extremes that you can accept, even though they are not as good as you would like (fallback positions). When negotiations first begin, you will present your well-thought-out initial position, working from that to come to an agreement with the target of your advocacy. A common approach to negotiation is to have the other party begin by describing its initial position. In this way, you know if you can agree to some things that you did not think you could achieve without a struggle. But the other party will be trying to get you to reveal your initial position first as well, so even this becomes part of the negotiation process.

An important point about advocacy negotiation is that advocates are often working with collaborations or in coalitions. In these cases, negotiation is with their allies, not an opponent. The negotiation process is to decide what the joint position of the collaboration or coalition will be. Some partners may want to advocate for less; some may want to advocate for more. Each member of the coalition should come to the table just as prepared when negotiating with friends as with adversaries.

In almost all cases where both sides to a negotiation are working hard for their position, none of the parties comes out with their initial position intact. Each party gives in on some points to achieve others. Because of this, a prepared negotiator will prioritize the various positions within the larger array of possible positions. When you can achieve a higher priority point at the cost of a lower priority item, it is usually a trade worth making. In the end, however, you did not get everything that you wanted, and most likely, neither did anyone else.

It is usual that policy entrepreneurs use all three styles of advocacy in their work. Thus, it is important to be conversant with and capable in all three: education, persuasion, and negotiation.

So far in this chapter, we have covered why program designers need to understand advocacy and the different styles of advocacy. Next, we turn to a brief description of the different stages that an advocacy effort goes through.

STAGES OF ADVOCACY

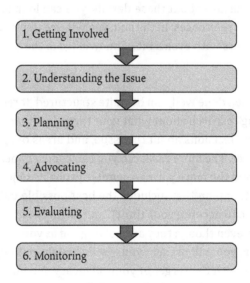

FIGURE 3.1 **Six Stages of Advocacy**

Stage 1: Getting Involved

For each new advocacy effort, a policy entrepreneur must answer the question "Why do I want to get involved with this issue?" With so many potential ways to spend time and energy, it is easy to become overcommitted and overwhelmed. An advocate who is burned out is not likely going to be effective. Thus, in Stage 1 it is important to focus on your own abilities and needs as well as the potential for positive achievement and change.

Stage 2: Understanding the Issue

Before moving along in the advocacy process, it is important to truly understand the issue you are getting involved with. You may find this related to Kingdon's (2010) policy stream described earlier in the chapter. How do you want to define the issue, and how is it different from others who are involved?

Hoefer (2019) argues the process of understanding an issue involves five steps. They are to (a) define the issue; (b) decide who is affected and how they are affected; (c) decide what the main causes of the issue are; (d) generate possible solutions to the issue (based on what the causes are); and (e) review the proposed solutions to determine their impact on social justice. By going through all five steps, you can be certain you have a grasp of not only what you are trying to fix (the problem) but also on what appropriate solutions are in your mind. In this way you combine the roles of the policy entrepreneur with a solutions entrepreneur. In keeping with our ideas on understanding community needs (Chapter 3) and empowerment practice, the process of understanding the issue must include client input. If you find an open policy window, you may be able to see your ideas adopted by relevant decision makers.

Stage 3: Planning

The planning stage of advocacy practice is fun, exciting, and a bit challenging. In Stage 2, you developed at least one proposed solution and judged it according to how well it would promote social justice. In this stage, you determine the steps you are going to take to implement the chosen solution. You can think of the planning stage as mapping out how to get from here (the current situation) to there (where you want to be).

The first thing to do in any journey is to decide where you want to go, what your final goal is. You also need to determine who the decision makers are who can get you where you want to go. Which specific individuals or decision-making bodies (e.g., a city council, a legislature, or a nonprofit board of directors, your supervisor) have the power to grant your request or withhold approval? Once you determine who has the authority to move your case forward, you know who your target is.

Stage 4: Advocating

At this point, you and collaborators have an understanding of the issue and a plan to put into effect. Now all you have to do is get the decision you want from your target. Naturally, this may be a long-term process, as when a new law or change in policy is the desired outcome of your advocacy efforts. Still, this is the time to gear up for the actual education, persuasion, and negotiation processes that advocacy entails.

Stage 5: Evaluating Advocacy

Once the advocacy is completed, it is tempting to say that the fun (or work) is over and it is time to go on to something else. But this would be like playing a game and not keeping score. Sure, you can play just for the fun of it, but usually, you want to know how well you did, and you know that by looking at a score. To improve in any skill, after the effort is over, it is important to review what went well and what could have been done better. Advocacy is an activity that has a purpose beyond just doing advocacy—you are trying to improve the state of the world for your clients and yourself. Thus, it is crucial that you find a way to "keep score" or evaluate your efforts and the outcomes you achieve. Although many ways exist to evaluate your advocacy efforts, the one suggested here is to compare your actual progress to your mental roadmap you developed earlier in the advocacy process during the planning stage. You can determine which milestones you reached and the extent to which you achieved your planned outcomes.

Stage 6: Monitoring

The final stage of advocacy is monitoring the results of your work on a longer term basis. Evaluating advocacy (as in the previous stage) is necessary to get better at the planning and implementation of advocacy. But most policy change is slow, and once the new policy is ratified, the hoped-for results may take a while to occur. Thus, advocates should devote themselves and some resources to keeping track of policy change and evolution. Any program change can become derailed over time. Funding can be incrementally decreased or cut all at once, so monitoring budget and personnel resources over time is vital.

All of these steps require practice and a considerable amount of effort. Yet, as we have seen, program developers need to be aware of the styles and stages of advocacy. If your program idea is truly helpful to your community, it is an ethical imperative for you and your organization to try to get it in operation. Obtaining the resources to do so requires honing your advocacy skills.

 SPOTLIGHT ON DIVERSITY

The information in this chapter is general and is intended to be accurate in most situations. Still, we should highlight two reasons to consider diversity and inclusion efforts in any advocacy effort (including for program development). The first is that such inclusion of diversity is a professional ethical responsibility. In Chapter 4, Understanding Your Community, this point is stressed. In addition, the literature indicates that including diverse voices makes for a more effective advocacy effort. Not all techniques of education, persuasion, and negotiation work equally well with everyone or within every group. Having "guides" to work with you who are familiar with how "things get done" in various contexts and with different stakeholders may be the difference between success and failure.

Habursky (2019), for example, notes that showcasing diverse voices in any advocacy effort indicates the broad appeal of the proposal. Decision makers are more likely to listen to the information presented if they believe the proposal is supported by many elements of their constituency, not just one or two. Policy entrepreneurs and program developers who have only considered their ideas from their own perspective may find moving beyond their single focus will lead to better proposals and more success.

Junk (2019) also finds that diverse coalitions are more successful than homogeneous coalitions when the issues addressed are salient. This finding implies that advocates who can put together a diverse set of voices for a proposal should work to make the issue better known to potential beneficiaries and decision makers.

DIFFICULTIES AND JOYS

Advocacy is a process that will always entail difficulties and joys. Even though we use examples from political systems in this chapter, program designers and agency leaders are working to improve their communities in concrete ways with specific funding and policy proposals. They bring to the table passion and commitment.

Still, becoming a successful policy entrepreneur is not an easy process (Minton, 2019). Minton (2019) states, for example, "Efforts to drive policy innovation might involve introducing wholly new policies within specific jurisdictions or they might involve making significant advances upon particular policies that are already in place" (p. 308). Bringing together all the required skills and strategies is challenging. Progress can be slow and fragile. Gains can be lost quickly. It is not for the faint of heart, Minton (2019) reminds us:

> Policy entrepreneurship is tough work. It often takes a lot of courage. By definition, the pursuit of change—unless it is a very tame kind of change—is highly disruptive. Against that backdrop, most policy entrepreneurs will be viewed by a few people as heroic and by everyone else as troublemakers or crazies. That is because change makes many people feel uneasy. (pp. 308–309)

At the same time, the joys of working together with others who have a common vision is exhilarating. Victories, even small ones, are high points in policy entrepreneurs' lives, along with their supporters. One does not need to change the lives of millions to achieve worthwhile progress; even to improve the situation in one community for a small number of people is to be lauded. With practice and increasing skill levels, it is likely to become more common.

LESSONS FROM THE PANDEMIC

What we have learned during the COVID-19 pandemic is that advocacy can be done in a socially distanced way. Many of these techniques will become part of the business as usual in the advocacy world.

The foremost advantage is that you have easy access to the internet and web-based tools and programs. This brings several benefits to you. First, in a few minutes of artful searching, you can find information that could have taken weeks or months to find looking through paper records in a large library or government repository. Huge volumes of government documents and the latest in scientific research are, literally, at your fingertips. News reports, historical information, and opinions of millions of other people can be searched and downloaded within seconds, perhaps giving you just the bit of information or compelling story that can drive your point home as you advocate for a new or revamped program to address a situation in your community.

Platforms and communication technology, such as Slack and Zoom, became omnipresent during the pandemic. Competitors brought out their versions with enhancements that were then matched by the original technology. Despite the "never off duty" element that such communications platforms entail, being able to communicate, plan, and make progress was a welcome fallback approach to meeting in person when social distancing was necessary.

A third benefit of the web is the ability to garner publicity in ways that are otherwise beyond the scope of most individuals or small groups. For example, a strategically promoted, entertaining YouTube video may be the start of an advocacy campaign that shows how a current problem could be addressed with a new program. Working to make a video go viral and motivate government officials to support legislation and funding for organizations willing to work on that problem can be effective.

The challenge for all advocates in an information age (that was also a year of pandemic) is to understand and use all the tools (old and new) available to make their most persuasive case; promote their views to opinion leaders, interested stakeholders, and the public; and to gain access to the correct target. This is done not for personal gain or public glory, but to ensure social justice.

CONCLUSION

We started this chapter with the somewhat unusual argument that program development is ultimately based on advocacy. Decision makers and potential funders must be convinced of the need and desirability of beginning a new program or revising a current one. Because resources are always limited, allocating money and time to the program you want to develop means that other ideas will not be funded. This situation impels program developers (who we also call policy or program entrepreneurs) to understand and use advocacy techniques.

With this conviction as the foundation of the chapter, we covered the definition of advocacy, theories that help show why advocacy is vital to program development, and Kingdon's multiple streams model of policymaking. We also provided information about the three styles of advocacy (education, persuasion, and negotiation) and the stages of an advocacy effort.

Once advocacy has been successful, authorization and resources for a new program will be available. The next step for a program designer is to understand the community that will be impacted. What type of program is truly needed, and how can it be developed with the assistance of a wide group of stakeholders from the community?

 SUMMARY/KEY POINTS

This chapter addressed two primary key points relating to the organizational and programmatic context of social program design and development.

First, we explored the rationale for all organizational leaders and program developers to have skills in advocacy so that this becomes an expected part of understanding the context and process of the program creation. In this way, they will be able to change the organizational context using theoretical concepts. They will not need to simply accept the status quo, which may be harmful to their community and potential clients.

Second, we addressed three aspects of advocacy (education, persuasion, and negotiation) to provide a range of approaches to use in your organization's specific situation. By having many practical tools in their repertoire, advocates are better able to match the correct approach to their situation.

KEY TERMS

Advocacy: A process of education, persuasion, and/or negotiation to achieve the goal of acquiring sufficient resources (of all kinds) to allow the creation of programs addressing specific social issues.

Advocacy target: A correctly chosen advocacy target is a person who (alone or together with others) has the power to impact the distribution of resources to your organization or program ideas. These people can be legislators and their personal and committee staff members, people working in the executive branch of any level of government, regulators, businesses, nonprofits, other organizations, and people within your own organization.

Bridging: A type of strategy an organization can use to reduce dependence on another organization for supply of a required resource by finding alternative sources for the resource, reducing the need for the resource, or changing somehow to supply the resource itself.

Buffering: A strategy an organization can use to reduce dependence on another organization for supply of a required resource by building up a reserve of that resource.

Decentralization of programmatic responsibility: This is a process in which a more central level of government shifts responsibility for a program or for solving a problem to a different level of government. An example is the shifting of the responsibility for COVID-19 vaccination implementation ("shots in arms") from the federal government to state government or from state government to local government.

Load shedding: A process by which governments declare they are not responsible for solving certain problems because those expenses would overload government's ability to pay for the services.

Policy entrepreneur(s): "Energetic actors who engage in collaborative efforts in and around government to promote policy innovations" (Mintrom, 2019, p. 307).

Policy problems: One of the three streams that Kingdon (2011) describes. This one reflects the fact that "problem descriptions" are ambiguous and contested.

Policy solutions: One of the three streams that Kingdon (2011) describes. This one indicates that solutions exist independently of problems and are promoted across topics by people who support the potential solution for reasons other than it being a clear way to solve the problem.

Policy window: A period of time during which a problem definition exists and an acceptable solution has been connected to it as a viable solution. In addition, political will exists to take action.

Political economy perspective: The political economy perspective states that for organizations to survive and to produce services, they must secure legitimacy and power, as well as production or economic resources. From this perspective, *political economy* refers to a system of distribution not only of resources but also of status, prestige, power, legitimacy, and related social amenities. The political economy perspective views the organization as a collectivity that has multiple and complex goals, paramount among them being survival and adaptation to the environment (Hasenfeld, 2000). The capacity of the organization to survive and to provide services depends on its ability to mobilize power, legitimacy, and economic resources—for instance, money, personnel, and clients (Wamsley & Zald, 1976).

Political conditions: One of the three streams that Kingdon (2011) describes. This one refers to the level of openness to change and willingness to take action that exists within decision makers and other policy actors. When the political stream is "ready," it is more likely that a problem and a solution will be connected, and an authoritative decision will be enacted.

Privatization of service provision: When government declares that private organizations should take on the running of programs. It may be that government maintains the funding of programs but pays private nonprofits or for-profits to conduct the programs.

Resource dependence theory: Resource dependence theory posits that the greater any organization's dependence is on resources controlled by another entity, the more dependent it is on that other body and the stronger is the influence of external interests on processes within the organization (Schmid, 2000). The theory assumes that organizations and their leaders prefer to be more independent than more dependent and so will exert effort to be as independent as possible, knowing that some dependence and interdependence cannot be avoided.

ADDITIONAL RESOURCES

Advocacy and Persuasion

Cialdini, R. (2021). *Influence. New and expanded: The psychology of persuasion.* Harper Business.

Hoefer, R. (2019). *Advocacy practice for social justice* (4th ed.). Oxford University Press.

Multiple Streams Model

Jones, M., Peterson, H. L., Pierce, J. J., Herweg, N., Bernal, A., Lamberta Raney, H., & Zahariadis, N. (2016). A river runs through it: A multiple streams meta-review. *Policy Studies Journal, 44*(1), 13–36.

Kingdon, J. (2010). *Agendas, alternatives, and public policies* (Updated 2nd ed.). Little, Brown & Company. (Original work published 1984.)

DISCUSSION QUESTIONS

1. Suppose you run into colleagues who say that advocacy is definitely not a part of what program designers and developers should be doing. What would you say to convince them to adopt this book's viewpoint?

2. Thinking about your background and current skills, where are you strongest in the realm of being an effective policy or program entrepreneur? Where do you feel you need to improve?

3. Kingdon's multiple streams model is simple in some ways and complex in others. Given space limitations, the material in this chapter is not a complete explanation. What questions do you have about the model and its application to the work of a program development professional?

 YOUR TURN

"The Runaway and Homeless Youth Act, passed in 1974, authorized the Basic Center Program (BCP), which enables community-based organizations to operate short-term, emergency shelters to provide crisis care to runaway and homeless youth (RHY) not already receiving services from the child welfare or juvenile justice systems. Today, FYSB funds the BCP under provisions of the Reconnecting Homeless Youth Act of 2008 (Public Law 110-378)" (Administration for Children and Families, 2020).

Your organization is a recipient of funds through this program, but you find that there are ways you would like to improve your services to this population. Of particular importance is the need to enhance your outreach efforts to "youth who may need assistance, as well as to public and private agencies that work with youth and families," one of the core services for the program (Administration for Children and Families, 2020, Services section).

Put together a short presentation that you could give to your organization's board of directors. It should describe an advocacy plan that you could use to convince local elected officials and community groups to support such an effort. Here are some questions you may wish to answer as you think about your plan:

- Who are the targets of your effort?
- Who are the individuals, friendly organizations, and community groups who you might work with on your advocacy effort?
- Will you prioritize education, persuasion, or negotiation in your plan (while understanding you may need to use all three styles)?
- Be sure to sketch out what will be included in the first four stages of advocacy in your plan.

REFERENCES

Administration for Children and Families. (2020). *Basic center fact sheet.* https://www.acf.hhs.gov/fysb/fact-sheet/basic-center-program-fact-sheet

Aldrich, H. E., & Pfeffer, J. (1976). Environments of organizations. *Annual Review of Sociology, 11*(2), 79–105.

Bedell, G. (2002). *Three steps to yes: The gentle art of getting your way.* Crown Books.

Charleton, B. & Miles, A. (1998). The rise and fall of EBM. *Quarterly Journal of Medicine (QJM), 91,* 371–374. https://doi.org/10.1093/qjmed/91.5.371

Cialdini, R. (2021). *Influence. New and expanded: The psychology of persuasion.* Harper Business.

Commission on Private Philanthropy and Public Needs. (1975). *Giving in America: Toward a stronger voluntary sector.*

Congressional Research Service. (2021). *Unemployment rates during the COVID-19 Pandemic: In brief.* Summary R46554.

Habursky, J. (2019). *The power of diversity in advocacy.* Campaigns and Elections. https://www.campaignsand elections.com/campaign-insider/the-power-of-diversity-in-advocacy

Hasenfeld, Y. (2000). Social welfare administration and organizational theory. In R. J. Patti (Ed.), *The handbook of social welfare management* (pp. 89–112). Sage.

Hoefer, R. (2019). *Advocacy practice for social justice.* Oxford University Press.

Hwang, H., & Suárez, D. (2019). Beyond service provision: Advocacy and the construction of nonprofits as organizational actors. In H. Hwang, J. A. Colyvas, & G. S. Drori (Eds.), *Agents, actors, actorhood: Institutional perspectives on the nature of agency, action, and authority* (pp. 87–109). Emerald Publishing Limited. https://doi.org/10.1108/S0733-558X20190000058007

Junk, W. (2019). When diversity works: The effects of coalition composition on the success of lobbying coalitions. *American Journal of Political Science, 63*(3), 660–674. https://doi.org/10.1111/ajps.12437

Kingdon, J. (2010). *Agendas, alternatives, and public policies* (Updated 2nd ed.). Little, Brown & Company. (Original work published 1984.)

Madsen, D. (2020). Have the reports of TQM's death been greatly exaggerated? A re-examination of the concept's historical popularity trajectory. *Administrative Sciences, 10*(32). https://doi.org/10.3390/admsci10020032

Mintrom, M. (2019). So you want to be a policy entrepreneur? *Policy Design and Practice, 2*(4), 307–323. https://doi.org/10.1080/25741292.2019.1675989

Pfeffer, J. (1992). *Managing with power: Politics and influence in organizations.* Harvard Business School Press.

Prochaska, J., Norcross, J., & DiClemente, C. (1994). *Changing for good: The revolutionary program that explains the six stages of change and teaches you how to free yourself from bad habits.* Putnam.

Ruggiano, N., & Taliaferro, J. D. (2012). Resource dependency and agent theories: A framework for exploring nonprofit leaders' resistance to lobbying. *Journal of Policy Practice, 11*(4), 219–235.

Schmid, H. (2000). Agency–environment relations: Understanding task environments. In R. J. Patti (Ed.), *The handbook of social welfare management* (pp. 133–154). *Sage.*

Schneider, R. & Lester, L. (2001). *Social work advocacy: A new framework for action.* Brooks/Cole.

Wamsley, G. L., & Zald, M. N. (1976). *The institutional ecology of human service organizations.* Indiana University Press.

Figure Credits

CHAPTER FOUR

Understanding Your Community

In this chapter, you will learn one of the most important aspects of creating or revising a program—learning what it is your community needs, wants, and can develop based on its assets and strengths. We cover different meanings of the word "need" and how to measure this surprisingly slippery concept. This is important because funders often are looking for "problems" to solve, so program developers must understand how to demonstrate need. More and more, however, solutions offered by program designers must acknowledge and incorporate **community assets** in their plans. Getting the support of community stakeholders from the start of planning is essential. Working to achieve this connection carries program staff beyond the walls of their offices, to the benefit of all.

People who develop human services programs have many duties to balance. Depending on the amount of specialization your organization can afford, you may be required to hire and train staff members, watch the budget carefully, attend meetings with stakeholders, keep up on the latest trends in your field, and much more. Often, overseeing the creation of a new program comes as an additional duty to what you are already doing. While it can sometimes be easy to set aside the reasons for all your work, keeping the overarching mission and vision of the organization is vital when planning a new program. No matter who is designing the program, some of the questions that need to be answered are "Why is the program being created?" "What are you trying to achieve?" and "Who is it designed to benefit?" Even questions such as "Where should it be located?" need to be asked and answered. The answers to all such questions relate to the underlying need that you want to address that exists within your community. Any program must be built on the foundation of solving a problem that is experienced by people in your area.

While it seems logical that a problem-solving rationale is always behind any effort, often that is not true—remember the multiple streams model we learned about in Chapter 3? Sometimes organizational interests prevail in choosing a program to advocate for. This situation can be created when organizations seeking to maintain or increase their resources believe that the most important reason to start or to continue funding a program is that they are already doing it or something similar. Another reason is that they believe there is a lack of a certain type of service that it wants to provide but the agency does not have enough resources to provide more. When the focus of a planning process is on organizational survival, program developers often merely seek to maintain programs that already exist. Doing so may ignore what community members and other stakeholders desire. Such "dollar-chasing" motives may even contradict evidence showing that another approach to the issue would be more effective. Clearly, this is not an approach that we condone, but it happens.

As a program developer, you must work closely with others in your organization, particularly the fundraiser. A clear synergy needs to exist between people in these two roles, as noted in Chapter 2's discussion of roles for the program development team. One role is the program specialist/planner who researches situations that can be improved and who figures out methods to make the world a better place. Another role is the fundraiser who locates the resources to enable program ideas to be made real. (Remember, this may be the same person, maybe even *you*!) That is why we place these steps of "finding funding" and "planning program" in the same box in the process diagram we introduced in Chapter 2.

This chapter, along with Chapter 5, will help you see how these two aspects of the program development cycle occur and the different roles at work. You will learn how to determine what community needs are using data and a view of the world informed by understanding systemic inequalities bound up as cultural and economic issues. In addition, you will be introduced to understanding community assets that can be incorporated into new program ideas. Chapter 5 looks in detail at fundraising for the program being developed. These two processes (program development and fundraising) often occur at least somewhat simultaneously and iteratively. This means that steps that have been taken in one area may need to be revisited. In the end, the amount of funds and the "amount of program" need to be commensurate with each other.

In understanding the context of the situation, one of the initial steps is to complete an assessment. This ensures that you will be able to explain to one or more potential funders what your and your community stakeholders' views of the situation are and why they should be addressed.

COMMUNITY AND PROGRAM NEEDS AND ASSETS ASSESSMENTS

Many descriptions of needs assessments gloss over the different purposes they can fill and the scope of inquiry necessary to fulfill the various possible roles. If students and practitioners only learn about the most rigorous types of community assessments, they may feel overwhelmed with the level of detail and amount of resources typically described in a comprehensive, community-wide assessment. Understanding that such an effort is beyond most individual agencies' abilities, they may resort to a very cursory process just to check off the box on that part of the program development process.

We believe that individual agency program designers need to understand that developing a "perfectly decent" assessment for a competitive grant proposal or program plan, to be run in their organization, focusing on only one problem, can be accomplished within their time and resource limits. At the same time, agency-level program planners should be acquainted with the standards of the best community-level needs assessments so that they can judge the quality of information that they gather secondhand from others' assessments.

Communities often have programs to address needs that are left out of "assets assessments." Program developers need to search for these programs to understand the community better.

Community-Wide Assessments

Before moving forward, let us make a distinction between community-wide (or comprehensive) assessments and the type of assessment you will likely use in a grant proposal or when planning to develop an individual program. **Community-wide assessments** are (more or less) comprehensive examinations of the state of a community, including needs (deficits) and assets (strengths), parts of which can be incorporated into individual agency-level program planning. These reports can also be conducted at the state level (Johnson et al., 2020), at a regional level (Pantoja, 2020), or even at a local level. Comprehensive assessments are generally undertaken by government bodies or broad-based community-based nonprofits, such as United Way. These efforts usually have significant monetary backing and will employ many types of approaches: community forums, focus groups, key informant interviews, meetings with many different stakeholders, wide-scale data collection tools such as online surveys, use of secondary data sources, and other data collection processes. The goal is to be as comprehensive and open to community input as possible, identifying concerns and issues within the entire locality. They examine as many community issues as possible given resource and time limitations. These efforts usually result in a report or website with results made available to everyone in the community. These can be used by individual organizations to use in their own funding proposals. An example of such a community-wide needs assessment is the *United Way of Tarrant County Community Assessment, 2018–2019* (Tarrant County United Way, 2019a; https://www.unitedwaytarrant. org/communityassessment/).

The report describes how the assessment was conducted and what the major findings were. It was sponsored by a local foundation and used personnel from a local university as well as United Way staff and graduate research assistants.

Through our partnership with the University of North Texas Health Science Center, we conducted numerous interviews and focus groups with key informants. We also analyzed and extracted key findings from existing research and publicly available statistical indicators. We found five major areas needing significant investment: housing and homelessness; health, mental health and wellness; transportation; education/early childhood/youth; and basic needs, emergency assistance and financial stability. (United Way of Tarrant County, 2019a, p. 2)

The report also states that these areas of need are interconnected. The root cause of them all is poverty. Based on this assessment, the United Way of Tarrant County decided to target all five major areas by targeting intergenerational poverty. Very helpfully, a second document (Rohr et al., 2019) provides a detailed technical report showing all the public data sources used and much of the actual data tables as well. Anyone reading it can find the information and could also look up the agencies listed for future reports as well, when updates are available. (See Box 4.1.) The technical report sometimes shows breakdowns of the larger information sets by gender, race and ethnicity, or different cities within the county (Rohr et al., 2019).

BOX 4.1	Public Data Sources for Community Assessments

Here are the public data sources listed in the United Way of Tarrant County Community Needs Assessment. When you conduct a needs assessment, you may find these (or similar) sources helpful. The Texas-based agencies listed here are equivalent departments in other states.

- Robert Wood Johnson Foundation (https://www.rwjf.org/)
- Texas Education Agency (https://tea.texas.gov/)
- Texas Health and Human Services (https://hhs.texas.gov/)
- Texas Department of Public Safety Law Enforcement Support (https://www.dps.texas.gov/section/law-enforcement-support/law-enforcement-support)
- United States Bureau of Labor Statistics (https://www.bls.gov/)
- United States Census and the American Community Survey (https://data.census.gov/cedsci/)
- Local school districts, health systems, and municipalities

Source: Rohr et al., 2019, p. 4.

In addition to public data sources, such as those in Box 4.1, Tarrant County United Way conducted its own research efforts. They conducted 25 key informant interviews and ran 20 focus groups, using volunteers who were invited by United Way staff and outside stakeholders (Rohr et al., 2019). These sessions were recorded, transcribed, and divided into more than 4,000 passages, which were then analyzed to identify perceived needs and issues as described in the reports (Rohr et al., 2019, p. 5).

The Tarrant County Community Assessment also reported information on community strengths (Tarrant County United Way, 2019, p. 21). About 15% of the comments made in key informant and

focus group interviews identified positive aspects of the community (see Box 4.2). Looking at what the community *offers* as well as where it has *needs* is vital in understanding the entire situation.

BOX 4.2	**Tarrant Count Strengths, According to Participant Comments**

Researchers with the United Way Community Assessment identified six main categories of community strengths.

General Social Services
Nonprofits, faith organizations, community centers, etc.

Community Relations
Compassion, friendliness, neighborhoods

Education
Early childhood initiatives, school district partnerships with community organizations, career readiness

Recreation
Cultural activities, arts, entertainment, bike trails, restaurants and shops

Health
Healthcare systems, children's services, health programs for underserved

Basic Needs
Food pantries

Source: United Way of Tarrant County, 2019, p. 21.

A comprehensive community assessment is very helpful for all the agencies in the area who are applying for funding in the areas of need identified. It also includes demographic information for the county and state, thus easing the pressure on individual organizations to locate that information, which is required in almost every grant or program proposal. State and federal funders, as well as foundations or even donors of significant amounts of money, are likely to trust the assessment because the data being used is from reliable and reputable sources. The data collected and reported by United Way represents a considerable amount of cost and effort. It may be beyond the resources (monetary and human) of any one human service organization.

Program Needs Assessment

When people in the program developer and fundraising roles begin to work together, they must align their expectations of what problem they want to address. This decision is based almost entirely upon the terms decided upon by the funder. In most cases (including the example case we are using throughout the book), funders describe what must be given to them in the proposal. It is common to need to ask questions so that unclear expectations can be clarified, but it is the funder that provides the answers regarding what they will allocate resources for.

A program-justifying needs assessment will more likely use secondary data—that is, information that someone else has collected, such as a local United Way's community-level assessment. The individual agency will need this secondary information to show a strong rationale for the proposed program. Most agencies do not have funding or skills to conduct a full community assessment and must therefore work to find whatever information is already available through other nonprofit or government sources. A funder will want to know the reason why its money should be allocated to your organization for the purposes that you describe. This seems reasonable given the intense competition for the limited resources any funder has.

The needs assessment contained in a grant proposal will be targeted and limited to one or a very limited number of problems directly related to the funding opportunity. Even in the situation where you rely on secondary data, you should learn how to use additional methods (such as key informant interviews or focus groups) in order to get deeper insights about your community. Due to resource and staff knowledge limitations in individual human service organizations, the process will likely be less systematic than in most community-wide assessments. They are still worth doing, however, because they can provide vital local information about what is acceptable for the program's target population and your community. By including more stakeholders in this way, when funding is received, the agency will already be prepared to move forward.

With this background, we now turn to the conceptual issue of what "need" is. After you learn about program needs assessments, community assets, and how to understand a community using data, we will look at the needs assessment section of the request for proposals that our example agency responded to and see how they wrote their answer. After all this, you will be prepared to tackle your own community and needs assessment.

WHAT IS "NEED"?

If you are doing a needs assessment, it is easy to assume that everyone understands the concept of "need" in the same way. After all, you might think, a need occurs when something important is missing. We can easily think of many needs: good physical and mental health, positive interaction, nourishing food, clean water, safe shelter, and so on. When these are not present, a deficit exists and "should" be ameliorated.

Yet, it is widely understood that needs have a hierarchy—some are more basic than others. Without liquid intake, humans usually die within a few days, so it is the ultimate need. Without food, people languish and die within weeks. On the other hand, people can live decades without being around other humans or being "self-actualized."

The idea of a codified hierarchy of needs is now most commonly connected with Abraham Maslow's (1943) formulation. Maslow (1970) originally had five levels but in later years added three more for a total of eight (see Figure 4.1).

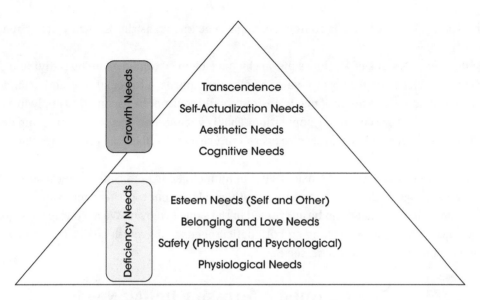

FIGURE 4.1   Based on Maslow's Hierarchy of Eight Needs (1970)

In Maslow's view, one can understand needs as motivations for human behavior. When these needs are not met, most people, most of the time, will do what they can to achieve them. If you are thirsty or hungry, for example, you will try to find water and food. Naturally, if you are conducting a hunger strike for social justice, you will change the order of needs within the hierarchy, but much research has been conducted using the concepts of **Maslow's hierarchy of needs**, and they are very useful in understanding human behavior, in general.

Maslow (1970) begins with basic physiological needs. These are the biological needs for survival. Next is the need for safety, both physical and psychological. Third are the needs for belonging and love. Humans are social in nature and so are motivated to be with others and to create positive relationships. This helps explain maintaining friendships, grouping with like-minded others, and all other forms of association, including intimate and family ties. The fourth level is called "esteem needs," which consist of both self-esteem needs (dignity, achievement, and independence) and respect or esteem from others (status and prestige). As a group, these first four types of need have been labeled **deficit needs**.

The next four levels are grouped as **growth needs**. Fifth are cognitive needs. They include knowledge, meaning, and predictability. Sixth are aesthetic needs, such as searching for and appreciating beauty. Self-actualization needs come in the seventh level. These are the needs for realizing one's potential and seeking personal growth. Finally, Maslow posited transcendence needs at the top of the hierarchy. These are the needs that go beyond the self—desires to live outside of oneself to see one's values and ideals become real. People who zealously promote social justice or religious experiences can be said to be living transcendently.

Maslow clarified in his later years that the levels are not as rigid or orderly as he might have intimated early on. Also, people do not need to be fully accomplished at one level in order to be motivated by higher levels of need. One example of this is you might experience hunger sometimes but still want to express your artistic impulses before "buckling down" and getting a job or "selling out" to produce "popular" works. (This situation is common enough to be known as the "starving artist syndrome" [Phillips, 2017].)

All the different versions of Maslow's hierarchy have been critiqued as being individualistic and culture-bound. Societies or groups that value a collective approach to social interactions may find it inaccurate and strange. The order of needs posited should thus not be assumed to apply in every circumstance and with every culture or population. That is yet another reason why program designers must incorporate representatives of service users' culture into the planning process (Fallatah & Syed, 2017; King-Hill, 2015).

The main reason to understand Maslow's list of human needs (and thus people's motivation for behavior) is that program designers can tune into them as they put together their programs, remembering how more than one need can be addressed in the same program. We encourage designers and funders to seek out programs working on both deficit needs and growth needs. (For an example of going beyond addressing deficit needs, see Box 4.3.)

BOX 4.3	**Going Beyond Addressing Deficit Needs in Program Design**

How does Maslow's hierarchy of needs matter for a program designer? Often, we think of programs being designed to remedy only the deficit needs of potential clients. Human services programs designed to reduce hunger (food pantries), child abuse, drug addiction, and other social concerns spring to mind as highest priority because they target basic physiological and safety needs. People, however, are multidimensional, and programs can be designed to address more than one level of need, including growth needs. For example, Turtle Creek Manor, in Dallas, Texas, ran a program to assist people who had substance abuse and mental health issues and often were homeless. Typically, such programs provide housing, food, clothing assistance, dental and health care, and other services addressing basic needs of this population. The director, Robert Stewart, had an idea, however, that the program could also address higher level needs, such as cognitive and aesthetic needs. Mr. Stewart began working with another organization, the Dallas Institute of Humanities and Culture. Together, the two organizations developed a program to have moderated reading clubs for clients. The books they chose were some of Western civilization's most enduring, such as Homer's *The Odyssey*. The moderators helped clients realize that they, too, were adrift among tumultuous circumstances, much as Odysseus was tossed about by the gods during his trip home from foreign countries. The program sought to appeal to the growth needs of clients, promoting their desire to express curiosity, gain knowledge, and increase understanding of their meaning. These are needs that often are ignored by programs focused only on deficit needs. Clients reported feeling "human" again and valued for their ability to think about deep subjects (R. Stewart, personal communication, November 18, 2014).

With a better conceptual understanding of what needs are, we now turn to discussing how to assess the level of a particular need. We quickly run into issues that show how important clarity is in measuring need.

Approaches to Measuring Levels of Need

The unfortunate truth is that most communities have a large number of problems. Many areas of our country, rural and urban, have high poverty and unemployment rates, inadequate schooling opportunities, and lack of access to the broader world through digital inequality. Some have frequent violence in the neighborhood or high numbers of death through suicide with few high-level medical personnel or care facilities. Other areas have more economic resources but experience high rates of substance abuse, teen delinquency and truancy, lack of affordable housing, and so on. These needs tend to fall into Maslow's physiological and safety needs categories, but we can also describe other types of needs. One example is that of older adults who are single and live far from relatives or have few, if any, friends. These people can be physically healthy but may feel lonely and forgotten. An even more extreme situation is described as the *unbefriended elderly* living in long-term care settings who "lack decision-making capacity and family or friends to act as their legal representative" (Chamberlain et al., 2019, p. 359). This can lead to "alarming issues in quality of life and quality of care" (Chamberlain et al., 2019, p. 359). Another situation of a growth need is when educational institutions contribute to deficits in esteem needs for children who are bullied or lack adequate preparation and support for doing well in school.

We must remember that the way a problem or need is defined shapes the solution that is devised to address it to a great extent. A poorly defined problem will almost always lead to a program that does not do as much good as it should. It is not difficult to look around at almost any community and discover problematic situations (needs) that might be addressed with a properly designed and implemented program. (You may recall the discussion of the problem stream in Chapter 3 and how definitions of problems are often ambiguous and contested.)

When we say "a properly designed program," we mean one that relates to a clear understanding of the problem being addressed and then matches the intervention logically to that problem. Thus, we must assess the need in terms of its extent (how many people are affected), its depth (the degree to which people are affected), and its duration (how long it lasts). Needs vary along these parameters. We also want to determine at what level we want to assess problems. Commonly, decision makers look at needs of individuals. They also could envision problems at a community, state, or national level. (See Table 4.1 for examples of analyzing problems at the individual level and at the community level.)

TABLE 4.1   Social Problems Assessed Along 3 Dimensions (Example of Dallas, Using Data from 2020)

Problem	Dimension		
	Extent	Depth	Duration
Homelessness (Individual Problem)	Affected 26,000 people in January 2020 (.0099 of Dallas' population; KERA, 2020).	Being homeless is an all-encompassing and all-consuming problem for the individual experiencing it.	Varies widely depending on multiple factors, including lack of affordable housing, unemployment, mental illness, and substance abuse.
Homelessness (Community Problem)	Homelessness is concentrated in a few areas in or near the downtown area. Areas with a concentration of homelessness are few but have wide impact in that area and beyond.	Homelessness in a neighborhood is connected with negative outcomes, such as residents not feeling safe, driving businesses out, increased visibility of street drug use, etc. Economic prospects for everyone who lives in that neighborhood suffer, and more tax dollars are spent for security and public health services.	Homelessness in a neighborhood can be slow to grow but once established may be difficult to decrease. Large-scale sweeps to move people who are homeless are seldom successful for long and may violate people experiencing homelessness's rights.
Poverty (Individual Problem)	In July 2019, 498,112 people, or 18.9% of Dallas population, are poor (U.S. Census Bureau, 2019a).	Different types of poverty exist, such as temporary voluntary poverty (college students, for example) and long-term poverty caused by individual and/or social factors. These can cause poverty to have different levels of "depth."	Most people who become poor are not poor for a long time—often less than half a year. But people who are poor for a long time account for the bulk of all poverty at any one time.
Poverty (Community Problem)	Poverty tends to be concentrated into smaller areas of a community. Concentrated poverty in only some neighborhoods has impacts of social and racial justice because our cities' neighborhoods tend to be segregated by race and ethnicity.	Concentrated poverty leads to strongly detrimental impacts on residents. Businesses tend to be few and sell less expensive products. Food deserts emerge so access to nutritional fresh foods decreases. Health care becomes more difficult to find. Mortality rates at all ages increase.	In many communities, certain areas have been "the poor side of town" for generations, often due to systemic housing discrimination. Rural areas without access to wage labor opportunities may be among the most destitute places in a state or region.

As the problem is being explored, we must ensure that this process is driven in large part by members of the community the program will touch. It is far too easy to be a professional program designer in charge of the assessment but then neglect outreach efforts to bring in other people and viewpoints. (See Box 4.4 for an example of a mistake in conducting an appropriate needs assessment.) Looking at Table 4.1, it is easy to ignore that the problems of homelessness and poverty do not have the same levels of extent, depth, and duration in all racial, ethnic, sexual orientation, or gender groups. This same dynamic holds true outside of the problems of homelessness and poverty. Therefore, as program developers do their work, representatives of a variety of groups should help determine the way the program is put together.

BOX 4.4	**Do Not Help a Good Program Go Bad: A Faulty Needs Assessment Process**

When I was a MSW community practice intern, I was embedded for some of my hours with the Lawrence, Kansas, Police Department as a crime prevention specialist. This was a look inside a world most civilians never get. One day, another intern and I were looking through a week's worth of crime reports and spotted a crime we had not seen before: An older adult retired school teacher had been arrested for shoplifting at a grocery store. What was most odd was that she had more than enough money with her to pay for the hidden items. My colleague and I decided that this would be a problem we could address through the Crime Prevention Unit. We spoke with our immediate supervisor who encouraged us to come up with something.

A couple of weeks later, we had a court diversion program outlined, a program that would allow for all senior citizens to enter a deferred prosecution agreement so that no stains on their record would exist if no further crimes were committed. Many such programs for various groups of citizens had been developed in recent years. We studied the research, pulled out best practices, and believed the program would work. We showed it to our supervisor, who passed it on to the assistant chief of police.

The assistant chief came to our Crime Prevention Unit's office (somewhat unusual in itself). He asked one question: "How many cases like this have happened?" We indicated that "so far, one case." He snorted and dismissively said, "Let me know when it's a *real* problem" and left muttering under his breath.

While it was an extremely embarrassing turn of events, we had to admit he had a point. The upside of the situation is that I certainly learned something about needs assessment that day, more than I had in the classroom. And last I heard, that was the only time anyone heard of the Senior Citizen Court Diversion Project in Lawrence, Kansas!

—Richard Hoefer

Bradshaw's Definitions of Need

Maslow's (1970) work is tremendously important in understanding what motivates human actions. Yet his work does not describe how to define or measure need. As Bradshaw (1972) notes, "One of the most crucial problems facing the social services is how to identify social need" (p. 71). Rather than deciding on one approach, Bradshaw provides four answers to this difficult problem, thus underscoring how difficult a task it is.

Normative need is when "a desirable standard" is created and compared to the real situation. The current poverty threshold in the United States is such a definition, whereby the cost of a minimal diet determined by the U.S. Department of Agriculture (the "Thrifty Food Plan") is multiplied by three. If any family household's income falls below that income level, they are "poor." Otherwise, they are not. One problem with this approach is that different standards for the same issue are put forward, each having different outcomes on service provision. Some antipoverty programs in the United States, for example, use a different level of income for eligibility than others, though all say they are trying to decrease poverty.

The second definition is felt need. *Felt need* emerges when a population is asked whether a service is needed. If the answer is "yes," then the program designer's response is to say that there is a need. This is a straightforward approach. Still, some people may deny their own need exists (people addicted to illegal substances, for example, may deny they are addicted), or detractors may argue that those claiming need are inflating the situation for their own benefit.

The third definitional approach is expressed need. *Expressed need* is seen as the extent to which people are demanding or queuing up for a service. They are behaviorally indicating that they want a service by receiving it or by signing up to receive the service as soon as it is available to them. Being put on a waitlist in this way indicates unmet need in the population. In early 2021, for example, when the COVID-19 vaccine was first delivered across the country, governments devised ways to ration the doses, leaving millions of people with an expressed need who nonetheless had to wait for a dose to become available. Another example of expressed need is people waiting for years to receive a housing voucher for affordable housing.

The fourth definitional approach is comparative need. According to Bradshaw (1970), *comparative need* means that if one group of people or a community receives a service and others that are similar do not receive it, those without the service are in need regardless of whether they are below any particular standard (normative need), want the service (expressed need), or feel they are deprived (felt need). People who were not considered eligible but did not want to receive a vaccine against COVID-19 anyway might be put into a category of comparative need by public health officials who wanted nearly the entire population to be inoculated.

More recent authors (Armson et al., 2020) have added a fifth type of need, *unperceived needs*. These are needs that we do not know we have or deny their existence. On a personal level, an unperceived need may be treatment for high blood pressure; on a community or organizational level, the unperceived need may be the elimination of unconscious bias. While it is difficult to plan how to determine levels of unperceived needs, using open-ended measures and being attuned to the possibility that unacknowledged needs may emerge are important steps to take (Armson et al., 2020). Knowing that there are needs that are unperceived helps us stay open to information from community members and others as well.

The information from Maslow and Bradshaw, when combined, provides answers to why people desire a new program ("Which one of Maslow's needs is being addressed?") and how to define need for the program ("Which definition of need is to be used in addressing the problem?"). For example, suppose you conducted a survey of nutrition concerns in your urban community. You learned that respondents wanted the same kind of access to healthy fresh food as was found in the suburbs. You would be addressing a physiological need (Maslow) using a "felt" or "comparative" need (Bradshaw) definition. Based on this, you might decide the best program was to create a farmer's market or subsidize a grocery store chain to locate in the area. Perhaps, though, you wanted to use Bradshaw's normative need approach. In this case, you might have done a diet diary to have respondents write down all the food they ate for a couple of days. This could be compared with what nutritionists say are the requirements for a healthy diet (use of a standard as the norm). Upon finding that most people were not eating well, you might have decided on a program emphasizing increasing knowledge of healthy eating rather than focusing on the lack of healthy food choice opportunities. The different ways needs assessments are structured will lead to different outcomes. Thus, the ability to think about need from multiple perspectives is important. Working with local informants can help you design the most appropriate processes and questions for your needs assessment, whether it is a community-wide assessment or **program-level community assessment**.

APPROACHES TO MEASURE NEEDS

No matter the category of need one is exploring (Maslow's, Bradshaw's, or any other) or where the information you want is located, you will need to access appropriate and convincing information. We focus here on locating appropriate statistics and demographic information, interviewing key informants, running focus groups, and surveying current clients. These approaches are useful in seeing the situation from all of Bradshaw's approaches. Gathering statistical data helps when using a normative definition; interviewing key informants is helpful from a relative approach.

Locating Statistics

The United States Census Bureau is the preeminent source for detailed information for demographic and other data. The Census Bureau has information available at almost all levels of political jurisdictions (counties, towns, cities, townships) and statistical areas (census blocks, ZIP codes, and more) that may or may not correspond to smaller, locally recognized areas. When you are looking for statistics on these smaller areas, you may need to use census tracts, block groups, and census blocks. Census tracts contain between 1,200 and 8,000 people; block groups are subdivisions of census tracts, generally containing between 600 and 3,000 people. Census blocks vary in size. In rural areas they may cover scores of square miles, while in urban areas they tend to be the size of a city block. These are only available in the major decennial census data but can be very helpful because you can group these to cover very particular areas within the United States. Another important resource for program planners is the American Community Survey (designed and run by the Census Bureau), which allows you to use census tracts and block groups when using the 5-year estimates (United States Census Bureau, 2013). Program planners should learn to use the Census Bureau's many resources and data sets in order to locate much of the information needed to support grant proposals and describe community characteristics. The quickest entry point is located at the webpage Explore Census Data (https://data.census.gov/cedsci/).

States and local organizations may also publish data they collect (as the United Way of Tarrant County [2019] did in their community assessment). Much of their data come from official sources (as noted in Box 4.1). You may be able to locate more specific data by running your own queries on the Census Bureau website, which includes a robust geographic information system accessing different levels of data, such as poverty by race and gender, within specific census tracts. The more specific you can be, the more clearly you can show your community's situation.

Interviews with Key Informants and Focus Groups

Key informant interviews and focus groups are similar in that they are interview situations where the organization's staff or consultants work to gather information from community members. They have a similar set up required: recruitment of respondents, development of questions, conducting the interview/focus group (which should be recorded, with participants' permission), data analysis, and, finally, reporting of conclusions.

A **key informant interview** is defined by the United States Agency for International Development (USAID, 1996) as "qualitative, in-depth interviews of people selected for their first-hand knowledge about a topic of interest. The interviews are loosely structured, relying on a list of issues to be discussed" (p. 1). Two of the key reasons to use this technique are to provide information about attitudes about relevant topics and to generate recommendations (USAID, 1996). A *focus group* (usually 5–10 people in each one), on the other hand, is used

Image 4.2

When using interviews to gather detailed information, program developers should probe deeply with follow-up probes, such as "Tell me more."

when participants with certain characteristics are asked to provide their perceptions and views on topics that they are especially knowledgeable about (Krueger & Casey, 2015).

Recruitment

Researchers compiling information for the Agency for Healthcare Research and Quality (2011) conducted key informant interviews with researchers who were considered experts in key informant interviewing. The study respondents listed a number of tips for recruitment of participants for key informant interviews, which also apply for focus groups recruitment (Agency for Healthcare Research and Quality, 2011):

- "Defining appropriate stakeholders to include is not easy and can cause controversy" (p. ES-3).
- "Often, interviewers reached out to people they already knew but also conducted recruitment using media and the internet" (p. ES-3).

- "Snowball sampling (asking a respondent to recommend potential respondents) was one of the most common ways to find additional appropriate interviewees" (p. ES-7).
- "Following up with potential interviewees is vital to obtain participation" (p. ES-3).
- "Researchers preferred to use one-to-one meetings and small group meetings. These techniques led to more attention to the interview, helped develop stakeholder relationships, and led to better understanding of different stakeholders' opinions" (p. ES-3).
- "Researchers interviewing consumers used similar methods but had to consider that reaching service users or community people takes additional time and attention" (p. ES-3).

Development of Questions

The questions asked must be guided by the purpose of the session. It is a great deal of work to make the arrangements for the conversation, so you must ensure that every question will provide information you can use to understand the community and its situation as well to help design a program, using existing assets whenever possible. Tips here include:

- Begin by providing background information and asking for questions.
- Start with factual questions, then move to opinions and judgments.
- Ask open-ended questions.
- Use probes to get more details.
- Be neutral.
- Use translators when needed.
- Ask about resources and assets as well as problems and needs.

Conducting the Interview or Focus Group

It is best to record the session, but be sure to gain approval from everyone. You can assure participants that their information is being used only for the purposes of improving services. If anyone objects to being recorded, do not try to change their mind. Be sure to have someone taking detailed notes so that all views can be retained. When focus groups are composed of people from a specific racial or ethnic group, it can be very helpful to have an interviewer or moderator of the same group. When conducting more than one key informant interview, use similar topics, if not identical questions. The same is true for focus groups. Be flexible with the questions, but ensure that the questions asked will provide useful information aligned with your purposes. If you have recordings, have them transcribed for ease in reading for analysis.

Data Analysis

Academics and well-trained consultants may use strict protocols for analyzing the data from interviews and focus groups. These procedures have valid reasons for their use, but it may be unreasonable to expect an average human service agency to have such expertise and required software on hand. Organizations may also not have resources to pay someone to do such analysis, but it can be worth looking into hiring someone. Remember, if the analysis is done poorly, it is possible that it will not be accurate. Hiring outside expertise may also be more convincing to potential funders. In the end, time and other resources may not permit a full, detailed analysis that is in line with academic standards. But the information and opinions shared, particularly from otherwise unheard voices and groups, can still be helpful, and that is the key to the program design process.

Reporting

As with analysis, results reporting can range from the high-level standards needed for publishable journal articles to a quick, impressionistic conversation after reading a transcript of the focus group or interviews. While we do not wish to hold you to academic standards, we also do not want the process to be completely without rigor. Where you end up will depend on your resources, particularly time. Many grant proposals and program ideas, for example, are written by someone who already has a full-time job and is just trying to get the information uploaded before the deadline. Remember, however, that review committees are looking for high-quality ideas. Rushed proposals or unclear information will hardly ever be funded.

Surveying Current Clients

Another approach to understanding views of potential clients is to ask current clients receiving services. Staff people can explore program improvement ideas with clients and solicit feedback on which elements are working and which are not. When you hear something negative, take that as a valuable bit of information. A single complaint may lead to considerable improvements if taken seriously. Clients, because they are probably not "professionals in the field," can often see situations in ways that trained staff do not. This outside view can plant seeds for important modifications and changes in standard operating procedures.

Mapping Assets

Just as planners find and document problems or weaknesses in needs assessments to lay the foundation for new programs, planners also must learn to uncover strengths and assets. The most prominent developers of this idea are John Kretzmann (1993) and John McKnight (2005), who founded the **Asset-Based Community Development Institute (ABCD)** at Northwestern University. The concept is simple—uncovering and using a community's strengths as building blocks for improvement is a better way to reinvigorate a locality than only finding needs and weaknesses. Assets include people, parts of the built and natural environments, formal institutions (e.g., businesses, places of worship), and informal organizations. Kerka (2003) indicates the process of assets-based community development (ABCD) "involves the community in making an inventory of assets and capacity, building relationships, developing a vision of the future, and leveraging internal and external resources to support actions to achieve it" (p. 1). Dorfman (1998) created an easy-to-use workbook to guide communities through the process of creating an asset map and discusses how asset mapping shows not only the individual resources in the community but also explicates the relationships between them. The relationships are important to understand because they serve as access points. Any individual working to improve a community might not know the person who can take the project to the next level, but through a series of relationships, it is possible to connect (Dorfman, 1998).

The ABCD framework has gained widespread acceptance and its use has been reported for decades. Recent publications show the approach being used to assist in early recovery populations (Best et al., 2017); to promote change efforts in universities (Biscotte & Mouchrek, 2020); and to tackle social isolation and loneliness in London, England (Pang, 2019), to name a few. Given the large number of research publications, it is likely possible that you can find an instance of the ABCD approach in practice for a topic you are interested in. Locating such information will assist you in understanding how to use the framework and overcome potential challenges.

Once assets are listed, it can be helpful to add them to an actual geographic map, or perhaps to a conceptual map. Ask questions such as:

- How do these assets connect to each other and to understanding the community we are hoping to improve?
- Are some areas relatively rich in assets, while others are poor?
- Can any of the strengths we know about be moved?
- Can we add links between them to increase their value?

Once you have mapped the assets in these ways, you can return to a systematic approach to understanding the needs in your community as they relate to a particular funding opportunity.

THE 4 DS OF UNCOVERING NEED

Every grant application or other program design effort must make a case for why the organization submitting the application should receive resources to tackle one or more community problems. The actual terminology varies. Sometimes applicants write a "needs statement," sometimes a "statement of need," and, occasionally, a "statement of the problem." No matter how it is phrased, the point of this section of your grant application is to convince the reader that something is wrong. In a later section of the application, your agency will make a case that the organization can do something to improve the situation. But first, the you must create a picture of the community where life is less than ideal even though strengths and assets exist. In short, you must uncover a pressing need in the eyes of the proposal reader. The process for doing this has four steps, which we call "the 4 Ds of describing need" (Hoefer, 2017; depicted in Figure 4.2):

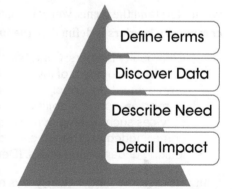

FIGURE 4.2   The 4 Ds of Describing Need

1. <u>Define the terms</u> explicitly in the same way as the funder does: What do you mean when you say "Y"?
2. <u>Discover data</u> that show the extent of the need in your community.
3. <u>Describe the need</u> in your community, possibly compared to other communities.
4. <u>Detail the impact</u> of the need or problem on people in your community.

Once you have gone through these four steps, you will have written a compelling statement that uncovers an important need for your community. This is the foundation for a successful fundraising effort.

Step 1: Define the Terms

One situation that is frequently encountered by grantwriters and program planning personnel is that they "know" there is a problem, but it is not clear exactly what they mean when they talk about it to others. For example, you might hear a board member say that there is a problem with poverty in your community and that you, as a grantwriter, should work on obtaining resources to combat it. When you question the board member more closely, however, it is not clear whether the problem is "too many poor people," "not enough jobs in the neighborhood for everyone who wants one," "too many government programs that destroy a will to work," or a host of other possibilities. All of these might be considered a "problem with poverty" in your community. Here is where it is useful to know the types of programs and activities that funders are interested in addressing now so that you can respond with a plan to write a grant on some aspect where resources are actually available.

Often, the literature can give you a precise definition of a problem. For example, many government programs are set up to assist people who are experiencing poverty. In this case, the term "poverty" has a precise meaning, which you should know and use in your grant writing. You may refer to Bradshaw's four approaches to defining problems discussed earlier in this chapter to think about how to define the terms.

In program planning efforts we have been involved with, proposals have included a statement similar to this one: The department "seeks to fund projects that address the personal and community barriers that must be overcome to help low-income individuals become self-sufficient" (Department of Health and Human Services, 2013, p. 1). To be competitive to win this grant, your organizational staff must understand all the terms here, such as "personal and community barriers" and "self-sufficiency." These terms may be defined in the request for proposals, or they may not. It is vital for you to be able to link our program ideas to this statement and the ways the funder understands the concepts. Once you understand the terms, you can relate your program to the funder's goals. As it happens, the term **community barriers** is defined by the funder:

> Community Barriers: Conditions in a community that impede success in employment or self-employment of low-income individuals. Such conditions may include: lack of employment education and training programs, lack of public transportation, lack of markets, unavailability of financing, insurance or bonding; inadequate social services such as employment services, child care or job training; high incidence of crime; inadequate health care; or environmental hazards such as toxic dumpsites or leaking underground tanks. (Department of Health and Human Services, 2013, p. 4)

In this case, the funder clearly lays out what appropriate indicators of a community barrier are. But what happens when the funder does not provide such clear definitions for the key terms? You still need to define your terms carefully and let the reader know where your definition comes from. Ideally, this will involve going to the research-based literature on the subject. For example, if you are addressing the issue of depression in middle-school aged girls, you would use a definition from a medical or psychological assessment source, such as *A.D.A.M. Medical Encyclopedia* (2013), not just *Webster's Dictionary* or some online, unattributed source.

Once you complete the step of defining terms, you turn to the second of the 4 Ds: In this case, you wish to discover the data you need to support the existence of community barriers. As you move forward, you begin to examine your data sources, looking to substantiate that barriers exist in your community.

Step 2: Discover Data that Show the Extent of the Need in Your Community

When you use standardized definitions of terms, you will find it much easier to find official statistics related to those terms. This is undoubtedly the best way to uncover need in your community to put into your grant applications. We have earlier noted the Census Bureau and other governmental sources for information that would allow you to show need, if it exists.

This section will point you to some of the major government data sources.

Of course, not all information is going to be available from any one source. As a program developer needing specific indicators of need, you may have to develop good relationships with researchers in various government offices at the state, county, city, school district, and other levels in order to get that one elusive bit of information that will make your case as strong as can be. Remember that you can create your own data as well, through key informant interviews and focus groups. If

Program developers need to search for and display data in comprehensible ways in their community assessments.

questions have been well-designed, they will help you know what perceptions exist regarding community barriers or whether many people are on waitlists for services. Going with more than one type of data shows you are using various Bradshaw's approaches: Statistics are normative needs, residents share their felt need, and waitlists show expressed need. Data from other communities can be used to show relative need as well.

Information that is useful to uncover need can also be found in other venues. Legislative hearings, community needs assessments conducted by nonprofit organization such as a local United Way, newspaper or magazine articles, conversations in hallways at meetings of nonprofit leaders—all these can help to open your eyes to needs that might be addressed. It is up to you to be ready to dig deeper for reliable information to support a diagnosis of a true need in your community.

Once the information has been discovered, it is time to put it together into a coherent whole. That is the process completed in Step 3.

Step 3: Describe the Need in Your Community, Possibly Compared with Other Communities

There is an important difference between Step 2, discovering data about a need, and Step 3, describing the need. It is the difference between a mere collection of facts and a compelling story about your community. Think about this difference carefully. Facts are often derided as factoids because they are small in scope, isolated, and unconvincing on their own. The key to turning a set of individual facts into a story is adding context.

Your job, in uncovering needs, is to tell a great story about why your community, organization, or group has reason to seek assistance to solve a clear problem. Your job, at this stage, is to get the reader to look up from the text and say, "This situation is truly intolerable."

The way to do this is to master the difference between reciting facts (such as unemployment and poverty rates) and truly describing the needs of your community in the context of the goals of the funder. It is one thing to write that your community has a high poverty rate, which is a problem. It is another thing to describe the high poverty rate as a result of a lack of educational and employment opportunities. Connecting the basic fact of having many community members being poor to the facts of high numbers of school dropouts or a dearth of jobs in the community within easy reach of residents provides the reader with an idea why a problem exists. This context allows readers to understand the "why" as well as the "what." If you think about the issue well, you are also adding in an understanding of assets in the community that can be used to address and solve the problem. You are saying the infrastructure for a specific new education program exists (a strength) but needs a new vision for how to succeed. That is what your program idea is. In this way you are now building up the community rather than tearing it down.

A very useful tool in understanding connections and context is to create a concept map. Originally developed to help understand children's knowledge of scientific ideas (Novak & Canus, 2006), a **concept map** is a graphical representation of connections and links between ideas. Words describing specific concepts are usually placed in circles or boxes, and lines are drawn between the concepts that are related. It can be helpful to write one or a few words next to the connecting line to describe the nature of the relationship between the two concepts. Because of the contextual nature of how concepts are connected, it is helpful to have a focusing question. Figure 4.3 shows a concept map that relates to the example we have been using in this chapter.

This is not a complicated example but does clearly show the funder's goal of economic development as a catalyst for individual self-sufficiency. Also shown are both community barriers and personal barriers that block the attainment of individual self-sufficiency. The four community barriers were identified from among those listed by the funder as being applicable to the community, while the three personal barriers were also identified as being important as blocks towards self-sufficiency by the Office of Community Services.

As shown here, one can imagine finding data to support all or almost all these barriers being present in a community. Information about (a lack of) employment opportunities could be found in the Census Bureau's surveys of economic activity. A community survey done by United Way, or even an examination of a phone book, might disclose the number of training programs and licensed child care centers in the community. Also, statistics on unemployment and poverty can be found quickly from the Census Bureau.

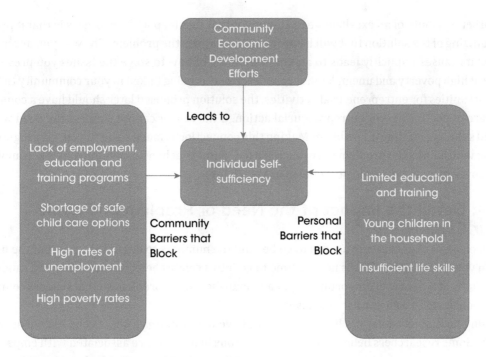

FIGURE 4.3   Self-Sufficiency FOA Concept Map

Information on personal barriers might not be as easy to find, but it is probably available. The Census Bureau has information about educational levels as well as the number of children below the age of 5 years at the community level. Key informant interviews and focus groups could be helpful in underscoring this situation, if questions have been asked and answered. Making a case that residents in a community have insufficient life skills may prove a challenge unless there has been a special survey taken on the topic in your community. Still, working with local schools, churches, or other institutions may turn up evidence along this line.

The concept map has been introduced to systematize the variables being examined and their relationships to each other. The concepts in the example shown in Figure 4.3 could be further linked to each other, such as the concepts of lack of education and training programs, unemployment, and poverty. Even a basic concept map such as this one can move the program development process along quickly. A concept map also serves as a graphic reminder of the main ideas being worked on by the funder and the applicant. The data that need to be collected and connected are also quickly referred to. In line with Bradshaw's (1970) idea of relative need, compelling descriptions of need often compare two locales with one another.

An excellent statement of need also does something else that marks the difference between a decent writeup and an excellent one. It looks forward to other parts of the funding plan or grant application. This is done in two ways. First, an excellent statement connects the problem being discussed in the application to the types of problems that the organization typically addresses. This is important because the funder wants to give resources to organizations with some expertise and experience in effectively addressing the problem at hand.

The other attribute of an excellent need statement that sets it apart from others is that it provides foreshadowing of the solution that will be proposed to address the problem. The way you describe the need and its causes implicitly leads to an understanding of how to solve the issues you present. For example, if high poverty and unemployment are described as being linked in your community to having few opportunities for entrepreneurial activities, the solution proposed later should have a component to increase opportunities for entrepreneurial action. If the reader cannot connect the need with the proposed solution, funding is less likely. Making this connection is made easier if you use a logic model, a graphic which links the problem to resources used, outputs achieved, and outcomes accomplished. We will cover how to create a logic model in a later chapter.

Step 4: Detail the Impact of the Need or Problem on People in Your Community

The final element of uncovering need is to go beyond the numbers to detail the impact of the need on people in your community. This is not the time to go into a comprehensive case study of a random set of individuals. It is, however, important to put a human face to the problem so that readers connect on an emotional level as well as a rational level.

Knowing human physiology is helpful here. We have in our brains a set of cells known as "mirror neurons." Some researchers believe that mirror neurons in humans are associated with empathy and the ability to understand other people's motives. Painting a verbal picture of others' actions can, they assert, trigger a response of empathy on the part of the reader (Winerman, 2005). If this is true, evoking such a reaction through detailing the impact of the problem on people in your community may trigger a higher emotional connection with the grant proposal, with the possibility of receiving a higher score when it is assessed. While this is a controversial aspect of both brain chemistry and fundraising, there is no doubt that clear writing filled with accurate, interesting, context-laden prose keeps the reader's attention, creating a better chance for thoughtful critique and judgment on the application's merits.

The key to detailing the impact of the problem is to show how it affects people and to link it very explicitly with the funder's intentions and goals. Connecting with the funder's stated desires through the facts and emotions you evoke are vital characteristics of successful grantwriting and in building support for new program development.

 SPOTLIGHT ON DIVERSITY

Community strengths may not be obvious to outsiders in some places—areas of deep urban poverty or isolated rural living are examples of seemingly asset-poor situations. Just as deserts can seem barren and lacking in life-sustaining elements but be fully developed and thriving ecosystems, all communities have at least some assets and a way of surviving, against all odds. Program developers must learn to locate strengths as well as problems and respect what they find. Too often, however, program developers may be unaware of the assets that exist because of cultural, ethnic, and socioeconomic differences between themselves and the communities they seek to serve.

The concept of coproduction shows how community members and program beneficiaries contribute to program development and operations, both informally and formally (Benjamin, 2021). By ensuring that plentiful opportunities exist before, during, and even after formal involvement is complete, information and opinions that would otherwise not be heard can have a considerable positive impact on programming. Such background information helps ensure that the program will be accepted in the community and be able to assist in solving an important problem.

Diversity is an important consideration in all aspects of community assessments:

- Recruitment of participants for information requires tailored outreach and encouragement (Johnson et al., 2020).
- Development of questions must ensure the community has an opportunity to include questions that will ascertain information important to all stakeholders and that the wording is clear and nonoffensive (Dorfman, 1998; Mannix et al., 2018).
- Focus group facilitators should be people who the participants can relate to by being similar in age, race, ethnicity, gender, and/or other connecting characteristics (Krueger & Casey, 2015).
- Data analysis can be done by any competent person, but diverse views should review the conclusions and reporting of results (Lumbantobing, 2020). If the review by members of the affected populations does reveal gaps in what was analyzed and discussed, release of the final report should be delayed until additional analysis and other revisions can be completed.
- As with all other aspects of community assessments, all stakeholders should be involved in discussion regarding future research needs (Agency for Healthcare Research and Quality, 2011; Pang, 2019).

The underlying principle we emphasize is that meaningful participation of people from the community is necessary in all aspects of program development, including assessments; being in the room where decisions are being made is only a first step (Benjamin, 2021). Explicitly committing to having a community-engagement approach is vital, as is the follow-through (Everhart, 2020).

DIFFICULTIES AND JOYS

"Where's the information I need?" is a common difficulty in this aspect of program design. You want to know these things, but the information does not seem to be available. Even in the vast recesses of the internet, you may run into significant barriers in accessing the data that will truly paint a clear picture of both needs and strengths. People may not return calls, emails may go unanswered, and the deadline for funding draws nearer.

Still, for anyone who loves research and working to solve community problems, the process of identifying community needs and strengths is potentially a joyful exercise. Capturing these important aspects of community life and bringing together the facts to show what a clear description can highlight is like directing an orchestra to ensure beautiful music comes out! In the same way, the program designer in the role of community assessment person also brings together a diverse set of talents and knowledge to ensure the most positive result. Particularly when working outside of your own organization to receive help from the community and potential beneficiaries to design a program that will really hit the mark, the rewards can be great.

LESSONS FROM THE PANDEMIC

A good needs and asset assessment will retain much the same structure and approaches during a pandemic as in nonpandemic times. The methods may be somewhat different, but all community assessments have their challenges and adaptations that are made from initial plans. Still, Lumbantobing (2020) makes these specific recommendations:

- Start where you are. By this he means that you can continue using the expertise you have built up over time in your community.
- Ask questions. Despite your knowledge, things have probably changed. It is important to find out what has changed and for whom. This demonstrates both culturally humility and a willingness to be led by the expressed needs of the community.
- Start with who you know. Outreach is important to get beyond a small group you are already connected to, but the best way to be welcomed is through introductions. In uncertain times, personal connections already established open more doors (literally and figuratively) than cold calls.

CONCLUSION

The purpose of an assessment is to help you, as a program developer, to understand your community better. This allows you to see both the needs to be decreased and the assets that are available to be used in creating improvement. In order to understand, you will need to use some of the advocacy skills you learned in Chapter 3 to contact stakeholders who may support your efforts. When you understand the concepts and measures of different aspects of your community, you will be able to make a stronger case for developing a workable program that is in line with local norms, traditions, and values. Such a program design will have a better chance, we believe, both in gathering the necessary resources and in being supported by the community within which it operates.

 SUMMARY/KEY POINTS

- Program design and program funding usually move forward together. The program design cannot promise a program that costs more than what the fundraiser can bring in. At the same time, the program design must be complete enough that the fundraiser can determine how much the funding needs to be.
- Needs assessments come in both community wide and program levels of detail and breadth. Many community-wide assessments are commissioned by large organizations or universities that will cover many topic areas. Programs are then free to take the information they need for a specific problem-based fundraising effort.
- Finding ways to use community members and potential beneficiaries in the program design stage will ensure that the solutions proposed are likely to be acceptable for recipients and that community strengths will be recognized and used in support of the program.

- The concept of need is not a single idea. Different types of need are discussed, including Maslow's hierarchy of needs, whether the problem is located at the individual or system level (or both), as well as the perceived extent, depth, and duration of the identified need.
- Measurement of potential need is a complex and multifaceted issue and is described by Bradshaw. Long discussions can be had in this area, but often, the program developer is limited by the difficulty in finding information more than not knowing what the most desirable information would be to have.
- Several different methods of measuring and collecting information to make the case for your proposal are provided, including both needs and assets.
- A four-step process of uncovering need is provided: defining the terms in the same way the funder or other stakeholders do, discover data to make your case, describe the need in your community, and detail the impact of the need on the people of your community.

KEY TERMS

Asset-based Community Development Institute (ABCD): "ABCD involves the community in making an inventory of assets and capacity, building relationships, developing a vision of the future, and leveraging internal and external resources to support actions to achieve it" (Kerka, 2003, p. 1).

Community assets: Community assets include people, parts of the built and natural environments, formal institutions (businesses, places of worship), and informal organizations.

Community barriers: "Conditions in a community that impede success in employment or self-employment of low-income individuals. Such conditions may include lack of employment education and training programs, lack of public transportation, lack of markets, unavailability of financing, insurance or bonding; inadequate social services such as employment services, child care or job training; high incidence of crime; inadequate health care; or environmental hazards such as toxic dumpsites or leaking underground tanks" (Department of Health and Human Services, 2013, p. 4).

Community-wide assessment: A comprehensive examination of the state of a community, including deficits (needs) and assets (strengths) that can be incorporated into program planning. These are often sponsored by an organization, such as United Way, or a governmental/university planning office because of the amount of cost and scope of the project.

Concept map: A concept map is a graphical representation of connections and links between ideas. Words describing specific concepts are usually placed in circles or boxes, and lines are drawn between the concepts that are related.

Deficit needs: Within Maslow's 1970 version of his hierarchy of needs, the needs that are labeled physiological, safety, belonging and love, and esteem.

Focus group interviews: Focus group interviews usually have 5–10 people in each one. These are used when participants with certain characteristics are asked to provide their perceptions and views on topics that they are especially knowledgeable about (Krueger & Casey, 2015).

Growth needs: Within Maslow's 1970 version of his hierarchy of needs, the needs that are labeled cognitive, aesthetic, self-actualization, and transcendence.

Key informant interview: This is defined by the United States Agency for International Development (USAID, 1996) as "qualitative, in-depth interviews of people selected for their first-hand knowledge about a topic of interest. The interviews are loosely structured, relying on a list of issues to be discussed" (p. 1).

Maslow's hierarchy of needs: A description of needs that result in motivation to act. The original version (1943) consisted of five types of needs: physiological, safety, love and belonging, esteem, and self-actualization. His updated version (1970) modifies the original five and adds three to become eight levels: physiological, safety, love and belonging, esteem, cognitive, aesthetic, self-actualization, and transcendence.

Program-level community assessments: A less-comprehensive examination of the state of a community, including deficits (needs) and assets (strengths) that can be incorporated into making a case for a particular program idea. This type of assessment is often almost entirely comprised of secondary data drawn from comprehensive community assessments.

ADDITIONAL RESOURCES

Community Toolbox. (n.d.). *Assessing community needs and resources.* University of Kansas Community Health and Development. https://ctb.ku.edu/en/table-of-contents/assessment/assessing-community-needs-and-resources/develop-a-plan/main

Everhart, R., Haley, A., Regan, G., Romo, S. Dempster, K. W., Barsell, D. J., Corona, R., Mazzeo, S. E., Schechter, M., & The Engaging Richmond Team. (2020). Engaging with the Richmond community to reduce pediatric asthma disparities: Findings from a community-engaged needs assessment. *American Journal of Community Psychology*, *66*, 222–231. https://doi.org/10.1002/ajcp.12439

Heaven, C. (n.d.). *Section 1. Developing a plan for assessing local needs and resources: Checklist.* https://ctb.ku.edu/en/table-of-contents/assessment/assessing-community-needs-and-resources/develop-a-plan/checklist

Mannix, T., Austin, S., Baayd, J., & Simonsoen, S. (2018). A community needs assessment of urban Utah American Indians and Alaska natives. *Journal of Community Health*, *43*, 1217–1227.

United States Bureau of Labor Statistics. (n.d.). *Home.* https://www.bls.gov/

United States Census Bureau. (n.d.). *Explore census data.* https://data.census.gov/cedsci/

United Way of Tarrant County. (2019). *Community assessment.* https://www.unitedwaytarrant.org/community assessment/

DISCUSSION QUESTIONS

1. What are some of the important differences between community and program needs and assets assessments? When should you expect to do one or the other?
2. Although the chapter provides arguments for why agencies should rely on comprehensive needs assessments when writing or discussing grant proposals, why might they *not* want to?

3. Have several people in your class talk with community agency leaders who have conducted community assessments, either comprehensive or not. Share the results of your discussions. What have been these leaders' difficulties and joys when doing so?

 YOUR TURN

The information in Box 4.5 is from the request for proposals that we are using as a case example (emphasis is added to focus what is most related to the need or problem).

Read the information and answer the questions about this abbreviated needs assessment.

As you see, the funder requires a clear demonstration of the problem, possibly using demographic data, information about the program participants, or target population and service area—using reputable data sources and literature. What follows is *part of* the response to the RFP by the agency in its successful grant proposal. Here are some things to note as you read through the material:

- What type of definition of need is being used (explicitly or implicitly)?
- What types of data are offered as proof of need? What sources were used? (Make a table or list to keep track. How would you characterize each data source?)
- What information do you believe is missing that would be helpful? (Remember, this is not the full submission from the grant.)

Assessment of proposal information:

- If you were grading this needs statement, given what you have read in this chapter, what would you say are its strengths and its weaknesses?
- Assume you could give from 0 to 10 points for this section (0 = worst rating, and 10 = best rating). What score would you give it, and why?
- Locate up-to-date information on this same topic for a location of your choosing or that is assigned to you.

BOX 4.5	**Objectives and Need for Assistance from Grant Request for Proposals**

Clearly identify the physical, economic, social, financial, institutional, and/or other problems requiring a solution. The need for assistance including the nature and scope of the problem must be demonstrated and the principle and subordinate objectives of the project must be clearly and concisely stated; supporting documentation, such as letters of support and testimonials from concerned interests other than the applicant may be included. Any relevant data based on planning studies should be included or referred to in the endnotes/footnotes. Incorporate demographic data and participant/beneficiary information, as well as data describing the needs of the target population and the proposed service area as needed. When appropriate, a literature review should be used to support the objectives and needs described in this section.

Source: From the RFP (p. 19)

AGENCY RESPONSE (NOTE: Some details have been changed.)

1. <u>Thorough depiction of conditions of youth and families in the proposed service area</u>: ACH

   LBJ Emergency Youth Shelter ("Shelter"), located in Johnson County, is the only Basic Center Program and/or emergency shelter for RHY in ACH's five-county service area of Eisenhower, Ford, Johnson, Kennedy, and Nixon counties. Most youth served are from Kennedy County, an 897-square-mile area, home to 1,814,667 residents. Kennedy County, Texas's third most populous county, has 33 cities. A 26-year Basic Center Program grantee, ACH has substantial experience serving RHY. In 2013, almost half of RHY served came to the Shelter due to family conflict. Shelter staff made a Child Protective Services report for neglect or abuse on 28% of RHY served. 11% had no home to return to. Here are recent RHY statistics:

TABLE I Recent Conditions of RHY Served, Basic Center Program

Clients	2022 Grant	2021 Grant	2020 Grant	2019 Grant
Total RHY Served	119	97	72	190
Home Counties				
Kennedy County	103	88	54	160
Eisenhower, Ford, Johnson, and Nixon Counties	0	3	3	10
Other counties	16	6	15	20
Other Client Info				
Presenting due to family conflict (includes abuse, neglect, family violence, youth and/or family substance abuse)	57	38	25	97
No home to return to	13	18	12	17
On whom Shelter staff made a CPS report of abuse	34	23	13	46

The 2020 *Kennedy City Youth Priority Issues Report*, published by the United Way of Kennedy County, studied issues affecting youth ages 12–18 in Kennedy City, Kennedy County's second most populous city. The study surveyed homeless youth served in the Kennedy City Independent School District's Families in Transition program, a specialized program for homeless students and their families. The survey asked, "What causes young people to leave their homes?" Of those asked, 93% said family problems, 63% said abuse/neglect, 52% said substance abuse, 29% said school problems, and 27% said poverty. These local findings mirror national findings. The National Runaway Safeline's *2021 Reporter's Source Book on Runaway and Homeless Youth* states that strong predictors for running away include abuse, contact with the juvenile justice system, failing in school, and parental substance abuse. The National Conference on State Legislatures reports that youth who were in the foster care system are more likely to become homeless at an earlier age and remain homeless for a longer period of time than their non–foster care peers. The same body reported that in non–foster care families, economic problems contribute to youth running away or becoming homeless, since financial instability has a domino effect on families, particularly those with a single head of household. The Kennedy County Area Food Bank, which distributed 22% more food in 2013 versus 2012, reports that 1 in 4 local children are hungry. Kennedy County risk factors appear below, correlated with national averages. (Texas rates were used when national rates were unavailable.)

TABLE II Risk Factors for Youth Becoming RHY (all stats are most recent available)

	Kennedy County	TX
2021 Confirmed child abuse victims per 1,000 children	10.9	9.3
2020 Children in foster care per 1,000 children	3.3	4.3
2010 Referral rate, juvenile population per 1,000 children	34	36
2021 Public high school attrition rate	29%	25%
		U.S.
2021 Children living in poverty	22.6%	23%
2021 Child food insecurity	23.5%	22%
2021 Children receiving free/reduced lunch	61.4%	68%
2021–2022 Children living in single-parent homes	29.7%	35%
2021 Children receiving SNAP	24.9%	26.9%
2022 High school dropout rate	7.3%	4%
2022 Unemployment rate	6.6%	8.1%

The National Runaway Safeline reports 5,416 2012 crisis calls/crisis chats from Texas, the third highest number after New York and California. 2021 crisis calls/crisis chats from Kennedy County totaled 1,059—20% of all incoming crisis calls and crisis chats from the entire state of Texas.

2. <u>Definition of number of runaway, homeless, and street youth in proposed service area</u>: Because RHY are notoriously underrepresented in official homeless counts, Kennedy County offers the following data to estimate the possible number of RHY and street youth in Tarrant County.

2021 Point-in-time count of homeless persons under age 18 (trans. housing: 462, emergency shelter: 232, unsheltered: 0)	694
2017 ACH RHY programs Basic Center Program RHY served Street Outreach Program RHY and street youth received youth assessments, case management, or psychoeducational services	119 260
2021–22 Arlington Independent School District homeless	1,392
2021–22 Fort Worth Independent School District homeless students	1,518
2021 Tarrant County Juvenile Services runaway referrals	33
Estimate (not counting "couch surfers")	4,016

REFERENCES

A.D.A.M. Medical Encyclopedia. (2013). *Major depression.* http://www.ncbi.nlm.nih.gov/pubmedhealth/PMH 0001941/#adam_000945.disease.causes

Agency for Healthcare Research and Quality. (2011). *Engaging stakeholders to identify and prioritize future research needs.* U.S. Department of Health and Human Services. https://www.ncbi.nlm.nih.gov/books/NBK62565/pdf/ Bookshelf_NBK62565.pdf

Armson, H., Perrier, L., Roder, S., Shommu, N., Wakefield, J., Shaw, E., Zahorka, S., Elmslie, T., & Lofft, M. (2020). Assessing unperceived learning needs in continuing medical education for primary care physicians: A scoping review. *Journal of Continuing Education for Health Professionals*, *40*(4), 257–267. https://doi.org/10.1097/ CEH.0000000000000300

Benjamin, L. (2021). Bringing beneficiaries more centrally into nonprofit management education and research. *Nonprofit and Voluntary Sector Quarterly*, *50*(1), 5–26. https://doi.org/10.0899764020918662.1177

Best, D., Irving, J., Collinson, B. Andersson, C., & Edwards, M. (2017). Recovery networks and community connections: Identifying connection needs and community linkage opportunities in early recovery populations. *Alcoholism Treatment Quarterly*, *35*(1), 2–15. https://doi.org/10.1080/07347324.2016.1256718

Biscotte, S., & Mouchrek, N. (2020). Bringing an asset-based community development (ABCD) framework to university change work. In K. White, A. Beach, N. Finkelstein, C. Henderson, S. Simkins, L. Slakey, M. Stains, G. Weaver, & L. Whitehead (Eds.), *Transforming institutions: Accelerating systemic change in higher education.* Creative Commons. http://openbooks.library.umass.edu/ascnti2020/chapter/biscotte-mouchrek/

Bradshaw, J. (1972). A taxonomy of social need. In G. McLachlan (Ed.), *Problems and progress in medical care: Essays on current research* (pp. 71–82). Oxford University Press. https://eprints.whiterose.ac.uk/118357/1/

Chamberlain, S., Duggleby, W., Teaster, P., & Estabrooks, C. (2019). Characteristics and unmet care needs of unbefriended residents in long-term care: A qualitative interview study. *Aging and Mental Health*, *24*(4), 659–667. https://doi.org/10.1080/13607863.2019.1566812

Dorfman, D. (1998). *Mapping community assets workbook.* Northwest Regional Educational Laboratory. https:// files.eric.ed.gov/fulltext/ED426499.pdf

Fallatah, R., & Syed, J. (2017). *Employee motivation in Saudi Arabia.* Palgrave Macmillan. https://doi.org/ 10.1007/978-3-319-67741-5_2

Hoefer, R. (2017). *Funded! Successful grantwriting for your nonprofit.* Oxford University Press.

Johnson, K., Allen, K., West, W., Williams-Kirkwood, W., Wasilewski-Masker, K., Escoffery, C., & Brock, K. E. (2020). Strengths, gaps, and opportunities: Results of a statewide community needs assessment of pediatric palliative care and hospice resources. *Journal of Pain and Symptom Management*, *60*(3), 512–521. https://doi. org/10.1016/j.jpainsymman.2020.04.009

KERA. (2020). *Dallas has the largest homeless population in Texas.* https://www.keranews.org/texas-news/2020-01-07/ dallas-has-the-largest-homeless-population-in-texas

Kerka, S. (2003). Community assets mapping. *Educational Resources Information Center Trends and Issues Alert, 47.* http://www.virtualcap.org/downloads/VC/US_Needs_Assessment_ERIC_Community_Asset_Mapping.pdf

King-Hill, S. (2015). Critical analysis of Maslow's hierarchy of need. *The STeP Journal, 2*(4), 54–57. https://ojs. cumbria.ac.uk/index.php/step/article/view/274

Kretzmann, J., & McKnight, J. (1993). *Building communities from the inside out: A path toward finding and mobilizing a community's assets.* ACTA Publications. http://www.povertystudies.org/TeachingPages/EDS_PDFs4WEB/ABCD-Bldg-communities-from-inside-out.pdf

Kretzmann, J., & McKnight, J. (2005). *Discovering community power: A guide to mobilizing local assets and your organization's capacity: A community-building workbook.* Asset-Based Community Development Institute. https://staging.community-wealth.org/sites/clone.community-wealth.org/files/downloads/tool-ABCD-capacity%20bldg.pdf

Krueger, R., & Casey, M. (2015). *Focus groups: A practical guide for applied research* (5th ed.). Sage.

Lumbantobing, N. (2020). *How to perform a needs assessment for your community during COVID-19.* https://blog.ioby.org/how-to-perform-a-needs-assessment-for-your-community-during-covid-19/

Mannix, T., Austin, S., Baayd, J., & Simonsoen, S. (2018). A community needs assessment of urban Utah American Indians and Alaska natives. *Journal of Community Health, 43,* 1217–1227. https://doi.org/10.1007/s10900-018-0542-9

Maslow, A. (1943). A theory of human motivation. *Psychological Review, 50,* 370–396.

Maslow, A. (1970). *Religions, values, and peak experiences.* Harper & Row.

Novak J., & Canus, A. (2006). *Theory underlying concept maps.* http://cmap.ihmc.us/Publications/ResearchPapers/TheoryCmaps/TheoryUnderlyingConceptMaps.htm

Pang, H. (2019). *Leveraging community assets to tackle social isolation and loneliness: A needs assessment of the London Borough of Hammersmith & Fulham* [Executive summary]. Imperial College. https://spiral.imperial.ac.uk/bitstream/10044/1/80602/2/Leveraging%20Community%20Assets%20to%20Tackle%20Social%20Isolation%20%26%20Loneliness%20in%20LBHF%20%28v1.%2020%20Sep%202019%29.pdf

Pantoja, L. (2020). *Community needs assessment: Opioid use within the Central Connecticut Health District.* [Master's thesis, University of Connecticut]. Opencommons.uconn.edu. https://opencommons.uconn.edu/gs_theses/1501/

Phillips, L. (2017). *The starving artist syndrome & how to cure it.* Americans for the Arts. https://www.americansforthearts.org/2019/05/15/the-starving-artist-syndrome-how-to-cure-it

Rohr, D., Morgan, K. B., Spence-Almaguer, E., Deahl, C., Sanderson, B., Aiken, J., Hardin, E., & Miank, A. (2019). *United Way of Tarrant County Community Assessment 2018–19: Technical report.* www.unitedwaytarrant.org/communityassessment

United States Agency for International Development, Center for Development Information and Evaluation. (1996). *Performance Monitoring & Evaluation TIPS.* from http://pdf.usaid.gov/pdf_docs/PNABS541.pdf

United States Census Bureau. (2013). *Finding data for my community.* https://www2.census.gov/geo/pdfs/education/brochures/MyCommunity.pdf

United States Census Bureau. (2019a). *Dallas city quick facts.* https://www.census.gov/quickfacts/fact/table/dallascitytexas,dallascountytexas/IPE120219

United States Census Bureau. (2019b). *Poverty thresholds.* https://www.census.gov/data/tables/time-series/demo/income-poverty/historical-poverty-thresholds.html

United States Department of Health and Human Services. (2013). *HHS-2013-ACF-OCS-EE-0583.* http://www.acf.hhs.gov/grants/open/foa/files/HHS-2013-ACF-OCS-EE-0583_1.pdf

United States Department of Health and Human Services. (2021). *Poverty guidelines.* https://aspe.hhs.gov/poverty-guidelines

United Way of Tarrant County. (2019). *Community assessment 2018–2019.* https://s3.amazonaws.com/ll. media.storage001/content-management-file-uploads/customers/11365/CommunityAssessmentFull. pdf?AWSAccessKeyId=AKIARYB632YRTHZCHAHW&Expires=1611458616&Signature=QUoU6sCkZXRei98qp-8WcgiSAbm8%3D

United Way of Tarrant County. (2019b). *Community assessment 2018–2019*: *Technical report: An overview of data sources.* https://s3.amazonaws.com/ll.media.storage001/content-management-file-uploads/customers/11365/CommunityAssessmentTechnicalReport.pdf?AWSAccessKeyId=AKIARYB632YRTHZCHAHW&Expires=1611459692&Signature=Ktj6o%2B6HShS%2ByZlDXfNj9IqkWDE%3D

Winerman, L. (2005). *The mind's mirror.* American Psychological Association. http://www.apa.org/monitor/oct05/mirror.aspx

Figure Credits

CHAPTER FIVE

Grantwriting and Fund Development

Finding and Applying for Funding

OVERVIEW

"Without funds, there are no programs" is a mantra of all fundraisers. Program funds can come from many different sources. Grantwriting and fund development are two major skills needed to secure program funds. Contracts and fees for service, or earned income, are other sources of funding for human service programs. This chapter presents the basics of a fundraising and grant writing program and the competencies you will need in this area of practice. You will learn

- the three major components of fund development;
- where to look for funding; and
- how to apply for funding or to raise money for your program.

In this chapter, we will take the first steps to developing our sample proposal by identifying an appropriate foundation funding source and examining their proposal guidelines and requirements. Your assignment at the end of the chapter is to find an appropriate funding source for your project.

WHERE DO YOU LOOK FOR FUNDING?

Hoefer (2017) describes the three main legs of nonprofit fundraising as individual giving, foundation giving, and government grants and contracts. We will explore each of these areas and will present several approaches to securing individual gifts, including the annual campaign, direct mail, special events, major gifts, and planned gifts. There is a lot of charitable gift money out there. American individuals, estates, foundations, and corporations gave an estimated $449.64 billion to charitable causes in 2019, according to Giving USA Foundation (2020). You will need skills in each of these areas to be effective in your role as an administrator. Of course, fundraising is not the only source of income for nonprofits or human services. Fees for service are a large part of the budget for many human services organizations. Figure 5.1 shows the mix of income streams for the nonprofit sector as a whole. The human services sector relies more heavily on government grants, fees, and contracts and private contributions but less on fees for services income from private sources. In this chapter, we focus on the skills that support fundraising to secure private contributions (individual and foundation) and government grants.

THE THREE MAIN LEGS OF FUND DEVELOPMENT

Individual Giving

For a few years during the Great Recession of 2008, individual giving decreased considerably across the nonprofit world. Fortunately, in 2013, the tide turned and overall charitable giving increased for many years in a row, with giving increasing across most types of donors each year at least until 2019 (figures for all of 2020 are not yet known, but for the first three quarters of the year, the trend continued, despite the effects of the COVID-19 pandemic; Hrywna, 2020).

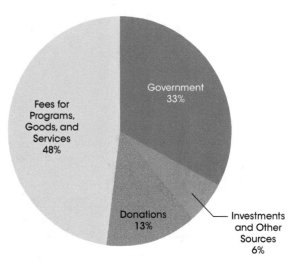

FIGURE 5.1   Sources of Nonprofit Revenues 2020

The problem for nonprofits is that no one can be sure just how well the economy is going to do in the next few years. Some economists argue that there will be a stock market correction, with a resulting loss of stock portfolio value, causing individuals to again lose significant ground financially. If this occurs, they will be less likely to give, just as they gave less during the other economic downturns, including the Great Recession that lasted from December 2007 to June 2009. In addition, income inequality is continuing to grow, with the percentage of Americans in the middle class declining. According to the Pew Research Center, U.S. income inequality has been increasing steadily since the 1970s, and now "the wealth gap between America's richest and poorer families more than doubled from 1989 to 2016" (Schaeffer, 2020, Section 5). Thus, it is not clear what will happen with individual donor giving. Blackbaud (McLaughlin, 2020) reports that the average age for a donor is 62 and that for those giving over $1,000, the median gift is $2,049. For those giving less than $1,000, the median gift is $20. The average online donation was $147. Online giving and social media fundraising are important emerging areas of fund development strategies.

In times of crisis, donor contributions may increase to meet the challenge. For example, Fidelity Charitable (2020) conducted a study of philanthropic individuals to understand their response to the COVID-19 pandemic. The study found that most donors will maintain or increase their charitable contributions in 2020. The findings indicate that 25% will increase their contributions, and 54% plan to maintain their current giving level (Fidelity Charitable, 2020). Early indicators of the impact of the pandemic in 2020 showed about a 6% lower level of giving in the first quarter of the year (Hrywna, 2020), but donations actually increased in both the second and third quarters of 2020, compared to 2019 (Fundraising Effectiveness Project, 2020).

Foundation Funding

According to Candid (2020), there were almost 119,800 foundations in the United States, based on Internal Revenue Service filings in 2020, up from 86,203 in 2015. They are responsible for 17% of all private giving in the United States (Hrywna, 2020) and gave approximately $75.7 billion in 2019 (Giving USA Foundation, 2020). Human service organizations received about 12% of total foundation giving (Hrywna, 2020). Giving by foundations has increased in 9 of the past 10 years after falling to its lowest point in 2010 (Giving USA, 2020).

Government Grants and Contracts

When government grants and contracts decline, the nonprofit sector feels the pinch quickly because of the extent of government funding for nonprofits. For example, in 2018, government grants and contracts provided one third of revenue for public charities (32%; Hrywna, 2019).

The federal government still provides tens of billions of dollars of funding per year, but as with other sources of income, competition is greater, and the need to have an excellent grantwriter is heightened if a nonprofit is relying on the federal government for support.

DEVELOPING GIFTS FROM INDIVIDUALS

There are several different approaches to soliciting donations from individuals. These include the annual campaign, direct mail, special events, major gifts, online campaigns, and planned gifts. The concept of moving donors from annual giving to major gifts and planned gifts will be presented. This chapter will also explore donor motivation and present a fundraising strategy based on the concept of providing donors with opportunities rather than approaching fundraising as a "begging" activity.

Begging is not an effective strategy to raise funds. The alternative to begging for funds is to have a well-developed fundraising program. Even if the organization employs a professional fundraiser, the administrator is still the chief fundraising officer and, as such, will develop professional fundraising skills or risk becoming the chief beggar for the organization. Securing resources for the organization is ultimately the responsibility of the board of directors, but it is the administrator's responsibility to develop and oversee a well-developed fundraising program.

There are many truisms in fundraising, but the most important one to remember is that "people give to people, not to organizations." This is another way to say that fundraising is really "friend-raising." The people that will give money to your organization are those who share a passion for the mission of the organization and who trust that their money will be used wisely. It is the responsibility of the administrator to develop and nurture relationships that will financially sustain the organization.

Another truism is that people will not give anything to meet your agency needs, but they will give when presented with the opportunity to invest in an organization that will make a difference in the lives of others. People will give when they think they can make a positive difference in something they care about. At whatever level of fundraising activity, your approach should be to present opportunities that will make a positive impact in the lives of the people your organization serves and not to present the needs of the agency. You may need funds to hire a new counselor, but the fundraising approach should be to secure funds to serve more clients. You must tell the potential donor why the clients need this service and what difference it will make in their lives if the services are provided. The approach should *not* be that your organization "needs a new counselor."

Remember that people want to give to successful causes. You want to give the donor not only the opportunity to give but also a reason to contribute to a cause that will support success. Your appeal is not that your organization has great needs but that it is successful in meeting the needs of your clients.

Before we explore the many levels of activities in a fundraising program, we will look at the factors that motivate people to give.

DONOR MOTIVATION

Why do people give? Often, you will hear that most people give a donation because they will get a tax break. It is very seldom that tax donations are the major reason for making a donation.

BOX 5.1	**I Don't Want to Be Rich**

A new executive director was excited to learn that an elderly couple had decided to leave their 1,000-acre ranch to the organization in their will. The executive went to visit the couple and raised the possibility that they could use a planned giving vehicle to go ahead and make their gift to the agency and at the same time enjoy a tremendous tax advantage, plus increase their income for the rest of their lives. In fact, through this gift, the couple could become rich. After listening politely, the elderly woman said, "Young man, I don't want to be rich. I want to go to our ranch and hunt birds!" It is important to know what motivates a donor. In this case, it was certainly not a tax break or more income.

People will give only when they are interested and involved in your cause. Of course, there are different levels of giving. The new donor responding to a direct mail piece will be very different from a board member donor with years of experience with the organization. People will respond to different kinds of appeals because they have different reasons for giving. So why do they give? Different authors provide varying answers to this question. Giving behavior is just as complex as any other behavior.

In a review of over 500 articles on charitable giving, Bekkers and Wiepking (2011) found eight mechanisms to be the most important forces that determine a person's decision to give. These are (1) awareness of need, (2) solicitation, (3) costs and benefits, (4) altruism, (5) reputation, (6) psychological benefits, (7) values, and (8) efficacy.

In his book *Tested Ways to Successful Fund Raising*, George A. Brakeley Jr. (as cited in "8 Rules of Thumb," 2012) wrote that virtually every fundraising campaign and development program depends on the following eight factors in motivating donors to support their organization:

1. The right person or persons ask them, at the right time, and in the right circumstances.
2. People have a sincere desire to help other people.
3. People wish to belong to or be identified with a group or organization they admire.
4. Recognition of how vital their gifts can be satisfies a need for a sense of personal power in many people.
5. People have received benefits—often, personal enjoyment—from the services of the organization and wish to support it.
6. They "get something" out of giving.
7. People receive income and estate tax benefits from giving.
8. People may need to give; that is, altruism might not be an option but a "love or perish" necessity for many people.

Donor motivation research by Tsipursky (2017) found that most donors give to receive a feeling of self-satisfaction or social prestige. Some researchers disagree, but most of the research exploring why donors give concludes that they do so because it makes them feel good. For donors, how they feel about making a contribution is even more important than what can be accomplished by the donation. The feeling of self-satisfaction is most powerful when the donation is based on a deeply held personal value. A contribution to any worthy cause may produce a feeling of enhanced self-value, but a donation to an organization that is dear to the donor's heart and represents their deeply held values will produce an enhanced feeling of self-value. The donors who have a strong interest in your organization based on their value system are the donors who have the greatest potential to be the major donors to your organization.

The donor who sends in a few dollars from a direct mail appeal is very different from the donor who strongly believes in what your organization represents. Wright and Bocarnea (2007) found that the level of connection to an organization is a key factor in determining if the potential donor has a positive or negative attitude toward the organization. The way that the organization interacts with the donor will shape the attitudes toward the organization, and the more a donor is connected to an organization, the more likely it is that they will view the organization positively (Gorczyca & Hartman, 2017). Whatever their other motivations, people will give only when they are interested and involved and when they are asked. To determine how to ask for a gift, we must know where our donors fit on the donor pyramid.

THE DONOR PYRAMID

Fundraising professionals often use the donor pyramid to conceptualize the fundraising program (see Figure 5.2). Each level in the pyramid builds on the level beneath it. For example, direct mail solicitation is appropriate to attract new donors to your organization, but once they have responded with even a small gift, your goal is to move them up to the next level of the pyramid. You want your new direct mail donors to become major givers. Of course, some donors will always be small givers or even stop giving to your organization, but most of your future major gift donors of tomorrow are your small gift givers today. Also, remember that all those small gifts add up and are very important to your overall fundraising plan.

Venkatish (2020) describes a fundraising **donor pyramid** as a "visual that categorizes prospects by their engagement level. Further, it provides nonprofits a path to move donors from lower levels of giving to greater commitment" (What Is a Donor Pyramid? section). A useful element of a donor pyramid is that it shows how a nonprofit may have a broad base of donors giving a little bit but fewer and fewer people give at higher amounts of either money or time. The more you can make your "pyramid" look like a "cylinder," the more you have been able to move your donors to higher levels of giving. Everyone who donates is valuable, and no one should be neglected. About 55% of all first-time donors do not give to the same organization the next year (O'Connor, 2020). This donor attrition figure illustrates a huge waste of effort because it is usually much easier to get a second donation than it is a first donation, if the organization acknowledges and works with the donor. Nonprofits that have a higher donor retention rate are more easily able to move donors up the pyramid because the donors already know and trust the organization and its mission. In addition, for every $100 gained in new donations, donor attrition in the typical nonprofit causes losses of $94 (O'Connor, 2020). Thus, all the work being done to bring in new donors is almost entirely lost from gift attrition.

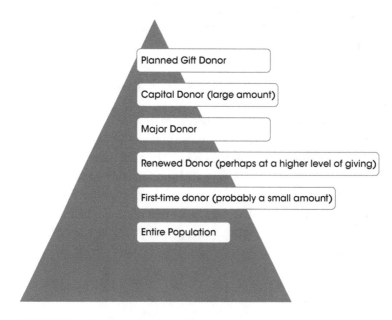

FIGURE 5.2   Sample Donor Pyramid

As you work through this chapter, refer back to the donor pyramid. In a sophisticated fundraising program, donors will be treated differently depending on where they are on the donor pyramid. Donors will move up the donor pyramid through involvement with the organization and through receiving personal attention from the board and staff of the organization. Notice that as you move up in the pyramid, the fundraising techniques become increasingly more personalized.

What seems to be a simple and obvious truism is "No one gives at any level unless they are asked!" As uncomfortable as it may be at times, eventually someone has to ask for the gift, but if you and your board believe in your mission and truly believe you are giving others the opportunity to participate in your important work, then the "ask" will be less difficult.

While the donor pyramid is a simple way to conceptualize a fundraising program, many professional fundraisers say that the pyramid is dead. Others describe the pyramid as a dinosaur that has had a good long run but is now extinct. Some of the objection to the old paradigm is that it is based on forcing donors to climb the pyramid to higher levels. The alternative is presented as "meeting people where they are." This should be an easy concept for human services administrators to grasp. We are all about meeting our clients where they are, and so it should make perfect sense that we would meet donors where they are.

Claire Axelrad (2014) says that the digital age has changed how people connect to and interact with organizations and that this offers new opportunities to connect and build relationships. She asks a legitimate question: "Are folks finding out about you through a letter you sent in the mail or through something they saw on the internet? Are they reading your email appeals at their desks or on a smart phone just before bed?" She suggests that the current conceptual model is more like a vortex into which donors enter and exit at different levels. For example, someone you have never heard of might make a major gift as their first gift to your organization. It is not unusual that an organization receives a major gift through a will from a person they have never encountered before. The pyramid is useful to think about categories of donors and to provide a road map for increased engagement and increased support, but the reality is that donors may come in at any level of support. The digital environment provides us with great new challenges and opportunities (Axelrad, 2014).

WHERE'S THE MONEY?

American individuals, estates, foundations, and corporations gave an estimated $449.64 billion to charitable causes in 2019, up from $410 billion in 2017, according to Giving USA Foundation (2020). Why do individuals, foundations, and corporations give so much? What motivates a person to give? "Donors' giving patterns evolve in response to changes in economic and social forces. In 2019, we saw solid, broad-based growth in almost all aspects of charitable giving by individuals due to strong growth in the S&P 500 and personal income" (Giving USA, 2020, para. 8).

Notice in Figure 5.3 that 69% of donations come from individual donors (Hrywna, 2020). While corporate, foundation, and planned giving are all important elements of a fundraising program, individual donors give the most every year. This is why it is critical to bring new individual donors into your organization.

When looking at the type of entities that receive donations, a wide variety emerges. Religious organizations receive the highest percentage (29%), and educational institutions receive the second highest percentage (14%). Only about 12% of donations go to human services activities, and another 12% are given to grantmaking foundations. These are thus tied for third place in terms of receipt of funding (Hrywna, 2020). It is important for you to know what other types of organizations are competing for the charitable dollars available.

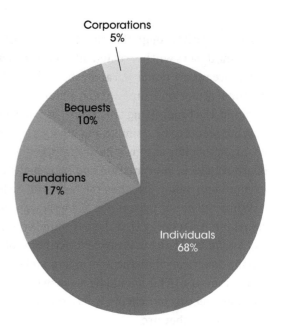

FIGURE 5.3   Sources of Contributions to Nonprofits 2019

Annual Campaign

The **annual campaign** consists of the fundraising activities that are conducted to support the organization's annual operating budget. Even though these funds will be used for the organization's operating budget, your approach will focus on the services to be provided, not on the need for things like staff raises or paying the electric bill. The operating expenses support the services your organization provides. Ask your donors to help serve your clients. Generally, the largest number of donors will be giving to the annual campaign. Some organizations may not think of their many and diverse fundraising activities as an "annual campaign," but whether it is thought of in these terms or not, mailings, special events, and similar activities are in effect the annual campaign for the organization. The approaches used in the annual campaign may include direct mail, social media appeals, phone-a-thons, or special events, such as golf tournaments or galas.

The defining feature of annual funding activities is that they are activities intended to raise gift income every year. It is expected that you will approach the same donors every year and, sometimes, several times within the same year. Funds donated to the annual campaign are intended to support operational costs, such as salaries, supplies, utilities, and client needs. The purpose is to support any part of the organization's operation that requires continuous and regular support.

Most donors will come into your organization through the annual campaign. It is possible but rare that a person's first gift to the organization will be a major gift. More likely, those who become major donors are those who have been consistent annual campaign donors.

Direct Mail

You probably know about **direct mail** fundraising from your personal experience. Direct bulk mail is used to ask millions of people for money, and most people receive solicitations in their mail on a regular basis. What rate of return should you expect from your direct mail campaign? Typically, the response is somewhere in the range of 1%. Even though the return is small, it is an economical way to get your message in front of thousands of potential donors. It is a key strategy in bringing new people into the bottom of your pyramid. The typical direct mail package includes the carrier (outside envelope), the letter, a reply device, and a return envelope.

The carrier, or outside envelope, should be designed with one objective in mind: to get the recipient to open it. If the piece goes into the trash, your chance of getting a donation is zero. The

Direct bulk mail is used to ask millions of people for money.

goal is to make the pieces look as much as possible like a personal letter and to make it look different from other solicitations in the mailbox that day. Ideally, the envelope could be hand addressed, but since direct mail is a strategy of large numbers, this is rarely possible. Precanceled bulk mail stamps give a more personal look than the standard postal indicia used on most bulk mail. The other strategy is to use an envelope other than the standard "number 10" business envelope that many fundraisers refer to as "the number 10 ugly." Choose an envelope that is smaller, larger, or a different shape. You may also want to consider using color or a see-through window to pique your potential donors' interest.

Once you get the potential donors to open the letter, your task is to capture their attention long enough to have them consider making a gift to your cause. The task here is not to write a scholarly piece or to impress anyone with your vocabulary. The letter should strike an informal tone and be easy to read and understand. Kim Klein (2000) proposes a set of principles to remember as you develop your letter:

- People have a very short attention span. Sentences should be short and take no more than 6–15 seconds to read.
- People love to read about themselves. The letter should refer to the reader at least twice as often and up to four times as often as it refers to the organization sending it. For example, "You may have read …" or "If you are like me, you care deeply about. …"
- People must find the letter easy to look at. The page should contain a lot of white space and wide margins and be in a clear and simple font. Paragraphs should be short—no more than two or three sentences. You should feel free to use contractions (e.g., won't, you're, can't, we're), as this will add a more informal tone to your letter.
- People read the letter in a certain order. First, they read the salutation and the opening paragraph, but then, no matter how long the letter is, they read the closing paragraph, then the postscript. Only a small number of people will read the entire letter.

The opening paragraph of your letter is critical. It must capture the attention of your readers and make them want to read on. Remember the truism that people will not give anything to meet your agency needs, but they will give when they have an opportunity to invest in a service that is of interest to them. Your letter must be about the people you serve, not the needs of your organization. Also, people do not relate well when you talk about the thousands of people you serve. Your letter should tell the story of one person helped by your organization and how this potential donor can make a difference in the life of someone else.

How long the letter should be is always a debate. Our natural instincts tell us that the letter should be short and to the point, but many fundraising consultants counsel that long letters are better, claiming that a two-page letter will get a better response than a one-page letter and that even three- and four-page letters will often outperform a shorter letter. There are many theories about why you should consider writing a longer letter. Some will say that it gives the impression that your organization has a lot to say, while others believe that more pieces of paper and longer letters give an opportunity for the potential donor to feel more involved with your organization.

In the closing paragraph, you ask for the money. Tell the reader what you want them to do. They have read your letter; now what do you want them to do about it? For example, say, "Send your gift of $25, $50, or $100 today." It needs to be direct and specific. No one gives unless they are asked.

The postscript is that small P.S. at the end of the letter. The reader will read the P.S. if they do not read anything else in the letter. This is your final opportunity to ask for the gift. Examples of an effective postscript are "Send your check today" or "Johnny needs your help."

Finally, the reply device is a small card that gives the potential donor the opportunity to respond. It will typically have a box to check that says something like, "Yes! I'll help" and then gives several options of giving—$10, $25, $50, $100, or more. The donor completes the card, encloses the check, and returns it in the enclosed return envelope. With that, your campaign is a success—at least with this donor.

Social Media

Social networking applications, such as Facebook, Twitter, and Instagram, offer new ways for nonprofits to engage the community in fundraising efforts. Today, these three are the most commonly used, but the landscape changes rapidly. LinkedIn, YouTube, and Pinterest are other platforms used in fundraising campaigns. Blackbaud Institute's Charitable Giving Report (MacLaughlin, 2019) shows that since 2016, online giving has grown 17%, and average online gift amounts have continued to increase. The percentage of total fundraising that came from online giving reached a record high in 2018. Approximately 8.5% of overall fundraising revenue, excluding grants, was raised online, and 24% of online transactions were made using a mobile device (MacLaughlin, 2019). Developing and maintaining a social media presence for your organization will be an important function for you as an administrator.

BOX 5.2	**Using Technology**

The QuickBooks Small Business Centre blog states:

> Technology is dramatically changing the rules of nonprofit fundraising. As more philanthropic supporters connect with causes they care about online, fundraisers have had to adapt their tried-and-true direct mail and phone solicitation strategies to cater to an online audience. Technology connects people to people, people to businesses, businesses to nonprofits, and so on. The great thing about this is that all the ways nonprofits use to connect with donors, volunteers, and other supporters online are the same ones those nonprofit supporters use to connect with the world around them. This is advantageous for nonprofits because most charitable organizations are constantly and sometimes urgently looking for ways to expand and retain their donor bases. The role of technology in connecting nonprofits with current and prospective donors cannot be overstated. Due to emerging technologies and social media in particular, donors have unprecedented "behind the scenes" access to the inner workings of nonprofit organizations. Giving donors access to special information such as client stories, emotionally compelling videos, and pictures of an average day at the office humanize a cause and put a face behind the organization. At the same time, nonprofits can engage with their donor base on a frequent, informal basis. Instead of just contacting donors after making a donation, nonprofits can interact with donors on social media at a moment's notice. To ensure you're connecting with your nonprofit's donor base, follow these best practices:

- Stick to a communications schedule to guarantee you're reaching out across multiple online channels.
- Engage with those interacting with you through email and social media.
- Create valuable, shareable content, and ask supporters to share this content on their own social media pages and profiles.

> With technology, nonprofits aren't just connecting with their own online audience, they're connecting with the friends, family, and other connections of their online audience. (Quickbooks Canada Team, n.d., "Pro" section)

Special Events

Special events are limited only by your imagination. The events may be galas, golf tournaments, walk-a-thons, performances—the possibilities are endless. Many times, special events do not raise large sums of money for the first few years but grow over time into major events that raise large amounts of money. When planning a special event, there are considerations other than the amount of money to be raised. The special event may be the activity that will raise the visibility of your organization in the community and an opportunity to involve more volunteers in your work.

Special events are by their nature very labor intensive and can take a great deal of your time and staff time. Before deciding on a special event, it is important to consider the volunteer and staff resources necessary for a successful event. Any special event will require a major investment of time in planning, marketing, and execution.

Major Gifts

Major gifts are the larger gifts that you will solicit for your cause. These gifts will typically come from those individuals, foundations, and corporations with whom you have developed a long-term, ongoing relationship. Many times, major gifts are solicited within the framework of a "capital campaign" (fund-raising for the purpose of capital improvement), such as building a new building or, in some cases, to develop or strengthen the endowment of an organization. An organization will often contract with a consulting firm to conduct a capital campaign. You, your board, and your staff will still have to solicit the gifts, but a good consultant can help structure and focus a successful campaign.

Major gifts require personal solicitation and the preparation of a proposal. A foundation may require a fully developed proposal, but an individual donor may prefer a short, well-developed statement of the purpose of the proposed donation. These donors are higher on the pyramid and, in most cases, know about your organization, believe in your work, and are willing to make a major contribution. When seeking a foundation or corporate gift, it is important to research the previous gifts and areas of interest of the foundation or corporation. As in all fundraising, finding a personal connection between your organization and the foundation or corporation is a great asset in your attempt to secure a gift. See the section below on foundations for a fuller discussion of foundation proposals.

Planned Gifts

Planned giving is a complex area. The bequest is the simplest form of **planned gifts**. This means that someone has named your organization in a will and that, on their death, a portion or sometimes all of that person's estate will come to your organization. As the administrator, you have an awesome responsibility to see that a person's life work is used for the intended purposes.

Other planned giving arrangements include charitable gift annuities, revocable and non-

Image 5.2

Planned gifts have tax implications for the donor and are often a part of estate planning.

revocable trusts, and other financial vehicles to transfer funds from the donor to the organization. These gifts have tax implications for the donor and are in many cases a part of the estate planning process. Any gift of this type will involve an attorney or certified public accountant. The role of the administrator is to see that the organization has the structure and the advisors necessary to accept gifts of this nature.

Say Thank You!

It is important to say "thank you" to any person or entity that donates to your organization, but it is especially important in dealing with individual gifts. It is impossible to say thank you too much to your donors. The acknowledgment or thank you is a vital part of your fundraising system. Donors should be thanked in writing as quickly as possible for their gift, and whenever possible, donors should be thanked with a telephone call. For large donations, you as the administrator or your board chairman should

You cannot say thank you too many times to your donors.

make a phone call or a visit to thank donors for their gifts. Since successful fundraising is based on relationships, it is important to nurture and sustain relationships by showing gratitude to those who invest in the mission of your organization.

DEVELOPING GIFTS FROM FOUNDATIONS

What are foundations? According to the Minnesota Council on Foundations (MCF, n.d.), "A foundation is a nonprofit organization that supports charitable activities in order to serve the common good" (Minnesota Council on Foundations, n.d., para. 1). There are several different types of foundations that exist under the law. The first, independent foundations, are the most common and typically are created by individuals or families that want to promote attention to a certain problem or approach to a problem. Independent foundations can be either family foundations or other independent foundations, although there is no precise legal definition of the term "family foundation," as they are part of the larger category of independent foundations (Minnesota Council on Foundations, n.d.). Giving to foundations and donor-advised funds (DAFs) continues to grow in response to supporter preferences and changes in incentives (Heisman, 2020).

The second type of foundation is the corporate foundation. These are set up by corporations as legally separate entities and are overseen by a board of directors, often made up of corporate directors and employees. Funding for corporate foundations varies but can include an endowment, contributions from current corporate profits, or even donations from employees. Some corporate foundations provide grants only to locales or states where the parent company has a strong presence; others have broader eligibility criteria. Corporate foundations are not the same as corporate giving programs, which often donate goods and services rather than cash or provide only small amounts of direct funding for nonprofit projects. Another difference is that corporate foundations are governed by Internal Revenue Service rulings and law, while corporate giving programs are entirely in the hands of the corporation.

Community foundations are the third major type of foundation. These are tied very closely to a particular geographic area and are usually funded by pooling smaller amounts of donations from people in the community. Donation decisions are made by a board of directors that is supposed to be representative of the community at large.

All private foundations are required to follow at least three very important regulations in order to maintain their standing as foundations, according to the Minnesota Council on Foundations (n.d.). First, they must pay out (donate) no less than 5% of the value of their investment assets. Second, they pay taxes of 1% or 2% of their earnings. Third, with rare exceptions, they can only donate to other organizations that are 501c3 (charitable) organizations. Not all organizations with the word "foundation" in their name provide grants to applicants. The Henry J. Kaiser Family Foundation (n.d.), for example, uses its resources to develop nonpartisan information on health care, so it is important when searching for foundation funding to carefully look up information on each prospective foundation.

Researching Foundations

It is critical that you conduct a thorough search to find a foundation that has interest in your area of service. As stated above, some foundations are restricted to a particular geographic area, and almost all foundations have a preference for the kinds of services they wish to fund. The number one source of information regarding foundation grants is undoubtedly the Foundation Center. According to its website, the Foundation Center has access to over three million funding records and opportunities from 90,000 grantmakers. The Foundation Center (http://foundationcenter.org) and GuideStar (https://www.guidestar.org/) have recently joined forces to become Candid, a 501c3 nonprofit organization (Guidestar, 2019). In their announcement, they state that "Candid connects people who want to change the world to the resources they need to do it" (Candid, n.d., What We Do section).

While this service can be extremely useful, the cost of access to Foundation Center information is outside the price range of some nonprofits that have only an occasional need to actually use this vast array of data. Fortunately, many public libraries carry a subscription at some level, and grantwriters can receive training from the library staff to use the Foundation Directory Online (FDO) on the premises. Sometimes access to the FDO is available through other entities, such as a nonprofit consortium, university, or government agency (Foundation Center, 2019).

While the trouble with using the Foundation Center's information is cost, the trouble with searching on your own is that, according to the Foundation Center, only 10%–15% of foundations have websites. Thus, you are not necessarily going to get as many results on your own as you may think you will. You are also not going to gain access to as much information as the FDO can give you if you use a search engine approach.

Writing the Proposal

Once you determine that your organization is within the guidelines of a foundation and that you meet all their eligibility requirements, it is time to write the proposal. So what should go in the proposal? The answer is, whatever they want. Most foundations will give you the guidelines for what they want included in their proposals. Some small foundations may want a one-page summary of your request. Other more-developed foundations may ask for a detailed proposal including your goal and objectives, your outcome data, and a detailed budget. Make sure that when they receive your proposal, they know that you have read and understood their guidelines for proposals.

Time to write the proposal.

Image 5.4

Relationships

Just like in individual giving, it is important to establish and nurture relationships to be successful in raising funds from foundations. You have the best chance of success if you have some personal connection with the foundation board members or staff. You should know if any of your board members have personal relationships with families who have family foundations or if they know people who serve on foundation boards. The same is true for corporate foundations. Do you have board members who are executives or employees of corporations that make corporate or corporate foundation gifts?

Takeaways of Foundation Funding

You should take away the following key lessons from this discussion regarding foundation funding. First, the Foundation Center's Online Directory (FDO) is most likely your best source for information on foundation grants. They have collected vast amounts of information that can be beneficial to your efforts. Because it is too costly for many nonprofits to order on their own, grantwriters should try to find a free way to use it through a public library or other source, such as a nonprofit resource center.

Second, whether using the FDO or your own online searches, constantly search for foundations that are active in areas you would like to apply for. Remember, applications may only be allowed for a short period once each year, so you must keep notes of when recurring deadlines are. Set up a "tickler" file or notices that will remind you to look up current proposal deadlines and requirements.

Third, knowing that foundations are more and more interested in working with a smaller number of nonprofits they already are aware of, you will need to be more proactive than ever before. Foundations can, and do, alter their own rules about allocating their funds. Be sure to publicize your organization's efforts year round, targeting people and finding connections to those who make foundation funding decisions.

Fourth, your organization should be conducting and publicizing rigorous program evaluation results, overseen by outside evaluators. Foundations are looking for successful nonprofits to partner with and soliciting applications only from them. You need to have evidence of effectiveness when you contact (or are contacted by) potential funders.

Fifth, keep an easily referenced set of notes on as many foundations as you can manage. Subscribe to any RSS or email lists from those foundations to keep up to date on what they are doing and the grants they are making.

GOVERNMENT GRANTS AND CONTRACTS

How do you find a government grant? This section discusses the primary ways of finding government funding sources, particularly at the federal level. While national government grants are perhaps the easiest to research, they are also therefore much more competitive to receive. Nonprofits looking for government funding need to be able to research and find ways to locate state and local government grant opportunities as well. The principles described in this chapter will work at the state and local levels, although the details will vary from location to location.

What Is the Difference Between a Government Grant and a Contract?

Nonprofit leaders may talk about receiving a government grant or a government contract as if they are the same thing. While both bring funding to an organization, they are different in many important ways. This section looks at the main ways they differ (see Table 5.1).

TABLE 5.1   Differences Between Federal Government Grants and Contracts

Characteristic	Grant	Contract
Purpose	Transferring money, property, services, or anything of value to a recipient (31 U.S.C. Section 6304)	Obtaining (purchase, lease, or barter) goods or services (31 U.S.C. Section 6303)
Goal	Accomplishing a public purpose	Achieving something for the direct benefit of the U.S. government
Amount of Government Involvement Once Awarded	Minor	Major
Who Sets Scope of Work?	Nonprofit	Government
How Regulated?	Through OMB Circulars A-21 (2 CFR 220) and A-110 (2 CFR 215)	Through Federal Acquisition Regulations (FAR) and Federal Agencies FAR Supplements

Source: Adapted from Woodward (2011).

First, the purposes and goals of a grant and a contract are not the same. A grant has the purpose of transferring "money, property, services or anything of value to a recipient (31 U.S.C. section 6304)," whereas the purpose of a contract is to "obtain (purchase, lease or barter) goods (property) or services (31 U.S.C. section 6303)." A grant's goal is to "accomplish a public purpose," while the goal of a contract is to achieve something "for the direct benefit of the U.S. Government" (Woodward, 2011).

Once a grant is awarded, there is only minor involvement with the operations of the grantee, and the grantee is given fairly free rein to accomplish the public purpose, although grantees must provide required reports and respond to performance issues. These are the main ways the government maintains contact with the grantee. When a contract is awarded, the government still has major involvement in the terms of the contract and how it achieves its purposes. Definite tasks, milestones, and deliverables expected are part of the contract between government and agency.

With grants, nonprofits generally set their scope of work in responding to the government agency's request for proposals (RFP). While the RFP lays out the general parameters of the applications, each responding nonprofit may define its own response. With a contract, on the other hand, the government is explicit in what it wants, and nonprofits have limited scope in determining what to offer other than the stated goods or services. Finally, grants are regulated through OMB Circulars A-21 (2 CFR 220) and A-110 (2 CFR 215), whereas contracts are regulated by the Federal Acquisition Regulations (FAR) and Federal Agencies FAR Supplements (Woodward, 2011). Examples of the two funding mechanisms can help clarify the situation.

Grant Example

A grant mechanism was used by a federal government agency, the Administration for Children and Families, Office of Community Services (OCS), to "address food deserts; improve access to healthy, affordable foods; and address the economic needs of low-income individuals and families through the creation of business and employment opportunities" (U.S. Department of Health and Human Services, 2013, p. 2). This does not have a fixed price; agencies can decide how much to request, up to the maximum amount allowed ($800,000), for up to 5 years. More specifically, OCS seeks to fund projects that will implement innovative strategies for increasing healthy food access while achieving sustainable employment and business opportunities for recipients of Temporary Assistance for Needy Families (TANF) and other low-income individuals whose income level does not exceed 125% of the federal poverty level. When talking about a grant, the government agency states the general purpose, but the way to achieve the stated purpose is left up to the organization making the application. Thus, a considerable amount of creativity is required within the grant application.

Contract Example

An example of a contract is the Centers for Medicare and Medicaid Services signing an agreement for "administrative management and general management consulting services" with the Health Research and Educational Trust for almost $76 million a few years ago. Again, a contract specifies definite tasks, milestones, and deliverables expected as part of the contract between government and agency. Another funding stream for many human service organizations is the fee for service. For example, a state agency may contract with a nonprofit agency to provide foster care and adoption placement or to provide vocational rehabilitation for citizens with disabilities. These arrangements are also a type of government contract and are a major funding source for many nonprofit organizations. State agencies will most often issue a request for proposals and will direct such requests to organizations already providing such services.

Finding Government Grants

The primary research tool to find grants (not contracts) at the federal government level is grants.gov (www.grants.gov). Some states have similar portals for state-level funding. If you live in a state that has a similar system, the information will be applicable there as well. An example is Texas eGrants Search (https://www.texasonline.state.tx.us/tolapp/egrants/search.htm).

The fact that all federal government grants can be accessed through one portal is a great boon to grant seekers. It does, however, place a premium on your ability to conduct an effective search there. Dr. Hoefer has developed a quick step-by-step video that's called "How to Use Grants.gov to Find Federal Grants," which is available on YouTube (http://youtu.be/yDbGerr5Oek). Other videos with helpful information are available on the grants.gov website and on YouTube if you search for "how to use grants.gov."

Astute grantwriters will not only look at the current grant opportunities but will also take the time to do a careful longitudinal analysis of several years' worth of the funding opportunity statements. These statements contain all the requirements, goals, and other information you must have in order to write your proposal. While these opportunities are closed, it will give you insight into what will be required when the next funding cycle is announced. The information available from such research will provide you with information about:

- who is eligible to apply
- deadlines for submission
- whether preapplication conference calls will be held for questions to be asked, and when
- contact information
- overview of the funding opportunity
- award information
- program scope, including purpose areas, priority areas, out-of-scope activities, and unallowable activities
- how to apply
- application contents, including formatting and technical requirements, application requirements, project narrative, budget detail worksheet and narrative, and more
- additional required information
- selection criteria, including review process, past performance review, compliance with financial requirements, and more
- post-award information requirements

While it sometimes happens that the contents of the funding opportunities change drastically from one year to the next, this is relatively rare. If you look at several years of the same funding announcement and the information is very similar, you have found a way to anticipate what is likely to be requested for the next round of applications. This way, instead of having about 6 weeks to get your 30–50 pages of application written, you have a year or more, with only small changes to be made based on minor changes in what is being asked.

TAKEAWAYS OF GOVERNMENT GRANTS AND CONTRACTS

Here are key points to recall regarding government grants and contracts:

- Differences exist between federal government grants and contracts, with grants providing the applicant with considerable latitude to propose their solutions to the pressing problem to be addressed, as described in the funding opportunity announcement or request for proposals.
- Grantwriters must learn how to use the advanced search features in grants.gov, the main portal to all federal grants and contracts. Using this process allows you to know which grant opportunities are currently open for applications and which are forecasted to be open in the near future.
- Beyond knowing which opportunities are forecasted and currently open, perusing closed and archived funding opportunities on the grants.gov site allows you to compare several years of grant announcements. Having access to this information lets you do two important tasks: It allows you to improve your planning by putting approximate dates on your calendar for when the next year's announcement will be posted and when the application will be due. If you do this for all the federal grant opportunities you are interested in, you can more effectively make long-range plans. The second task is to compare multiple years of grant application requirements so that you can determine what the likely requirements will be in the next round. Priorities often do not change much from one year to the next. Because one year's change in priority may be the next year's change in requirements, knowing what has stayed the same and what has been altered gives you a fantastic opportunity to get a peek into what may be coming around the bend before it gets there. If you can be 80%–90% sure of what the application is going to call for next year, you can already be putting together a coherent grant proposal now, giving yourself far more than 6 weeks to write a strong grant application.

 SPOTLIGHT ON DIVERSITY

> *"The people you need to listen to—to both correctly identify the problem you are trying to solve, and to come up with ways to address it—are those with lived experience. ... It means working alongside the communities you seek to impact and letting them shape and guide the direction of your work." (Raikes, 2019)*

The world of philanthropy is becoming more active with diversity, equity, and inclusion (DEI) initiatives. An example is the Minnesota Council on Foundations, which is working with its members to improve the situation in Minnesota and act as a model for other philanthropic organizations. One of their initiatives is called Transforming Philanthropy: Learning Community of Practice. This is a "members only intensive blended learning experience designed to help current and emerging leaders within the philanthropic sector to better identify and productively address white privilege and its consequences in their man different spheres of influence" (Minnesota Council on Foundations, 2020, About section).

DIFFICULTIES AND JOYS

Looking for funds and competing for funds is a very difficult task. It is a time-consuming and often frustrating exercise. The competition is great, and often times the chances of success are small. It is difficult to spend countless hours working with your staff to develop a solid proposal and then receive a one-page standard rejection letter. However, there is great joy in doing the research and identifying potential funders for your agency and the clients you serve. Developing a proposal can, and should be, a very creative process. It is a time to showcase your skills in many different areas and to highlight the good work of your agency. One of the greatest joys is getting the call from the foundation director or the government grants staff member to inform you that your proposal has been selected and that you will have new resources to expand your agency services. Those are great days in the life of an administrator.

LESSONS FROM THE PANDEMIC

A great deal changed quickly in fundraising during 2020. New ideas were required and found. How many of these stick once pandemic restrictions are in the past remains to be seen, but the spirit of innovation released will be impossible to eliminate, nor is there any reason to do so. Remote work is a long-term trend in most industries, including program development.

Much of the background work for fundraising was done remotely before COVID-19 hit. Accessing information from online databases, such as the Foundation Directory Online, or the federal government's site, grants.gov, was already regular practice. As before, it pays to learn as much from others about how to use these resources because a mentor will cut your learning time considerably. YouTube and vendor videos are extremely valuable and usually free to watch as often as you desire.

Video conferencing with tools such as Zoom and Teams has become a way of life for large numbers of program developers and other human service administrators. Collaborations have flourished due to necessity in this context. There is no reason it will disappear, as it is the "new normal" and few organizations have seen productivity declines.

Remote working is not the usual course of action when soliciting individual donations, as these are often built on personal relationships and getting to know the potential donor's desires. Using your contacts to facilitate introductions and internet-based meetings will be necessary when you are not able to meet in person. Electronic and telephone conversations can still set up or develop relationships that can be mutually beneficial later on, if they do not have immediate results. Dietz (2021) recommends creating a short virtual tour you can share with donors as well as a prerecorded video explaining the case for support.

Nonprofits engaged in fundraising during the first year of the COVID pandemic were advised to keep moving forward with their board-approved plan. These plans were undoubtedly modified but should not have been eliminated. Here are some key points:

Keep mailing and emailing donors and potential donors. People who support a cause want to continue supporting it. Be sure to note in your records how individuals are reacting. Track whether your emails are being opened and if embedded links are being clicked. This will help you hone your email campaigns in ways similar to regular mail efforts.

While financial issues and joblessness affected millions of people, others have been able to stabilize or even improve their economic situation.

People with investments in the stock market may have seen large gains in their portfolios and be willing to donate more than expected. Donor-advised funds have been found to be giving more grants worth more money to nonprofits clearly hurt by the economic and health crises.

Spend the time to check in personally with phone calls and individualized emails to your long-term donors, even if they are not giving a lot. The personal touch will be remembered with appreciation, especially if it is not seen as only a "dialing for dollars" call.

Ensure your digital platforms are operational and effective. Does your website have easily accessible and working "donate now" buttons? Is your website mobile friendly and able to receive donations of all sizes and amounts quickly and with no hiccups?

Special events have been hosted successfully in online formats. You may want to pause in-person events, but even small-scale efforts can raise funds. You may be able to host a cause-related interview, concert, or performance that people will pay to watch. It need not be much more difficult than any other Facebook or YouTube live performance. What would your audience like to be entertained with? Even if you choose to offer it without a fee, you will show that you are still interested in providing information and resources that benefit your community.

Even auction houses are now prepared to have remote auctions so if that is a special event you would like to hold, it should not be a problem. In fact, by spreading the news widely, you may access a larger audience and bring in more resources for your organization.

CONCLUSION

Effective grantwriters and fundraisers work from a strategic funding plan that is long term, has specific goals, and uses a variety of fundraising methods and techniques. The organization's financial strength can be developed and maintained only through a funding strategy that is diversified by using many different fundraising approaches appropriate for their various categories of donors. Fundraising must be approached like any other major project, in that it requires the administrator to set goals, allocate resources, develop action steps and timelines, and then evaluate the process. As the administrator, you are the chief fundraising official for the organization. You may have others that perform these daily functions, but it is your responsibility to understand what motivates the donors to your organization and to coordinate the efforts of everyone involved in the fund development task. A comprehensive development program will include individual giving, foundation giving, and government grants and contracts (Hoefer, 2017). You will need skills in each of these three areas.

 ## SUMMARY/KEY POINTS

- Hoefer (2017) describes the three main legs of nonprofit fundraising as individual giving, foundation giving, and government grants and contracts.
- In a review of over 500 articles on charitable giving, Bekkers and Wiepking (2011) found eight mechanisms to be the most important forces that determine a person's decision to give. These are (1) awareness of need, (2) solicitation, (3) costs and benefits, (4) altruism, (5) reputation, (6) psychological benefits, (7) values, and (8) efficacy.
- Just like in individual giving, it is important to establish and nurture relationships to be successful in raising funds from foundations. You have the best chance of success if you have some personal connection with the foundation board members or staff.
- Organization should be conducting and publicizing rigorous program evaluation results, overseen by outside evaluators. Foundations are looking for successful nonprofits to partner with and soliciting applications only from them.
- The Foundation Center's Online Directory (FDO) is most likely your best source for information on foundation grants.
- The primary research tool to find grants (not contracts) at the federal government level is grants.gov (www.grants.gov).

KEY TERMS

Annual campaign: The fundraising activities that are conducted for the purpose of supporting the organization's annual operating budget.

Direct mail: A fundraising approach using bulk mail to reach potential donors. The typical direct mail package includes the carrier (outside envelope), the letter, a reply device, and a return envelope.

Donor pyramid: A diagrammatic description of the hierarchy of donors by size of gift. The diagram reflects that as the size of donations increases, the number of donations decreases; as the number of years a donor is asked to renew increases, the number of donors decreases; as campaign sophistication progresses from annual giving to planned giving, the number of donors decreases; and as donor involvement increases, the size of the donor's contribution increases and the response to campaign sophistication increases.

Major gifts: The larger gifts that typically come from individuals, foundations, and corporations with whom the organization has developed a long-term, ongoing relationship. Some major gifts are solicited within the framework of a capital campaign, for the purpose of capital improvement, such as building a new building or, in some cases, to develop or strengthen the endowment of an organization.

Planned gifts: The bequest is the simplest form of planned giving. Other planned giving arrangements include charitable gift annuities, revocable and nonrevocable trusts, and other financial vehicles to transfer funds from the donor to the organization. These gifts have tax implications for the donor and are in many cases a part of their estate planning process.

Special events: Very labor-intensive activities that have the advantage of increased volunteer participation and the opportunity to increase the visibility of the sponsoring organization (e.g., galas, golf tournaments, walk-a-thons, performances, etc.).

ADDITIONAL RESOURCES

Association of Fundraising Professionals (AFP, https://www.afpnet.org).

Denver Public Library. (2019). *Foundation Center directory tutorial* [Video]. YouTube. http://youtu.be/tKlb8iurAK4

Dietz, V. (2021, April 15). *Watch and learn how to make the virtual ask in 2021* [Video]. The Curtis Group. https://curtisgroupconsultants.com/watch-and-learn-how-to-make-the-virtual-ask-in-2021/

Fundraising Effectiveness Project (n.d.). *The Fundraising Effectiveness Project.* https://afpglobal.org/FundraisingEffectivenessProject

Monell, M. (2021, April 8). *6 tips to adapt to the new fundraising normal.* The Curtis Group. https://curtisgroup-consultants.com/6-tips-for-new-fundraising-norm/

DISCUSSION QUESTIONS

1. Writing a funding proposal is a major undertaking. What process would you put in place, and who would you involve in the process to develop a strong proposal?
2. Sometimes agencies and agency directors are accused of "chasing the money." In other words, they see that there is money available and then design a program to go after the money. In the process described in this book, the process is to conduct a needs assessment and then look for the money. Do you think this is a realistic approach? Do you think it is a problem to chase the money?

REAL-LIFE EXAMPLE

In the following chapters, we will present a real-life example. This will provide an example of an actual proposal and will help you to develop the corresponding section for your proposal in the "Your Turn" exercises. The following is a modified program announcement from the Department of Health and Human Services for a program for runaway and homeless youth. The original full-length program announcment can be found online (https://ami.grantsolutions.gov/files/HHS-2018-ACF-ACYF-CY-1354_0.pdf). Take a few minutes to examine the full announcment to familiarize yourself with the look of a federal grant announcement. This federal proposal will require that we provide matching funds. These will come from the fundraising activities of Cornerstone Family Services.

Executive Summary

The Administration for Children and Families (ACF), Administration on Children, Youth and Families (ACYF), Family and Youth Services Bureau (FYSB) supports organizations and communities that work every day to put an end to youth homelessness, adolescent pregnancy, and domestic violence. FYSB's Runaway and Homeless Youth (RHY) Program is accepting applications for the Basic Center Program (BCP). The purpose of the BCP is to provide temporary shelter and counseling services to youth who have left home without permission of their parents or guardians, have been forced to leave home, or other homeless youth who might otherwise end up in contact with law enforcement or in the child welfare, mental health, or juvenile justice systems.

Project Goal, Vision, and Outcomes

Goal: The primary goal of the BCP is to provide temporary shelter and counseling services to youth, under the age of 18, who have left home without permission of their parents or guardians, have been forced to leave home, or other homeless youth who might end up in contact with law enforcement or in the child welfare, mental health, or juvenile justice systems.

Vision: Projects will have a vision to increase young people's access to safe and stable housing, connections to school and employment, enhance social and emotional well-being, self-sufficiency, and help them build permanent connections with families, communities, schools, and other positive social networks, as required by the BCP performance standards set forth in the RHY Final Rule and corresponding measures detailed in *Section VI.3. Reporting* of this FOA.

The Project's vision will describe how achievement of short-term outcomes will lead to achievement of specific intermediate and long-term outcomes.

- *Long-term outcomes* are outcomes that speak to a desired condition of the youth served. For the purposes of this FOA, the long-term outcomes may include, but should not be limited to, the estimated number and percent of BCP youth graduating high school with a GPA of 2.5 or higher, and the number and percent not convicted of a crime, or the number and percent maintaining lasting, healthy relationships with family.
- *Intermediate outcomes* relate primarily, though not exclusively, to sustained behavior changes in the youth served. For the purposes of this FOA, the intermediate outcomes may include, but should not be limited to, youth maintaining stable housing or pursuing education beyond high school or a GED.
- *Short-term outcomes* concern both the acquisition of knowledge, skills, and attitudes and with the achievement in the BCP Performance Standards (i.e., social and emotional well-being, permanent connections, education or employment, and safe and stable housing) discussed below and set forth in the RHY Final Rule and detailed in *Section VI. 3 Reporting*. For more details about associated performance measures related to the BCP Performance Standards, see details in *Section VI. 3 Reporting.*

Federal Award Information

Funding Instrument Type:	Grant
Estimated Total Funding:	$15,225,563
Expected Number of Awards:	89
Award Ceiling:	$200,000 Per Project Period
Award Floor:	$50,000 Per Project Period
Average Projected Award Amount:	$171,074 Per Project Period
Anticipated Project Start Date:	09/30/20xx

The Project Description file must include these items:

The cover letter: Gives a brief statement about the attached proposal and thanks the funding agency for their consideration of your request.

Abstract: A very brief description of the project that presents the project name the scope of the work to be accomplished, the major components of the project, and the expected outcomes.

The needs statement: A description of the community to be served and the identified problem or need that the project proposes to address.

Project description: This section of the proposal will describe the proposed program in great detail. In most cases the goals and objectives (both process and outcome objectives) will be presented.

Evaluation plan: What are the performance measures and the plan to evaluate the project? How will the funder know if the goals and objectives of the project have been met? Have the activities outlined been delivered, and more importantly, what impact has the project had of those it is designed to serve?

Budget request: An outline of how the requested funds will be used. This section will require a line item budget and also a budget justification statement to explain how the funding level request was developed.

Capacity statement: In this section, the applicant will assure the funding source that the agency has the experience and capacity to carry out the project. This will usually include biographical information of the agency leadership, the history of the organization, descriptions of past successful projects and the agencies standing in the community.

Sustainability: How will the program be continued after the initial funding has expired? Is there a plan for the long-term viability of the program?

Letters of support: Include letters of support from other agencies in the community who provide similar services or those whose clients can benefit for the program. Letters from community leaders and elected officials are often helpful.

Memoranda of understanding: This can be a key element to strengthening your proposal. Most funders want to have clear picture of how you cooperated and coordinate with other service providers in your community. It is usually as simple matter to develop such memoranda, but they can be invaluable to your proposal.

Appendix: In this section add any other pertinent information or other information requested by the funder.

 YOUR TURN

Your assignment is to locate an appropriate foundation for your proposal. We are using a federal grant proposal as our example to give you an overview of a government proposal. For your project, we recommend that you identify a foundation as your source of funding because they are generally less complex but will still give you the experience you need. Use the information on the Foundation Center to conduct your search. Once you have identified a foundation for your program, start developing the outline of your proposal. Use the major headings required in the project description file above as the headings for your computer file folders. You can start to put materials into each of these as you work through the chapters.

REFERENCES

Association of Fundraising Professionals. (n.d.). Donor pyramid. In *Association of Fundraising Professionals (AFP) Fundraising Dictionary.* Retrieved January 13, 2021 from https://afpglobal.org/fundraising-dictionary.

Axelrad, C. (2014, July 8). Yes, the donor pyramid is really dead: An open response to Andrea Kihlstedt. *Candid.* https://trust.guidestar.org/blog/2014/07/08/yes-the-donor-pyramid-is-really-dead-an-open-response-to-andrea-kihlstedt/

Bekkers, R., & Wiepking, P. (2011). A literature review of empirical studies of philanthropy: Eight mechanisms that drive charitable giving. *Nonprofit and Voluntary Sector Quarterly, 40*(5), 924–973.

Candid. (n.d.). *Mission and vision.* https://candid.org/about/mission-and-vision

Dietz, V. (2021, April 15). *Watch and learn how to make the virtual ask in 2021* [Video]. The Curtis Group. https://curtisgroupconsultants.com/watch-and-learn-how-to-make-the-virtual-ask-in-2021/

Dietz, V. (2021). *Making the ask—even virtually.* Giving USA. https://givingusa.org/making-the-ask-even-virtually/

Fidelity Charitable. (2020). *COVID-19 and philanthropy: How donor behaviors are shifting amid pandemic.* https://www.fidelitycharitable.org/insights/how-covid-19-is-shifting-donor-giving.html

Foundation Center. (2019). *Foundation Center directory tutorial* [Video]. https://foundationcenter.org/

Fundraising Effectiveness Project. (2020). *Charitable giving continues significant growth in third quarter despite pandemic.* AFP Global. https://afpglobal.org/charitable-giving-continues-significant-growth-third-quarter-despite-pandemic

Giving USA Foundation. (2020). *Giving USA 2020: Charitable giving showed solid growth, climbing to $449.64 billion in 2019, one of the highest years for giving on record.* https://givingusa.org/giving-usa-2020-charitable-giving-showed-solid-growth-climbing-to-449-64-billion-in-2019-one-of-the-highest-years-for-giving-on-record/

Gorczyca, M., & Hartman, R. L. (2017). The new face of philanthropy: The role of intrinsic motivation in millennials' attitudes and intent to donate to charitable organizations. *Journal of Nonprofit & Public Sector Marketing*, *29*(4), 415–433.

GuideStar. (2019). *Foundation Center and GuideStar join forces to become a new nonprofit entity named Candid.* https://learn.guidestar.org/news/news-releases/foundation-center-and-guidestar-join-forces-to-become-a-new-nonprofit-entity-named-candid

Heisman, E. (2020). *The 2020 DAF report.* National Philanthropic Trust. https://www.nptrust.org/reports/daf-report/#:~:text=For%202019%2C%20DAF%20donors%20contributed,12.7%20percent%20of%20individual%20giving.

Henry J. Kaiser Family Foundation. (n.d.). *About us.* http://kff.org/about-us/

Hoefer, R. (2017). *Funded!: Successful grantwriting for your nonprofit.* Oxford University Press.

Hrywna, M. (2019). 80% of nonprofits' revenue is from government, fee for service. *The Nonprofit Times.* Retrieved from https://www.thenonprofittimes.com/news/80-of-nonprofits-revenue-is-from-government-fee-for-service/.

Hrywna, M. (2020). Donors putting brakes on giving: 2019 went well, 2020 not so much. *The Nonprofit Times.*

Klein, K. (2000). *Fundraising for social change* (4th ed.). Chardon Press.

McLaughlin, S. (2020). *Charitable giving report 2019.* Retrieved from Blackbaud Institute: https://institute.blackbaud.com/asset/2019-charitable-giving-report/

Minnesota Council on Foundations. (n.d.). *What's a foundation or grantmaker?* https://mcf.org/whats-foundation-or-grantmaker

Minnesota Council on Foundations. (2020). *Transforming philanthropy: Learning community of practice.* https://mcf.org/events/transforming-philanthropy-learning-community-practice

National Council of Nonprofits. (2019). *Revenue sources.* https://www.nonprofitimpactmatters.org/site/assets/files/1015/revenue-sources-nonprofits.png

O'Connor, S. (2020). *4 surprising donor retention statistics.* Causevox.com. https://www.causevox.com/blog/donor-retention-statistics/#:~:text=1)%20Donor%20Retention%20Averaged%2045.5,non%2Dprofits%20was%2045.3%25.

Quickbooks Canada Team. (n.d.). *How technology is changing the rules of fundraising.* https://quickbooks.intuit.com/ca/resources/nonprofit-organizations/how-technology-changing-rules-fundraising/

Raikes, J. (2019). Can power be anything but zero-sum? *Forbes.* https://www.forbes.com/sites/jeffraikes/2019/06/17/can-power-be-anything-but-zero-sum/#2c0e5df546bd

Schaeffer, K. (2020). *6 facts about economic inequality in the U.S.* Pew Research Center. https://www.pewresearch.org/fact-tank/2020/02/07/6-facts-about-economic-inequality-in-the-u-s/

Tsipursky, G. (2017). The psychology of effective fundraising. *Psychology Today.* https://www.psychologytoday.com/us/blog/intentional-insights/201704/the-psychology-effective-fundraising

U.S. Department of Health and Human Services (2013). *Community economic development healthy food financing initiative projects:* HHS-2013-ACF-OCS-EE-0584. https://www.acf.hhs.gov/sites/default/files/documents/ocs/2013_ceh_hffi_foa_522013.pdf

Venkatish, S. (2020). *How to create a donor pyramid to raise more for your capital campaign.* Wealthengine.com. https://www.wealthengine.com/donor-pyramid/

Woodward, D. (2011). *Grants and contracts: How they differ.* https://www.cga.msu.edu/PL/Portal/DocumentViewer.aspx?cga=aQBkAD0AMgAxADQA

Wright, M. H., & Bocarnea, M. C. (2007). Contributions of unrestricted funds: The donor organization–public relationship and alumni attitudes and behaviors. *Nonprofit Management & Leadership, 18*(2), 215–235.

Figure Credits

Fig. 5.1: Source: https://prosper-strategies.com/2020-nonprofit-stats/.

Fig. 5.3: Adapted from Mark Hrywna, "Sources of Contributions to Nonprofits from 'Donors Putting Brakes on Giving: 2019 Went Well, 2020 Not so Much,'" *The Nonprofit Times*, pp. 1. Copyright © 2020 by Nonprofit Times Publishing Group Inc..

IMG 5.1: Copyright © 2011 Depositphotos/kelpfish.

IMG 5.2: Copyright © 2018 Depositphotos/designer491.

IMG 5.3: Copyright © 2013 Depositphotos/Karenr.

IMG 5.4: Source: https://pixabay.com/photos/woman-business-work-young-computer-3687084/.

CHAPTER SIX

Planning Programs for Your Organization

OVERVIEW

In this chapter we cover the important idea of creating a new program within the context of what is already in existence in the larger organization. Presumably, a considerable amount of effort has been spent on defining a mission statement, vision statement, and other foundational documents for the larger agency or the work of a department or bureau in a government body. The new program must fit within that context. Thus, we will discuss:

- what strategic and program planning are
- how to link program **goals** and desired **outcomes** to strategic and foundational documents
- what evidence-based programs (EBPs) are and where to find them
- what the differences are between core and adaptable components of evidence-based programs (EBPs)
- how to appropriately adapt an evidence-based program
- what to do if no EBP is available
- what the Campbell and Cochrane Collaborations are

By the end of the chapter, you will understand how to find and select an EBP. That, indeed, will be your task as you improve your program planning skills.

Planning can be used in human service organizations to chart the general direction of the agency (strategic planning) as well as smaller-scale decisions about the specific actions and programs to implement within the organization (program planning). As program planners/developers, you need to respect the work that has been done in the past for creating an organizational mission and vision. Programs new to your organization, such as the one you are designing or adapting, must fit within the current **foundational ideas** (vision, mission, and values).

These foundational ideas are part of a strategic planning process. Bryson (2018) defines **strategic planning** as a "deliberative, disciplined effort to produce fundamental decisions and actions that shape and guide what an organization (or other entity) is, what it does, and why" (p. 317). Box 6.1 provides more information on what these terms mean.

BOX 6.1	**Strategic Planning Process Outputs: Defining Foundational Statements**

When a strategic planning process is completed, most experts agree that several decisions will have been made. Vision, mission, and value statements will be agreed on. These will be used to plot the course of the organization's future. But what are these? *According to Bowen (2018),* a **vision statement** "drives the long-term goals that determine where the organization would eventually like to be" while a **mission statement** is "more concrete and ... [is] used to prioritize activities" (Abstract section). To clarify the difference a bit more, Bowen (2018) writes, "A vision statement thus specifies *where an organization is going* and a mission statement gives an organization direction *on how to get there*" (Abstract section). **Value statements** put parameters around the specific actions that employees of the organization are expected to abide by.

We define **program-level planning**, on the other hand, as deliberative effort to design a set of actions that an organization will conduct to achieve particular desired **outcomes** for program participants within the resource constraints provided and the vision, mission, and values of the organization. Any program conducted by an organization should contribute to achieving the vision and mission of the larger agency.

In Table 6.1 we show seven important differences between these two different types of planning efforts. All organizations should have the planning elements shown under strategic planning. These guide the elements listed under program planning operationalize or contribute to one or more of the strategic directions that have been approved by top-level organizational leaders. Decisions at the program level should not contradict strategic-level planning decisions.

These important differences (shown in Table 6.1) indicate that the time horizon, the goal focus, and the focus of decision makers are different in strategic as opposed to program planning. Strategic planning, because it focuses on understanding both external and internal elements that influence the organization's future, requires top-level administration and board involvement (in governmental agencies, this will be the purview of elected or appointed officials). It involves making decisions about what the organization hopes to achieve (the vision), its reason to exist (the mission), and what values will guide it (values statement). Decisions will be made regarding which sources of funding and other resources will be in line with the organization's mission, vision, and values; will be available in sufficient amounts; and will be most desirable to pursue. Monitoring of results is usually done quarterly or annually. Program planning, on the other hand, is almost wholly restricted to elements internal to the organization. Decisions at the program level are primarily regarding the best ways to use the resources (funds and personnel) allocated to the program or department as a result of strategic planning. Department directors and program managers monitor program processes and outcomes.

TABLE 6.1   Differences Between Strategic and Program Planning

Planning element	Strategic planning	Program planning
Time period	Looks at goals for next 3–5 years.	Looks at a shorter time period, typically 1 year.
Goal focus	Shows how organization will work toward its long-term vision and mission.	Shows how organization's programs achieve part of the strategic plan and the steps to take within the program to be successful.
Focus of decision makers	External and internal elements impacting organization.	Primarily internal elements related to resources, process, and outcomes.
Plan generation	The highest-level decision makers make final decisions.	Department or program leaders have responsibility for making program decisions on a frequent basis to ensure successful implementation.
Locus of monitoring and adjusting plans	Top-level decision makers in organization examine received high-level data quarterly or annually.	Mid-level administrators and managers create and disseminate reports to guide immediate actions on a weekly or monthly basis.
Budget	Funding comes from a special part of the budget to create and monitor the impact of strategic initiatives.	Funding comes from annual budgets and is part of the day-to-day activities of departmental or program managers.
Reporting	Updates occur at a high level of abstraction to examine how well overall goals are being achieved.	Frequent detailed updates on progress of implementation and achievement of outcomes.

Source: Adapted from Foley, A. (n.d.), with additions.

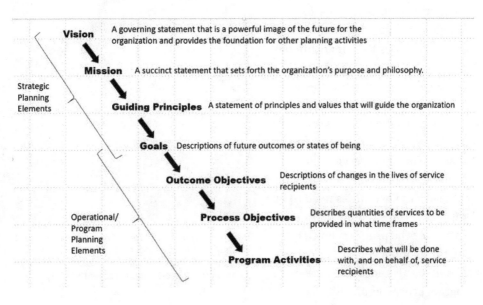

FIGURE 6.1   Strategic and Program Planning Elements

In strategic planning, administrators and/or other stakeholders provide leadership in describing why the organization should exist, what it wants to achieve, and the values that will guide it. Program planning is done at a different, more operational level. Once a general strategic direction is decided and codified in the strategic plan and other documents, the specific programs that will be continued or developed to reach the agency's strategic goals are created and implemented. This requires a more specific set of planning details.

As a program developer, you do not want to get "somewhere"—you want to get to a clearly defined future state. Strategic planning involves formulating a course of action that will move the organization from its present state to some desirable future state. Such planning is important for the agency to achieve its goals. It allows the board, administration, and staff to have an end-in-mind perspective that helps to orchestrate the day-to-day decisions that are made throughout the agency. Strategic planning minimizes the possibility of activity without purpose. Such planning involves creating and articulating a vision of a desirable and attainable future state, having a clear and concise mission, and articulating the guiding values of the organization. Once these are developed in the form of a vision statement, mission statement, and a statement of **guiding principles**, the organization can move on to identify appropriate goals at both strategic and program levels.

At the program level of planning, program developers derive outcomes, processes, and activities to accomplish these goals (see Figure 6.1). An important subtlety of Figure 6.1 is how program outcomes derive from and feed back into the strategic goals. In other words, programming is done with the intent to achieve strategic goals, but the program outcomes are not necessarily exactly the same as the strategic goals. When combined with other programs' goals and desired outcomes, however, all contribute to the overall mission and strategic vision of the organization. The concept of **process objectives** is also important. These include desired levels of clients served, classes held, contacts made, and so on. These are important because it is only by reaching these process objectives that program designers believe the outcomes for clients will be achieved.

The ongoing and constant question for all other elements of organizational life and decisions should be "Does this fit within our mission?" This question often arises in organizations when new funding opportunities arise. The alternative to evaluating funding opportunities considering the agency mission is to be involved in "chasing dollars." Just because funding is available or a new service opportunity emerges does not mean that it is right for the agency. All such opportunities need to be evaluated within the context of the mission of the organization. At the program level, however, you must think on a very practical and measurable level. You also need to differentiate between program processes and impact.

Guiding principles need to be well-understood before they can shape organizational and individual behavior. Make sure that your organization's mission, vision, strategy, and core values are discussed and implemented daily.

Image 6.1

BOX 6.2	**Mapping Strategic and Program-Level Information**

In this example, we use information from an actual agency (ACH Child and Family Services of Fort Worth) to map strategic and program-level information, as shown in Figure 6.1.

Vision:

"Through leadership, research, and training, ACH will set a recognized example for replicable programs in child welfare that dramatically strengthen families and reduce child abuse. Our vision is to be a leading agency in the communities we serve, so families thrive, and children experience safety, hope, and love" (ACH, n.d.a,) *Our Shared Vision.* https://achservices.org/en/about-ach/)

Mission:

"Protecting Children, Preserving Families. Since 1915. Through strengths-based partnership, ACH Child and Family Services brings resources and skills to children and families struggling with life's challenges. Together, we develop solutions that create safety, hope, love, and the capacity to thrive" (ACH, n.d.b,) *Mission.* https://achservices.org/en/about-ach/).

Values

"We strive to partner with families and support their efforts to provide environments for children to thrive. We work to secure a family setting when one is unavailable to children" (ACH, n.d., *Families.* https://achservices.org/en/about-ach/)

Strategic Goals

- thriving families
- children experience safety, hope, and love

Description of Program

Families Together: "Families Together provides transitional housing for single mothers and their children who are experiencing homelessness due to domestic violence. The program offers a safe and stable living environment while they work to overcome the trauma that led to their homelessness and return to independent living. Families receive intensive case management and therapeutic services designed to help them heal from the trauma and victimization they've experienced while gaining the skills they need to promote long-term self-sufficiency and obtain stable housing" (ACH, n.d.,d) (https://achservices.org/en/programs/families-together/).

Program Goals/Outcome Objectives

- heal from trauma and victimization
- gain skills to promote long-term self-sufficiency

Process objectives

- "provide transitional housing for single mothers and their children who are experiencing homelessness due to domestic violence
- "offer a safe and stable living environment
- "provide intensive case management and therapeutic services"

Source: Retrieved from ACH (n.d.ed). https://achservices.org/en/programs/families-together/.

Nothing in the program-level information contradicts the strategic-level information. The program designer clearly does not merely repeat what is in the strategic-level information but provides a closer look at how clients will be approached in the program and how they are expected to be different when they have completed the process. This is a good example of an agency with a thoughtful approach to designing programs for their organization and client population.

As shown in Figure 6.1, program planning is a continuation of the strategic planning process. The strategic goals decided upon by those leading the organization point to a string of steps at the program level. From this top-down approach, you determine first what long-term outcomes you want to achieve with a particular program. You then determine what the medium-term and short-term outcomes can be that must be achieved as prerequisites to achieve longer term outcomes. The planning process also includes developing the processes and activities that must occur to achieve the desired outcomes. (This is what a logic model shows. We cover logic models in the next chapter.)

Once the purposes of an individual program are determined by connecting with the strategic level of planning that has been completed, the question "How do we accomplish these desired outcomes?" naturally arises. Two primary ways to answer the question exist. As a program designer, you may turn to an existing evidence-based program (with or without adaptations) or you may design your own program. We examine both these approaches.

PROGRAM PLANNING: EVIDENCE-BASED PROGRAMS

Of the two possible approaches, we suggest you search for an evidence-based program that has already been shown to be effective in addressing the problems your clients are experiencing or in achieving the outcomes that you want to reach. Because these are model programs, you are more likely to find support for adopting them than an approach that has not been tried before. The EBP documentation will provide clear guidance on what **program activities** will be conducted, for how long, and under what conditions.

What Are Evidence-Based Programs?

The term **evidence-based program** refers to a program that has been designed to solve a particular problem and has been proven through research to reduce the problem in the desired way. As one arm of the United States federal government has stated, "An evidence-based program (EBP) is a program proven through rigorous evaluation to be effective" (Family and Youth Services Bureau, n.d., p. 1).

This concept emerges from evidence-based practice and derives from the term used in the field of medicine to denote practices that are effective in decreasing medical issues. In medicine, of course, double-blind tests of new drugs and procedures are standard practice, and the efficacy and safety of anything new needs to be proven through clinical trials before being released to the public. While the same level of proof is not usually available for social program interventions, this is the model on which evidence-based practices in social work, and human services in general, is based.

All programs are made up of various components that come together with the goal of trying to improve lives. In programs that are not evidence based, aspects or parts of the program are included because the designer feels or believes that they are important or will be effective. Evidence-based programs must meet a higher standard, with all parts of the program being tested to determine if they help achieve program outcomes. Evidence-based programs usually have two types of components: core and adaptable. **Core components** are based on theory and need to be implemented according to the program developer's guidelines if you wish to achieve the results that have been shown to result from the program. According to the Family and Youth Services Bureau (n.d.), "Core components of an evidence-based program are the characteristics that must be kept intact when the program is being replicated or adapted, in order for it to produce program outcomes similar to those demonstrated in the original evaluation research (i.e., the essential ingredients of an evidence-based program)" (p. 2). Core components are made up of the following:

- staff selection
- preservice and in-service training
- ongoing consultation and coaching
- staff and program evaluation
- facilitative administrative support
- systems interventions

The Family and Youth Services Bureau (n.d.) indicates that core components (for educational programs) fit into three categories: content, pedagogy, and implementation. Thus, important core components always include what *is taught,* how it is taught, and the logistics that go into making for a productive learning environment (Family and Youth Services Bureau, n.d., pp. 2–3). Similar distinctions can be made for other service sectors.

While core components are those that may not be changed, lest the efficacy of the intervention be lost, other aspects of the planned program may be considered adaptable because they can be changed to meet the needs of another locale, population, or culture. **Adaptable components** are ones that have been tested but are not necessarily vital to achieving positive results. Choosing a program based on the evidence that it is effective but then changing the core components of the program is quite unsound and can result in a waste of considerable time, energy, and other resources. Altering noncore or adaptable components, however, constitutes a reasonable effort to increase the fit of the evidence-based program to a new environment and situation. **Adaptations** tend to be in the areas of procedure, dosage, content, participants, and cultural relevance (Child and Family Research Institute, 2016). Program planners must be careful when they plan to change elements of any evidence-based program and should carefully plan how to monitor these changes (see Box 6.3). Developing a **fidelity monitoring plan** before you start the program is needed to document that you will include all required appropriate content and activities, deliver content as specified, and use the right type of staff (Banikya-Leaseburg & Chilcoat, 2013).

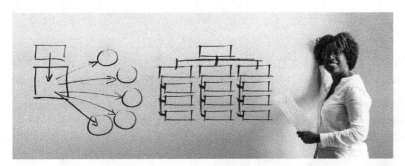

Image 6.2

Understanding your evidence-based program well will assist in implementing it.

BOX 6.3	**How to Plan and Implement an Adaptation to a Selected EBP**

Not all adaptations are acceptable [to a] program, especially if they are not informed by the EBP's core components. There are several theoretical approaches on how to make adaptations to EBPs in a planned and thoughtful way. ... Most include the following steps:

1. Assess: Analyze the results of assessments of the target population(s) and the organization's capacity. These will highlight the important factors to include in the program.
2. Know the selected program(s): Identify and review the goals, objectives, logic model, curriculum activities and cultural appropriateness of the selected EBP(s) and compare the factors addressed in the program (i.e., increasing negotiation skills) to the determinants most relevant to the target population (i.e., self-efficacy in negotiating with sexual partners). ...
3. Identify adaptation challenges: Assess fidelity concerns or adaptation challenges that emerge from considering how the curriculum activities may conflict with the target population needs and/or agency capacity and logistical constraints. Assess acceptability of the motives for these changes as well.

   In addition to having the appropriate motives for adaptations, there are only certain things that can be changed in an EBP in order to maintain fidelity to the core components and maintain the program's effectiveness in achieving identified behavior change and/or sexual health outcomes. ...
4. Select and plan adaptations: Using information about the EBP (i.e., curriculum, core components, logic model) and adaptation resources (i.e., adaptation guidelines, fidelity monitoring tools), determine whether or not each proposed adaptation is an acceptable change and maintains program fidelity.
5. Pilot and monitor adaptations: Before full implementation, pilot the entire curriculum and/ or pilot test the proposed adaptations with a subgroup of participants. This will serve as an opportunity to correct glitches and to test assumptions (e.g., how long an activity might take, whether the audience reacts as intended, whether concepts are clear, etc.). Then, gather feedback and make changes as needed. Use a fidelity monitoring tool to monitor and assess the success of the adaptations, and to provide feedback and continuous quality improvement for implementation, as well as evaluate the overall EBP implementation.

Source: Family and Youth Services Bureau (n.d.).

(For more information on making adaptations to enhance the fit for different cultures and communities, see the Spotlight on Diversity segment of this chapter, below.)

An example of the difference between core and adaptable components may be useful. According to Reconnecting Youth (2021), one of their program offerings is CAST (coping and support training):

> This program combines skills training and small group work (6–7 students per class). Students meet twice per week for six weeks—the schedule is rotated throughout the school day. Students work together to learn and practice skills to enhance

self-esteem, decision making, anger management, reinforcement of coping and help-seeking behaviors, and increased access to social support. (Reconnecting Youth, 2021, How Does it Work? section)

It is noted that CAST is appropriate for middle or high school aged youth and is used by "schools, community centers, and other youth-oriented agencies" (Reconnecting Youth, 2021, What Is Cast? section). CAST is appropriate for students who "are having a poor school experience; are behind in credits; have slipping grades; are skipping school or at risk of dropping out; and report depressed mood and/or have had thoughts about suicide" (Reconnecting Youth, 2021, Who Can Participate? section). In order to gain access to CAST materials, facilitators-to-be must pay for training at a cost of $1,499 for an online experience (in June 2021).

Core components of the CAST program are that 12 sessions are held over a 6-week period, covering specific topics in a specific way, as shown in the course curriculum notebooks (Reconnecting Youth, n.d.). If an organization changes the number, length, timing, or content of the sessions, it will be altering at least one core component, and this should be avoided. On the other hand, the age of the students may be adaptable. Currently, the information about the program indicates that positive effects are found when using the curriculum and program with youth who are of middle and high school age (approximately 13–20 years). Would this approach be as effective with "emerging adults" up to the age of 30? Perhaps even for children ages 10–12? No information is currently available, but a case might be made that this is a reasonable extension of the initial research, and so the age of the student could be seen as an adaptable component. No information is provided regarding the gender, race, or ethnicity of students who have been in the evaluations thus far. It may be possible that this program works better for some types of youth than others.

Certain government agencies have lists of programs that they believe have evidence to support their efficacy when implemented according to guidelines. These lists do change as new programs are added that have gained research support and old, "promising" programs are dropped as new evidence determines that the programs are not effective after all. A number of these directories are provided at the end of the chapter under Additional Resources. One is the Substance Abuse and Mental Health Services Administration's Evidence-Based Practices Resource Center (https://www.samhsa.gov/resource-search/ebp). According to their website:

> This new Evidence-Based Practices Resource Center aims to provide communities, clinicians, policy-makers and others in the field with the information and tools they need to incorporate evidence-based practices into their communities or clinical settings. The Resource Center contains a collection of scientifically-based resources for a broad range of audiences, including Treatment Improvement Protocols, toolkits, resource guides, clinical practice guidelines, and other science-based resources. The retooled EBPRC neither accepts open submissions from outside program developers nor rates individual programs. (SAMHSA, 2021, para. 1)

Before you definitively choose a new program to begin or include in a grant proposal, you will want to ensure that program manuals, guides, training, and evaluation tools are available so you can implement the program as intended. You should determine if the EBP is a good fit for your organization and community in other ways as well. Nine things to consider when you are in the process of selecting a program are the fit with:

- your population
- your setting
- your target population's culture
- availability
- values of the community
- values of the local power structure
- organizational mission, vision, and culture
- administrative feasibility
- capacity of staff
- availability of sufficient time, funding, and other resources

It is time consuming to assess all nine variables listed here, but you may be unpleasantly surprised if you and a group of stakeholders do not do so.

WHAT IF NO EBP IS AVAILABLE?

Sometimes you will want to start a program to address a particular need, but you cannot find an EBP listed in government directories (or elsewhere) that fills your organization's requirements. In this case, you need to become creative and put together the best program you can that has yet to be tested. You may have the goal of creating a program that can be rigorously evaluated so that it eventually becomes an evidence-based program itself. If so, you need to approach the design especially carefully. Advice on this matter is provided by Orlando et al. (2019) who describe a four-phase process (see Box 6.4).

Image 6.3

Look at all the components of a program's logic model and results before carefully deciding how to create your own evidence-based program.

BOX 6.4	**Four-Phase EBP Creation Process**

Phase 1: Conduct a literature review and information search. This phase should look at research, practice, and policy in the relevant area of program need. The results can be used to inform questions used in Phase 2.

Phase 2: Interview key stakeholder informants. Orlando et al. interviewed over 100 people individually and in focus groups to understand needs of potential future clients. Some groups can be oversampled because their experiences or needs are particularly important to capture.

Phase 3: Analysis. This phase uses qualitative analysis techniques to code the themes in the interviews.

Phase 4: Convene a development team to design a program using the information gathered. Team members may include an instructional design expert, faculty with expertise in the area, evaluators, agency workers, and others with experience in the field. The team engages over a lengthy period to conceptualize and create a program that is based on the prior literature and interview/focus groups information.

Source: Orlando, L., Barkan, S., & Brennen, K. (2019). Designing an evidence-based intervention for parents involved with child welfare. Children and Youth Services Review, 105, Article 104429. https://doi. org/10.1016/j.childyouth.2019.104429

When you create a new program, you want to locate the most current evidence, even if it is not already put into program form. Two sources of information that you can use are the Campbell Collaboration and Cochrane Collaboration websites.

The Campbell Collaboration (campbellcollaboration.org) showcases comprehensive literature reviews of program impact relating to social welfare and international development issues. The vision of the Campbell Collaboration (n.d.) is "better evidence for a better world," and the mission statement is that "the Campbell Collaboration promotes positive social and economic change through the production and use of systematic reviews and other evidence synthesis for evidence-based policy and practice" (Mission and Vision Statement sections).

The authors are top-notch, and the reviews are both deep and broad. All (or nearly all) relevant studies on the particular subject are found, analyzed, and discussed, with a clear conclusion being written, even if the conclusion is "We don't yet have enough good research to answer our question." As a source for results that are easy to find and apply, it is not as practical as some of the government sites that have prepackaged solutions in the form of actual programs. If you and/or your team are good at translating basic principles from a research setting to a programmatic setting, however, you can find valuable information for putting together an evidence base for a new or adapted program using the Campbell Collaboration library.

Another source of evidence for programs comes from the Cochrane Collaboration (cochrane.org). It is very similar to the Campbell Collaboration, although it has a different focus area. The Cochrane Collaboration focuses on health and mental health issues. Its vison is "a world of improved health where decisions about health and health care are informed by high-quality, relevant and up-to-date synthesized research evidence," and its mission is "to promote evidence-informed health decision-making by producing high-quality, relevant, accessible systematic reviews and other synthesized research evidence" (Cochrane Collaboration, n.d., Our Vision and Our Mission sections). The Cochrane Collaboration is about as easy to use as the Campbell Collaboration and has the same strengths and limitations.

As you explore the world of evidence-based programs, looking to select one for your organization, you need to go beyond "The program is on the list, so it must be good." Indeed, this approach will perhaps land you in hot water with community stakeholders or others involved in the project. You absolutely need to investigate the details on who was in the population when the program was evaluated.

Let us use an example from the Campbell Collaboration, "Voluntary Work for the Physical and Mental Health of Older Volunteers: A Systematic Review" (Filges et al., 2020). The review sounds at least somewhat promising, as the authors indicate that they worked with information on 47,000 participants from 24 studies conducted in different countries with different populations. Their conclusion is that older people who volunteered had improved physical and mental health outcomes, particularly lower levels of mortality. In addition, no adverse effects were found. Because there is little cost to run the program and nothing bad resulted from participation, the authors indicate that this may be a good program for adoption and expansion to include more older people (Filges et al., 2020).

What is disappointing about the writeup that we have access to is that there is no analysis of differential effects on different populations. A simple but important comparison (if one had original data) would be if differences existed between the impact on men versus women. We would also like to know if some effects were stronger and more beneficial for different racial or ethnic groups. Socioeconomic status and health status are not explored, either.

In fact, so little information is available on the constituent studies underlying the report that readers will have to do considerable digging to answer basic questions. It may be that the methodology of this systematic review prevents deeper analysis, but one cannot assume without more details that this program would work as well for every group.

ANOTHER OPTION FOR FINDING PROGRAM IDEAS

There is another approach that is less systematic but possible if you have already read the professional and academic literature for ideas and information about programs and been disappointed. You can be on the lookout for information on promising program ideas online and in the newspapers and magazines you read. These information outlets frequently want to showcase positive human-interest stories and often describe a program that helped a particular person achieve success in overcoming a problem. When you view a story that pertains to social issues similar to ones you want to address, be sure to note the program name and follow up with a search of the organization running it. You can gather additional information from its website and then email or call to find out more.

In addition, it is very useful to keep a digital or physical idea file where you can place summaries of programs that you discover in both professional and popular media. In your summaries, start with where you heard about the program so you can track it down again when you need to. Write in your summary what the goal of the program is, what program components you can uncover, and any other information that you have been able to find, including the organization running the program and a contact name if you have located one. If you file these in an organized way corresponding to how they connect with your organization's priorities and goals, you will have a good starting point for generating additional ideas when it comes time to writing a future grant.

The ideas in this short section may or may not be evidence based in any formal sense, so you will need to examine them carefully before suggesting that you want to emulate them or use them as a basis of a new program at your organization. They may, however, be helpful when nothing else has emerged.

 ## SPOTLIGHT ON DIVERSITY

A helpful resource for helping understand EBP adaptations for different cultures and communities is authored by Eric Wadud and Bill Berkowitz (n.d.) from the Community Tool Box. They make the point that "interventions are not always one-size-fits-all. When the setting is different, they may need to be adapted" (Wadud & Berkowitz, n.d., para. 4). They provide answers about why interventions should be adapted to fit different cultures and communities; when they should be adapted; and how they should be adapted (if at all). The process to make appropriate adaptations, they argue, may be time consuming and will require considerable openness on all sides. For program design professionals, especially when they have not worked much with a particular culture or community before, you should be mindful of the following questions:

- Is it your role to direct the adaptation, or would it be better for another person (likely from the culture or community itself) to lead the process? (If you feel it is your role, then move forward.)
- Are you personally ready to openly engage with the culture or community?
- Is the target group ready and able to work with you?
- Do research about cultural beliefs and practices, norms, and history before plunging in. (You can use many of the same tools and data sources discussed in Chapter 4.)
- Talk to a variety of people who are experts and/or key members of that group.
- Spend time in the setting.
- Only after you have done these above actions should you propose your intervention idea.
- Once you have proposed it, ask for feedback and take it into account.
- If all is a "go" at this point, find people from the culture and community who will work with you.

Even after you have done the work, you may not have the success you hoped for. Much can happen to derail even the best ideas. However, as Wadud and Berkowitz (n.d.) say, "When success does happen, the rewards can be great. ... And you may have set a precedent that can long outlast your own departure from the scene" (In Summary section).

DIFFICULTIES AND JOYS

The creation of an idea for a program based on the research you have done can be both frustrating and exhilarating. There will be gaps in your knowledge and the research base no matter how diligently you strive to fill them. You will have to work inside of a large zone of ambiguity and doubt. You will have to be persuasive in defending your nascent ideas even while being open to constructive criticism that makes your concepts clearer and more likely to both receive start-up resources and succeed once implemented. These are challenging but essential tasks in the job of a program developer.

However, when you uncover and apply both long-established information and the latest research findings or when you link ideas previously located in separate silos, you play the role of explorer, discoverer, and assimilator. Taking research-based information and molding it into a set of ideas for staff to implement and clients to use while maintaining integrity with your organization's mission, vision, and values is a daunting task. Obtaining and keeping community stakeholder and funder approval is definitely a challenge and will test your skills. Still, few things in your professional life will ever feel as sweet as when you use your policy entrepreneurial and other skills to make a new program come into existence. When you see the positive results from "your" program, you will know you have accomplished something worthwhile.

LESSONS FROM THE PANDEMIC

By the time you read this book, a great deal will be available in academic journals regarding impacts of the pandemic on various programs. COVID-19 led to a large number and great variety of impacts on individuals and program participants. The results of those studies may be accurate or they may need to be interpreted in the context that large numbers of people were living during an all-encompassing negative situation that impacted working conditions, income, stress, anxiety, health, and many other factors. We believe that research studies about client outcomes that were undertaken during 2020 and 2021 need to be examined with a skeptical eye. The impact of this once-in-a-lifetime situation may invalidate efforts to assess the generalizability of the results on client populations once pandemic-related conditions are reduced.

CONCLUSION

When describing your desired program, it is much easier to find a predesigned program with evidence to support its efficacy than to create one on your own. Such evidence-based programs can be hard to discover, however, when you have specific goals for a clearly defined population. Adapting an evidence-based program can get around some of the problems, but you must be careful not to change core components of the program or else you undermine the reason for choosing an evidence-based program.

SUMMARY/KEY POINTS

- Strategic planning and program planning are intertwined but different. Strategic planning points the way for the organization to go. Program planning is "closer to the ground" and helps clients achieve outcomes that benefit them. Seven important differences between these types of planning are discussed.
- With the information in this chapter, you now understand how to map the ways that strategic and program planning link.
- Finding and possibly adapting evidence-based programs to meet the needs of your intended clients is the approach we recommend in selecting an approach to assist your clients. This shortens the time to design the program. Still, you must consider very carefully if it should be implemented in your organization. Does it fit with your current organizational vision, mission, and values? Is it acceptable to your community stakeholders?
- Often you will need to adapt any existing EBP so that it is customized to work with your clients in your community. The chapter lays out a process for making the adaptations that are needed.
- If no EBP is available, you have learned about how to use the Cochrane Collaboration and the Campbell Collaboration as sources for empirical information about what sorts of interventions work on which problems.
- Other ways to find program ideas were presented as well.

KEY TERMS

Adaptable components: Adaptable components are elements of evidence-based programs that have been tested but are not necessarily vital to achieving positive results. These tend to be in the areas of procedure, dosage, content, participants, and cultural relevance (Child and Family Research Institute, 2016).

Adaptations: The changes that are made to the evidence-based program that are designed to improve fit between the program and the culture or community it is to be implemented in.

Core components: "The characteristics that must be kept intact when the program is being replicated or adapted, in order for it to produce program outcomes similar to those demonstrated in the original evaluation research (i.e., the essential ingredients of an evidence-based program)" (Family and Youth Services Bureau n.d., "Fidelity" section).

Evidence-based program: "An evidence-based program (EBP) is a program proven through rigorous evaluation to be effective" (Family and Youth Services Bureau, n.d., p. 1).

Fidelity monitoring plan: A method to monitor that all components of the evidence-based program you are using are implemented in the way the designer has indicated, including content delivered, activities completed, and staff qualifications ensured.

Foundational ideas (also known as governing ideas): The vision statement, the mission statement, and the statement of guiding principles (Senge, 1990).

Goals: Descriptions of future outcomes or states of being that typically are not measurable or achievable. Instead, goal statements are focused on outcomes and are ambitious and idealistic.

Guiding principles: See "Foundational ideas."

Mission statement: A statement that "gives an organization direction" for accomplishing its vision (Bowen, 2018).

Outcome: Answers the question "So what? What difference did it make in the lives of the people served?" Outcomes are stated as improved behavior, increased skills, changed attitudes, increased knowledge, or improved conditions.

Program-level planning: Deliberative effort to design a set of actions that an organization will conduct to achieve particular desired outcomes for program participants within the resource constraints provided and the vision, mission, and values of the organization.

Process objectives: Quantify the usage of the services and identify how much service will be provided. Process objectives are designed to determine whether the program is doing what it says it will do. It describes the services that are to be provided, in what quantities, and in what time frames.

Program activities: What will be done by program staff and volunteers with, and on behalf of, service recipients.

Strategic planning: A "deliberative, disciplined effort to produce fundamental decisions and actions that shape and guide what an organization (or other entity) is, what it does, and why" (Bryson, 2018, p. 317).

Value statement: A statement that puts parameters around the specific actions that employees of the organization are expected to abide by.

Vision statement: A governing statement that "drives the long-term goals" of an organization and "specifies where an organization is going" (Bowen, 2018, Abstract section).

ADDITIONAL RESOURCES

Sources for Evidence-Based Practices and Programs

California Evidence-Based Clearinghouse for Child Welfare. (n.d.). *Program registry.* https://www.cebc4cw.org/registry/

National Council on Aging. (n.d.). *Search for evidence-based programs.* https://www.ncoa.org/evidence-based-programs

Office of Juvenile Justice and Delinquency Prevention. (n.d.). *Model programs guide.* https://ojjdp.ojp.gov/model-programs-guide/home

Substance Abuse and Mental Health Services Administration. (2021). *Evidence-Based Practices Resource Center.* https://www.samhsa.gov/resource-search/ebp

Adapting EBPs

Child and Family Research Institute. (2016). *Developing strategies for child maltreatment prevention: A guide for adapting evidence-based programs*. University of Texas at Austin. https://txicfw.socialwork.utexas.edu/wp-content/uploads/2016/09/Guide-to-Adapting-an-Evidence-Based-Intervention.pdf

Wadud, E., & Berkowitz, B. (n.d.). *Section 4: Adapting community interventions for different cultures and communities*. Community Tool Box. https://ctb.ku.edu/en/table-of-contents/analyze/choose-and-adapt-community-interventions/cultural-adaptation/main

DISCUSSION QUESTIONS

1. Locate an agency webpage (or other source of information) and look for information to replicate what is shown for ACH Services. Analyze a program that fits well. Search also for a program that may not be as well integrated into the organization's strategic-level ideas. What would you tell the staff at that agency about their program's connection with the vision, mission, and values?

2. Decide on a client population and problem to be addressed by an agency you are familiar with. Then search for an evidence-based program using the resources provided in this chapter. What is the best program for your situation? Would you need to adapt it or simply adopt it as it is currently described?

 YOUR TURN

Review the material about Cornerstone Family Services, particularly its mission. The board has decided that it should apply to be a Basic Center Program so that it can access federal funding (https://www.acf.hhs.gov/fysb/programs/basic-center-program). Information on the program states:

The Basic Center Program (BCP) helps create and strengthen community-based programs that meet the immediate needs of runaway and homeless youth under 18 years old. In addition, BCP tries to reunite young people with their families or locate appropriate alternative placements.

BCP provides the following services:

- up to 21 days of shelter
- food, clothing, and medical care
- individual, group, and family counseling
- crisis intervention
- recreation programs
- aftercare services for youth after they leave the shelter

Please see the Basic Center Program Fact Sheet and Youth Profile for more details.

Using information from this and earlier chapters, complete the following tasks:

1. Create all the elements needed to complete a diagram similar to Figure 6.1 and what is shown for ACH. Some may be available in your information, and some may need to be written by you. Clarify the population you will serve with this program. Be specific regarding age, race, ethnicity, and so on.
2. Select one of the four required Basic Center Program elements from this list to complete the rest of this exercise:

    o   individual, group, and family counseling
    o   crisis intervention
    o   recreation programs
    o   aftercare services for youth after they leave the shelter

3. Find and describe in detail an evidence-based program that Cornerstone Family Services could use in a grant application. Be sure it is in line with the information in your version of Figure 6.1 and your answer in Question 1.
4. Critique the information you have (or do not have) on the EBP you have selected. How well does it describe the people who were in the evaluation used to determine it is evidence based? What more would you like to know?

REFERENCES

ACH Child and Family Services. (n.d.a). *Our shared vision.* https://achservices.org/en/about-ach/

ACH Child and Family Services, (n.d.b). *Mission.* ACH Child and Family Services. (n.d.). Mission. https://achservices.org/en/about-ach/

ACH Child and Family Services (n.d.c). *Families.* https://achservices.org/en/about-ach/

ACH Child and Family Services, (n.d.d). *Families together.* https://achservices.org/en/programs/families-together/.

Bowen, S. (2018). *Mission and vision* [Abstract]. Wiley. https://onlinelibrary.wiley.com/doi/epdf/10.1002/9781119010722.iesc0111

Bryson, J. M. (2018). *Strategic planning for public and nonprofit organizations: A guide to strengthening and sustaining organizational achievement.* Jossey-Bass.

Campbell Corporation. (n.d.). *Campbell's vision, mission, and key principles.* https://www.campbellcollaboration.org/about-campbell/vision-mission-and-principle.html

Cochrane Collaboration. (n.d.). *Our vision, mission, and principles.* https://es.cochrane.org/our-vision-mission-and-principles

Family and Youth Services Bureau. (n.d.). *How to plan and implement an adaptation to a selected EBP: Making adaptations tip sheet.* U.S. Department of Health and Human Services. https://www.acf.hhs.gov/sites/default/files/documents/prep-making-adaptations-ts_0.pdf

Filges, T., Siren, A., Fridberg, T., & Nielsen, B. (2020). Voluntary work for the physical and mental health of older volunteers: A systematic review. *Campbell Systematic Reviews, 16*(4), e1124. https://onlinelibrary.wiley.com/doi/full/10.1002/cl2.1124

Foley, A. (n.d.). *Strategic planning vs. operational planning: The 5 main differences.* ClearPoint Strategy. https://www.clearpointstrategy.com/strategic-planning-vs-operational-planning/

Orlando, L., Barkan, S., & Brennen, K. (2019). Designing an evidence-based intervention for parents involved with child welfare. *Children and Youth Services Review, 105*, Article 104429. https://doi.org/10.1016/j.childyouth.2019.104429

Reconnecting Youth. (2021). *Coping and support training (CAST).* https://www.reconnectingyouth.com/content/programs/cast

Senge, P. M. (1990). *The fifth discipline: The art & practice of the learning organization.* Doubleday/Currency.

Substance Abuse and Mental Health Services Administration. (2021). *About the Evidence-Based Practices Resource Center.* https://www.samhsa.gov/ebp-resource-center/about

Wadud, E., & Berkowitz, B. (n.d.). *Section 4: Adapting community interventions for different cultures and communities.* Community Tool Box. https://ctb.ku.edu/en/table-of-contents/analyze/choose-and-adapt-community-interventions/cultural-adaptation/main

Figure Credits

CHAPTER SEVEN

Logic Models and Program Evaluation

OVERVIEW

Nonprofit leaders and program developers must be skilled in both planning and evaluating programs. A logic model is useful for both these tasks, even though planning happens before the program begins and evaluation happens after it has been in operation. A good evaluation, however, is planned at the same time that the program is designed so that a clear process is in place to collect necessary data along the way, rather than after the program finishes. This chapter describes the process of logic modeling and then shows how to use the logic model to plan an evaluation. The programs chosen, as well as the evaluation methods you select, are elements of program planning and management.

Once you have selected a program to use as your starting point (whether it is an existing evidence-based program (EBP) or a program idea you have created yourself), it is time to create a logic model for it. Having a one-page illustration of the program in this way eases communication about what the program's purpose is and all the elements that are needed to make it effective. It also links processes and impacts clearly.

LOGIC MODELS

The idea of logic models as an adjunct to program evaluation extends back at least as far as 2000, when the Kellogg Foundation published a guide to developing logic models for program design and evaluation. According to Frechtling (2007), a **logic model** is "a tool that describes the *theory of change* underlying an intervention, product or policy" (p. 1). You can find many explanations describing how to construct a logic model, but not all demonstrate how it is a versatile tool to design programs, assist in their implementation, and guide their evaluation. This section describes one basic approach to logic modeling for program design and evaluation. We thus link the planning and evaluation aspects of human service administration.

You should understand that not all current programs, including EBPs, have been designed with the aid of a logic model. This situation, however, is becoming less common every year. Federal grants, for example, often require applicants to submit a logic model, and their use throughout the human services sector is growing through academic education and in-service training. If there is no logic model for a program you are considering or for a program you are designing, you need to create one yourself. That way you can bring the power of this tool to bear when changing a program or creating an evaluation plan. You will find

Logic models rely on "if-then" chains of statements to move from having resources to achieving program outcomes.

having a logic model leads to staff and clients understanding the program's purposes and processes better. Such greater understanding then usually results in a higher level of effectiveness.

Logic model creation uses system theory terminology. Because logic models describe the program's "theory of change," it is possible to believe that this refers to something such as social learning theory, cognitive behavioral theory, or any one of a number of psychological or sociological theories. In general, though, logic models have a much less grand view of theory.

We begin with the assumption that any human services program is created to solve a problem. Thus, the logic model should begin by clearly describing the negative situation that the program, intervention, or policy is trying to improve. The problem should be clearly stated in a way that does not predetermine how the problem will be solved. The usefulness of a logic model is to show how the resources used (inputs) are changed into a program (activities) with closely linked products (outputs) that then lead to changes (outcomes) in the short, medium, and long terms. The net effect of these changes is that the original problem is solved or at least made better. An example of a logic model is shown in Figure 7.1.

The problem being addressed by the example program is expressed in a **problem statement**: "School-aged youth have anger management problems, leading to verbal and physical fights at school and home." This problem statement is specific about who has a problem (school-aged youth), what the problem is (anger management problems leading to verbal and physical fights), and where it is a problem (school and home). It also does not prejudge what the solution is, allowing for many possible programs to address the problem. An example problem statement that is not as good because it states the problem in a way that allows only one solution is "There is a lack of anger management classes in schools for school-aged youth."

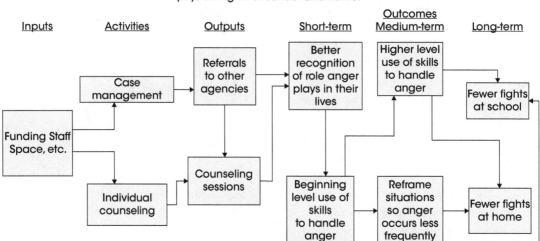

FIGURE 7.1   Example Logic Model

Another way to make the problem statement strong is to phrase the statement in such a way that almost anyone can agree that it is actually a problem. The example problem statement might make this point more clearly by saying, "There are too many verbal and physical fights at school and home among school-aged youth." Phrased this way, there would be little doubt that this is a problem, even though the statement is not specific about the number of such fights or the cause of the fights. Note that if the program personnel want to focus on anger management problems, this way of stating the problem might lead to a host of other issues that might be leading to fights being addressed instead— such as overcrowding in the halls, gang membership, conflict over curfews at home, or anything else that might conceivably cause youth to fight at school or home. Be prepared to revisit your first effort at developing the problem statement and seek input from interested stakeholders to be sure that you are tackling what is really considered the reason for the program. The problem statement is vital to the rest of the logic model and evaluation, so take the time to make several drafts to get full agreement.

After the problem statement, the logic model has six columns. Arrows connect what is written in one column to something else, in the next column to the right or even within the same column. These arrows are the "logic" of the program. If the column to the left is achieved, then we believe that the element at the end of the arrow will be achieved. Each arrow can be considered to show a hypothesis that the two elements are linked. (The example presented in Figure 7.1 is intentionally not perfect so that you can see some of the nuances and challenges of using this tool.)

The first column is labeled "inputs." In the **inputs** column, you write the major resources that will be needed or used in the program. Generically, these tend to be funds, staff, and space, but they can include other elements, such as type of funds, educational level of the staff, and location of the space (e.g., on a bus line), if they apply to your program. The resource of "staff," for example, might mean MSW-level licensed counselors. In the end, if only staff members with bachelor's degrees in psychology are hired, this would indicate that the staff input was inadequate.

The second column is "activities." In the **activities** area, you write what the staff members of the program will be doing—what behaviors you would see them engage in if you sat and watched them. Here, as elsewhere in the logic model, there are decisions about the level of detail to include. It would be too detailed, for example, to have the following bullet points for the "case management" activity:

- Answer phone calls about clients.
- Make phone calls about clients.
- Learn about other agencies' services.
- Write out referral forms for clients to other agencies.

This is what you would see, literally, but the phrase "case management" is probably enough. Somewhere in program documents, there should be a more detailed description of the duties of a case manager (such as a job description) so that this level of detail is not necessary in the logic model, which is, after all, a graphical depiction of the program's theory of change, not a daily to-do list.

The other danger when developing your logic model is being too general. In this case, a phrase such as "provide social services" would not be enough to help the viewer know what the employee is doing, as there are many activities involved in social services that are not case management. Getting the correct level of specificity throughout the logic model is important to help develop your evaluation plan.

As you can see from the arrows leading from the inputs to the activities, the program theory indicates that, given the proper funds, staff, and space, the activities of case management and individual counseling will occur. This may or may not happen, however, which is why a process evaluation or fidelity assessment is needed and will be discussed later in this chapter.

The third column lists "outputs." An **output** is a measurable result of an activity. In this example, the activity of "case management" results in client youth being referred to other agencies for services. The output of the activity "individual counseling" is counseling sessions. It is important to note that outputs are not changes in clients—outputs are the results of agency activities that may or may not then result in changes to clients. The connection between agency activity and outputs is perhaps the most difficult part of putting together a logic model because many people mistakenly assume that if a service is given and documented, then client changes are automatic. This is simply not true.

The next three columns are collectively known as "outcomes." An **outcome** is a change in the client. These changes occur in a client's knowledge, attitude, belief, status, or behavior. Outcomes are why programs are developed and run—to change clients' lives or decrease community problems. You can develop outcomes for any level of intervention—individual, couple or family, group, organization, or community of any size. This example uses a program designed to make a change at an individual youth level, but it could also target changes at the school or district level, if desired.

Outcomes are usually written to show a time dimension with short-, medium-, and long-term outcomes. The long-term

Outcomes should be clear to everyone who looks at a program's logic model.

Image 7.2

outcome is the opposite of the problem stated at the top of the logic model and thus ties the entire intervention back to its purpose—to solve a particular problem. The division of outcomes into three distinct time periods is obviously a helpful fiction, not a tight description of reality. Still, some outcomes are expected to come sooner than others. These short-term outcomes are usually considered the direct result of outputs being developed. On the example logic model, the arrows indicate that referrals and individual counseling are both supposed to result in client youth better recognizing the role that anger plays in their life. After that is achieved, the program theory hypothesizes that clients will use skills at a beginning level to handle their anger. This is a case where one short-term outcome (change in self-knowledge) leads the way for a change in behavior (using skills).

BOX 7.1	**Outcomes Versus Goals and Objectives: What's the Difference?**

People sometimes have difficulty understanding the difference between the terms "outcome" and "goals and objectives." Logic models use the term "outcome" to signify desired changes in clients, but many people use the term "goals and objectives" to talk about what a program is trying to achieve. What's the difference?

In reality, there is not much difference. Goals and **objectives** are one way of talking about the purpose of a program. This terminology is older than the logic model terminology and perhaps is more widespread. But it can be confusing, too, because an objective at one level of an organization may be considered a goal at another level or at a different time. A strategic goal is something tied to achieving an organizational mission. In this chapter, we are concerned with identifying **program goals** or, as we prefer, outcomes. In this sense, just as with an outcome, we are describing desired future states of client being.

Outcomes are easier to fit into the logic model approach by their relating to resources, activities, and outputs. This terminology avoids some of the conceptual pitfalls of goals-and-objectives thinking, particularly when thinking about the time dimensions involved. It is easier to think of which outcomes occur first, then second, and so on in your logic model than to worry about what is a goal and what is an objective and how they are related over time to other goals and objectives.

No matter which terms are used in your organization or by your funders, you need to feel comfortable with the concepts. Most importantly, you should realize that both sets of words are ultimately talking about the same thing: the actual changes an organization is working for to make people's lives better.

The element of "beginning-level use of skills to handle anger" in Figure 7.1 has two arrows leading to medium-term outcomes. The first arrow leads to "higher level use of skills to handle anger." In this theory of change, there is still anger at this point, but the youth recognizes what is occurring and takes steps to handle it in a skillful way that does not lead to negative consequences. The second arrow, leading to "reframe situations so anger occurs less frequently," indicates that the program designers believe that the skills youth learn will assist them in reframing situations they are in so that they feel angry less frequently. This is a separate behavior from applying skills to handle anger, so it receives its own arrow and box.

The final column represents the long-term outcomes. Often, there is only one element shown in this column, one indicating the opposite of the problem. In this logic model, since the problem is seen to occur both at school and at home, each is looked at separately. A youth may reduce fights at home but not at school, or vice versa, so it is important to leave open the possibility of only partial success.

This example logic model shows a relatively simple program theory, with two separate tracks for intervention but with overlapping outcomes expected from the two intervention methods. It indicates how one element can lead to more than one "next step" and how different elements can lead to the same outcome. Finally, while it is not necessarily obvious just yet, this example shows some weak points in the program's logic that will emerge when we use it as a guide to evaluating the program.

TABLE 7.1 **Attributes of SMART Objectives**

Attribute	Description
Specific	Clear and concrete
Measurable	How many, how much
Achievable	Can be achieved with appropriate program activity and resources
Realistic	High enough that there is a possibility that the objective will not be reached, and not so low that achieving the stated objective would be meaningless
Timely	Provides a time span within which the objective will be achieved

Adapted from Lewis, Packard, & Lewis (2011).

Many people use the objective-setting acronym **SMART** to help them develop their outcome statements, particularly at the short- and medium-term levels (see Table 7.1). (The example logic model in Figure 7.1 does not show a SMART format because of space limitations, but it can be used in the full program materials.) Outcomes need to be specific (S), measurable (M), achievable (A), realistic (R), and timely (T). Table 7.1 helps explain each of these attributes. An example of using the SMART format for the short-term outcome of "beginning level use of skills to handle anger" is "95% of program participants will successfully demonstrate one anger management technique in a role-play situation after 2 weeks in the program." The use of the SMART approach is clearly more specific and measurable than the more general statement. It is also longer and more difficult to fit into a small box in the logic model format. Remember that the purpose of the logic model is to show the overall rationale for the program elements and how they relate to each other, not to describe the details of the program. The SMART format can be used in expanding the description of program activities and outputs as well. An example is "During the first year of operations, program staff will provide a total of 100 individual counseling sessions to students in the program."

Conceptually, the logic model can be divided into two parts. The three columns on the left (resources, activities, and outputs) are about the *process* of running the program. What is shown in these columns represents what you have to do to reach your program outcomes, or to impact your clients. Although it can be confusing, the term "process objectives" is sometimes used to label statements about the quantity of services provided. **Process objectives** are designed to determine whether the program is doing what it says it will do. They describe the services that are to be provided and in what quantities in what time frames. For example, the process objective might be to deliver 250 counseling hours to 75 clients within a 6-month period.

The three columns on the right relating to how clients will be different after being in the program (short-, medium-, and long-term outcomes) indicate the impact of the program. Outcome statements answer the "So what?" question. If you deliver the 250 counseling hours to 75 clients, the questions you want to answer are "What difference will it make in the lives of the people served?" and "How are they different afterward?" The outcome objectives become the basis of the outcome evaluation for your program. Outcome objectives indicate what will be different after the service is delivered. These may be stated as improved behavior, increased skills, changed attitudes, increased knowledge, or improved conditions. The well-developed, complete outcome objective will follow the SMART formula and include the target group, the number of program recipients, the expected results, and the geographic location (Coley & Scheinberg, 2016). We stress that this complete objective is difficult to fit in the logic model, so use a shortened version there and have the complete version in the full program description materials for reference.

PROGRAM EVALUATION

As you can see from this discussion, we have used a logic model to represent what we believe will happen when the proper inputs are applied to the correct client population. In the end, if all goes well, clients will no longer have the problem the program addresses, or at least the degree or extent of the problem will be less.

Evaluation is a way to determine the worth or value of a program (Rossi et al., 2019). There are two primary types of evaluation: process *and* outcome. The first, **process evaluation**, examines the way a program runs. In essence, a process evaluation examines the first three columns of a logic model to determine whether required inputs were available, the extent to which activities were conducted, and the degree of output accomplishment. **Fidelity monitoring** is a process to ensure that the implementation of an evidence-based program conforms to the core elements of the program, even when adaptations are made. This planning occurs before the program begins and is ongoing throughout the program's existence. Another aspect of a process evaluation, called **fidelity assessment**, examines whether the program being evaluated was conducted in accordance with the way the program was *supposed* to be conducted. If all components of a program are completed, fidelity is said to be high. Particularly with evidence-based and manualized programs, if changes are made to the program model during implementation, the program's effectiveness is likely to be diminished. As you develop your evaluation plan, before any implementation begins, you will want to create a **fidelity monitoring tool** that is used to track how well the EBP is being implemented. While these are usually part of an EBP's suite of information, if you are creating your own program, you will need to also create your own tool. These are often as simple as a checklist or a count of resources and activities.

The value of the logic model for evaluation is that most of the conceptual information needed to design the evaluation of a program is in the logic model. The required inputs are listed, and the evaluator can check to determine which resources actually came into the program. **Program activities** are similarly delineated, and an evaluator can usually find a way to count the number of activities that the program completed. Similarly, the logic model describes the outputs that are expected, and the evaluator merely has to determine how to count the number of completed outputs that result from the program's activities.

Looking at the example logic model shows us that we want to have in our evaluation plan at least one way to measure whether funding, staff, and space (the inputs) are adequate; how much case management occurred and how many individual counseling sessions were planned (the activities); and the extent to which referrals were made (and followed up on) and the number of individual counseling sessions that happened (the outputs). This information should be in program documents to compare what was planned for with what was actually provided. Having a logic model from the beginning allows the evaluator to ensure that proper data are being collected from the program's start, rather than scrambling later to answer some of these basic questions.

Image 7.3

Evaluation is part of a series of ways of examining the value and accomplishments of programs.

As noted earlier, this is not a perfect logic model. A question in the process evaluation at this stage might be to determine how to actually measure case management. The output is supposed to be "referrals to other agencies," but there is much else that could be considered beneficial from a case management approach. This element may need careful delineation and discussion with stakeholders to ascertain exactly what is important about case management that should be measured. Also, additional editing may be needed to better differentiate between the "activity" of individual counseling and the "output" of counseling sessions.

The second primary type of evaluation examines program outcomes. Called an **outcome evaluation**, it measures the achievement of program outcomes and is shown on the right half of the logic model, where the designated short-, medium-, and long-term outcomes are listed. The evaluator chooses which outcomes to assess from among the various outcomes in the logic model. Decisions need to be made about *how* to measure the outcomes, but the logic model provides a quick list of *what* to measure. In the example logic model, the short-term outcome "better recognition of the role anger plays in their lives" must be measured, and this could be accomplished using a set of questions asked at intake into the program and after some time has passed after receiving services. The next section examines what measurement is and talks more about measures themselves.

Measurement and Measures

The basic premise of any program is that after being a part of the intervention, things will change—whether the change is at the individual, organizational, or community level. **Program evaluation** is the way we determine what changed and by how much. The logic model points to what we will measure—resources, activities, outputs, and, ultimately, outcomes.

Measurement is the act of operationalizing concepts (e.g., learning, behavior, and mental status) and assigning a score or value to the level of that concept. Is a person educated, well-behaved, or depressed? It depends very much on what the terms mean. Without defining the terms and then having a way to measure them, we cannot say precisely.

BOX 7.2	**Temperature Is an Easy Example of Measurement**

When someone asks you if it is cold outside, we can run into a problem. That person probably wants to know the answer to help them know how to dress for the day. Some people are "cold-blooded" and are seemingly cold all the time. Others are the opposite, and frequently feel overheated. Can we do anything about the different interpretations of the words "hot" and "cold"?

Fortunately, we can. We all have learned the concept of temperature as some number on a thermometer. Temperature is a number that is a more precise and objective operationalization of whether it is hot or cold. While people can disagree with whether it is hot or cold because the terms are relative to personal judgment, different people can agree that it is indeed 85 degrees.

A **measure** is one way to determine the level of the concept of interest. With temperature, we have different scales to use and they all have a different answer to something as simple as the question "At what temperature does water boil at sea level?" Using the Fahrenheit scale, the answer is 212 degrees. With the Celsius scale, 100 degrees is correct.

Temperature is easy; other concepts, such as "depressed," "angry," or "combative," are less easily defined and measured. But we make progress in assessing a program's success by doing our best to operationalize even tricky concepts as we measure them.

Evaluators should determine what scales they will use and what constitutes the amount of change needed to show a successful program *before* the program begins. Resources such as Fischer et al.'s (2020) *Measures for Clinical Practice and Research* are invaluable for selecting appropriate measures for clinical interventions. This ensures the highest amount of objectivity in assessing the program.

One standardized anger management instrument is called the "Anger Management Scale" (Stith & Hamby, 2002). A standardized instrument, if it is appropriate for the clients and program, is a good choice because it can help you find norms or expected responses to the items on the instrument. It is helpful to you, as the evaluator, to know what "average" responses are so you can compare your clients' responses to the norms. Sometimes, however, it can be difficult to find a standardized instrument that is fully appropriate and relevant to your program.

Another way of measuring is to use an instrument you make up yourself. This has the advantage of simplicity and of being directly connected to your evaluation. In this case, for example, you could approach this outcome in at least two ways. First, you could request a statement from the caseworker or counselor indicating that the client has "recognized the role that anger plays" in their life, without going into any detail. A second approach would be to have the client write a statement about the role anger plays in their life. Neither of these measurements will have a lot of practical utility. Going through the logic model in this way in the design stage can show that this link in program logic is difficult to measure and may not be necessary.

While it may seem startling to have an example in a text that shows a less-than-perfect approach, it is included here to show that a logic model is very useful in showing weak spots in the program logic. This link to better recognition is not a fatal problem, and it may indeed be an important cognitive change for the client. The issue for evaluation is how to measure it and whether it really needs to be measured at all.

Returning to the example logic model, the next link leads to "learn skills to handle anger." The evaluation must ensure that clients understand skills to help them handle anger and so document these skills. It is not enough to indicate that skills were taught, as in a group or individual session. Teaching a class is an activity, and so would be documented in the process evaluation portion of the overall evaluation, but being in a class does not guarantee a change in the client. In this evaluation, we would like to have a measure that can show a client's change in the ability to perform the anger management skill. This attribute of the measure is important because we expect the clients to get better in their use over time and have included more skillful use of the techniques as a medium-term outcome in the logic model.

The other medium-term outcome shown is that clients will be able to reframe situations so that they actually get angry less frequently. The program logic shows this outcome occurring as a result of both beginning- and high-level use of skills. Because this element is broken out from the "use of skills to handle anger," it will need a separate measure. As an evaluator, you can hope that an established, normed instrument is available or that this is a skill that is measured by a separate item on a longer scale. If not, you will need to find a way to pull this information from staff members' reports or client self-assessments.

The final links in the logic model connect the medium-term outcomes to the long-term outcomes of fewer fights at school and fewer fights at home. Because youth having too many fights was identified as the problem this program is addressing, we want to know to what degree fights have decreased. The measure here could be client self-reports, school records, or reports from people living in the home.

Implicit in the discussion of the use of this logic model for evaluation purposes is that measurements at the end will be compared to an earlier measure of the same outcome. This is called a *single group pretest–posttest evaluation* (or research) design. It is not considered a strong design, due to the ability of other forces (known as "threats to internal validity") to affect the results. The design could be stronger if a comparison group of similar youth (perhaps at a different school) were chosen and tracked with the same measures. The design could be much stronger if youth at the same school were randomly assigned to either a group that received the program or a different group that did not receive the program. Even if this were to occur, however, one can find reasons to criticize that approach. It is beyond the scope of this book to cover in detail all the intricacies of measurement and evaluation design, but we hope this brief overview whets your appetite to learn more. (For more information on research design issues, see the Additional Resources listing at the end of the chapter.)

Accurately measuring outcomes is an important part of any evaluation effort. If measures are not appropriate or have low validity and reliability, the value of the evaluation will be seriously compromised. We suggest that anyone designing an evaluation consult a book on evaluation (such as Rossi et al., 2019) or other research methods (such as Rubin & Babbie, 2017) and also have access to books about measures (such as Fischer et al., 2020). You may desire to access evaluation training exercises (such as Preskill & Russ-Eft, 2015) as well. (The cost of new books on these topics may be high, but recent used editions contain much the same information and usually cost considerably less.) You should also consider hiring a program evaluation consultant who can assist you with the process.

Sometimes program evaluations find evidence of outcomes occurring that are not expected to happen. These are called "unanticipated outcomes" (see Box 7.3).

BOX 7.3	**What Is an Unanticipated Outcome?**

Outcome evaluations also sometimes include a search for unanticipated outcomes. An *unanticipated outcome* is a change in clients or the environment (positive or negative) that occurs because of the program, intervention, or policy but that was not thought would result and so is not included in the logic model. Unanticipated outcomes are often missed because they are not being looked for or measured. Be open to the possibility that clients or others are reporting things that were not part of your original thinking. They can be very important to notice and report.

 ## SPOTLIGHT ON DIVERSITY

As with all aspects of the program design process, we must be mindful to seek out diverse opinions and obtain them from people who are more likely to become clients, or who have close connections with such people. This is true both when creating a logic model as well as when planning the evaluation.

While the process of developing a logic model may not seem to be a situation where diverse views are needed ("It's just logical, after all!"), few things are less true. Remember, the logic model is the basis for the evaluation plan. It lays out the process evaluation requirements and milestones in terms of resources, activities, and outputs. Each of these three columns on the left side of the logic model are critical for program implementation and success. Getting feedback on the logic model will help you with important questions:

- Is this a program that will meet with the norms of the populations, or will it be rejected for cultural reasons?
- Will the population the program is intended for mistrust the messengers and recruiters and therefore stay away?
- Do you need to build in some time for becoming acquainted with thought leaders in the community who can provide important introductions and legitimacy?

You may not know unless you receive feedback on a draft logic model.

Another aspect of the logic model is that the right side shows connections between all the levels of outcomes and how they emerge from the activities. It is possible that outside stakeholders see gaps and overly ambitious thinking about results to be achieved. These people may be able to temper expectations and therefore have more realistic thinking about what is probable or even possible.

Of course, the evaluation plan is the heart of telling the tale of success for the program participants and the agency putting on the program. A vital aspect is the way outcomes will be measured. Are the scales unwittingly culturally insensitive? Is the reading level incorrect for the population? Will the evaluation process hit snags because the data collectors work hours that are inconvenient for the majority of the service recipients? All the aspects of collecting information need to be viewed by potential program clients.

Recall that potential clients can be busy in their own recovery or working two jobs to keep a roof over their heads. Time is precious for us all, but especially if one of the elements of program eligibility is being a low-income individual. Are you offering a stipend for respondents' time? If not, you may want to rethink that position.

These issues are important regardless of gender, race, ethnicity, or many other defining character-istics. If you, as the program designer, are not well integrated into the client population, you may make serious errors in putting together the logic model and evaluation plan.

DIFFICULTIES AND JOYS

Creating logic models and evaluation plans are two elements of program planning that are especially creative and fun (for some people). Still, it is not everyone's cup of tea. Our experience indicates that developing a logic model entails a logical, rational choice type of thinking that can feel foreign to many people who consider themselves more creative in nature. Also, because logic models require a clear understanding of desired outcomes (as well as inputs, activities, and outputs), people may realize they are not truly clear on the problem they are addressing and why the draft program is expected to improve the situation. Thus, disagreements and acrimony may result when unexpressed conflict is brought to the fore. We consider this unfortunate, especially when outside stakeholders' and program developers' views diverge without final agreement. We also consider efforts for program planning that do not create logic models and evaluation plans to be at a higher risk of wasting time and resources because the reasons for the programs are not well-established. The programs become like a fabled "road to nowhere" that cost a lot, divert staff time, and do not help any clients.

On the other hand, joys are also many. Once you have a well-constructed logic model that has had helpful feedback from interested stakeholders of all types, you have achieved something akin to lead-ing an orchestra through a complex symphony. Everyone is now on the same page. The problem to be addressed is clear, the methods agreed to, the parts assigned, and desired results (outcomes) made clear. When the program is then implemented, everyone understands how to measure the progress made. In the end, agreement on how much good the program has done is easy. This is when program evaluation feels necessary, beneficial, and well worth the effort.

LESSONS FROM THE PANDEMIC

The outcomes from the pandemic that relate to creating logic models and designing evaluations are numerous. The considerable disruption of people's physical and mental health, work status, living situations, and so much more means that what had seemed "logical" connections between program activities and expected outcomes for clients suddenly became very uncertain. Think about how COVID affected your clients and program. If clients were not able to attend activities or if people in residential settings were isolated, did the EBPs in place automatically become "tainted" in terms of expected outcomes? Should the EBP implementation be considered "invalid," taking with it all hopes for usable data? Are all client results (good or not) acceptable or not?

The underlying lesson from the pandemic is to ensure that the agency has contingency plans for any large-scale disaster, ranging from weather events (e.g., floods, tornadoes, and hurricanes), to domestic terrorism and political upheaval. Widespread illness is just one thing most organizations were not prepared for in 2020 but found they needed to be extremely agile in responding to revised work expectations and problems.

Program models needed to change to take into account issues clients were suddenly and unexpectedly dealing with. On top of financial and health concerns, stress was felt by nearly everyone, to one degree or another. We must also consider the impact on program staff when such problems emerge. As eloquently stated by D'Brot (2020):

> Program evaluations are grounded in the contexts in which they are implemented. As the environments that affect out programs change, our evaluations will likely need to change with them. It is safe to assume that many of our assumptions pre-Coronavirus will need to be revisited, revised, or thrown out altogether. ("Program Evaluation" section)

D'Brot (2020) also notes the opportunities that exist when so much is disrupted. A fresh and flexible eye toward routines is necessary. Much may be learned or unlearned in the process, and better solutions may be identified and implemented.

CONCLUSION

This chapter covers a large amount of information regarding the two topics presented: logic models and program evaluation. Both clearly link to the previous chapter on program planning and need to be integrated into your skillset. Each topic is the subject of entire books you can read, but this chapter presents the key elements. Working through the exercises at the end of the chapter will help you solidify your competency in this material. The mutually reinforcing interconnections among these three topics will help you move forward quickly in your understanding and assist you in applying your knowledge.

SUMMARY/KEY POINTS

- Logic models are an important tool to communicate with stakeholders. It shows the "theory of change" the program exemplifies. On what is usually one page, you can show what the problem being addressed is, what resources are needed to conduct what activities, and how, in the end, the problem is diminished or eliminated for those who went through the program. The outcomes of the program are thus linked to the inputs.
- A problem statement is written so that all stakeholders agree. Once that has occurred, necessary resources are listed and activities of the program are described (briefly) along with the outputs of the activities.
- Outcomes are helpfully divided into short term, medium term, and long term. An outcome is a change in the client (at whatever level the program is aimed). The long-term outcome is the opposite of the problem initially stated.
- Program evaluation is a process that builds on the logic model. At the end of the evaluation, it should be clearer what impact the evaluation has had on clients.
- Measures and measurement are vitally important to evaluation. You must plan how you will determine what the level of the logic model's variables (at least) before and after clients have gone through the program. This allows you to judge whether the program is successful or not.
- As with other parts of the program planning process, incorporating an understanding of obtaining diverse opinions and views is important for creating logic models and also conducting an evaluation.

KEY TERMS

Activities: What is done in the program, intervention, or policy with the inputs allocated (also known as "program activities").

Fidelity assessment: A type of process evaluation specifically designed to determine the fidelity with which a program, intervention, or policy was implemented. In other words, fidelity assessment determines the degree to which the program was conducted in the way it was supposed to be conducted. (See also fidelity monitoring.)

Fidelity monitoring: A process to ensure that the implementation of an evidence-based program conforms to the core elements of the program, even when adaptations are made. This planning occurs before the program begins and is ongoing throughout the program's existence. (See also fidelity assessment.)

Fidelity monitoring tool: A tool, such as a checklist of core evidence-based program elements, used to track how well an EBP is being implemented. Appropriate tools are typically developed by the evidence-based program's developers to assist program implementers.

Inputs: Element of a logic model that describes the resources that will be used to address the problem described in the problem statement. Inputs typically include funding, staff, and space.

Logic model: A "tool that describes the *theory of change* underlying an intervention, product or policy" (Frechtling, 2007, p. 1). A logic model displays the relationships between program resources, activities, and desired outcomes.

Measure: A tool to determine the level of a concept of interest.

Measurement: The act of operationalizing concepts (such as a particular change in clients) and assigning a score or value to the level of that concept.

Objectives: The results that are expected as the organization works toward its stated program goals. Achieving objectives leads to reaching the desired goals. These can be process objectives (e.g., how many services were conducted) or outcome objectives (e.g., what will change in the service recipient's knowledge, attitudes, or behavior).

Outcome evaluation: A type of evaluation in which the focus is on answering questions about the achievement of the program's stated desired outcomes. Sometimes, efforts are included to measure unanticipated outcomes—that is, effects of the program that were not included in the logic model.

Outcomes: Elements in logic models that describe changes in recipients' knowledge, attitudes, beliefs, status, or behavior. These are often divided into short-, medium-, and long-term outcomes to show that some outcomes come before others. The description of outcomes is a way to describe the purpose of having a program—how will service recipients be different after they engage in the program? Writing outcomes are replacing having program goals and objectives because they are more clearly linked to program activities and outputs.

Outputs: Element of a logic model that describes the measurable results of program, intervention, or policy activities.

Problem statement: Element of a logic model that describes the negative situation that the program, intervention, or policy is trying to improve.

Process evaluation: A type or part of a larger evaluation that examines the way a program, intervention, or policy is run or is implemented. Much of the information to design a process evaluation is in the logic model's columns of resources, activities, and outputs.

Process objectives: These are statements that quantify the usage of program services. Process objectives are designed to determine whether the program is doing what it says it will do. It describes the services that are to be provided, in what quantities, and in what time frames.

Program activities: What will be done by program staff and volunteers with, and on behalf of, service recipients.

Program evaluation: The use of a set of research-based methods to determine the worth or value of a program.

Program goals: Descriptions of desired future outcomes or states of client being.

SMART: A useful acronym to remember when developing objectives. Objectives need to be specific (S), measurable (M), achievable (A), realistic (R), and timely (T).

ADDITIONAL RESOURCES

Logic Models

Hoefer, R. (2015). *Creating a logic model in Microsoft Word* [Video]. YouTube. https://youtube/Ph2jtBaVKMM

Learning for Action. (n.d.). *Define the outcomes.* http://learningforaction.com/define-the-outcomes

SAMHSA's The Evidence-Based Practices Resources Center (https://www.samhsa.gov/ebp-resource-center). Formerly the National Registry of Evidence-based Programs and Practices (NREPP), this new website was created to provide guidance regarding programs that have evidence to support their use.

The Office of Justice Programs' CrimeSolutions (crimesolutions.gov) and Model Programs Guide (www.ojjdp.gov/MPG) websites are resources to find information about evidence-based programs in criminal justice, juvenile justice, and crime victim services.

Program Evaluation

Hoefer, R. (2012). *Hiring an evaluator: 5 steps on how to hire an evaluator* [Video]. YouTube. https://www.youtube.com/watch?v=hMEEBZJT4uE

Research Design

Rubin, A., & Babbie, E. R. (2017). *Empowerment series: Research methods for social work* (9th ed.). Cengage.

DISCUSSION QUESTIONS

1. Design Your Own Logic Model

    Choose a program or intervention with which you are very familiar. With one or two other people who share your knowledge, develop a logic model (if you are a student, you might choose your educational program; if you are employed, use the program you are employed with). Be sure to construct a problem statement—what problem is being addressed? (Knowing the purpose is sometimes a difficult question to answer, but it is essential.) When you are done, show your work to another group or talk about it in class. What were the easier parts of the process, and which parts were more challenging?

2. Using a Logic Model to Plan an Evaluation

    Using the logic model that you created in Discussion Question 1, discuss how you would ideally evaluate this intervention. What are the most important process and client outcomes to measure? What measures will you use? Who will collect the information? How will it be analyzed to determine whether the recipients of the intervention changed? Which were the easier parts of the process, and which were the more challenging parts?

3. The Chocolate Chip Cookie Evaluation Exercise

    (This idea is adapted from Preskill and Russ-Eft [2015]. It is a student favorite.)

Have participants get into small groups of no more than four people. This works well in work settings as well as in classes. The task of each group is to develop an evaluation system to determine the "ideal" chocolate chip cookie. The only caveat is that all members of the group must agree to the process developed. Each group should develop a set of criteria that individual members will be able to use to rate how closely any individual chocolate chip cookie nears "perfection." This means the criteria must be understood similarly by all, with an agreed-on benchmark. (For example, one student group indicated that shape was an important attribute of the perfect cookie, but it was unclear from their work what shape was preferred. After all, all cookies have a shape.) Once all group members have agreed to a set of criteria, the leader gives each group a cookie from several different varieties of store-bought or homemade cookies. Group members must then individually go through all of the criteria for each cookie and, based on the criteria chosen, choose the "best" cookie from among those they were given.

Often, groups come up with very different criteria, and individuals using the same criteria rate the same cookie very differently. This variation in criteria and ratings provides a very good basis for understanding the underlying principles of criterion-based evaluation and measurement issues.

 YOUR TURN

The exercises for this chapter relate to the program you developed after reading Chapter 5 on Program Planning (or you may use any program that you are familiar with).

1. Develop a logic model for your chosen program. Be sure to begin with the problem statement. When you have finished, use this checklist to ensure all elements of a logic model are included.

    A. Is the problem statement written so that more than one solution is possible (including the program idea you have chosen)?
    B. Are the resources adequately described so that it is possible to know what they are and how much of each is needed?
    C. Can the activities be conducted given the level of resources listed?
    D. Do the outputs naturally emerge from the activities, and in appropriate amounts?
    E. Do the short-term outcomes logically link to the outputs and to each other?
    F. Do the medium-term outcomes logically link to the short-term outcomes and to each other?
    G. Do the long-term outcomes logically link to the medium-term outcomes and to each other (if more than one)?
    H. Are the long-term outcomes the opposite of the problem; that is, if you achieve the long-term outcomes, will the problem be solved (or at least decreased)?

2. Once the logic model is completed and refined through feedback from others, create an evaluation plan. Which elements are you going to measure and with what measurement instrument? You should create a table that summarizes each variable measured, how they will be measured, and what level of achievement will be considered a success (see the example table).

Sample Evaluation Plan Table

Variable	Measure	Instrument	Level to be a success
Process: Counseling sessions provided	Enrolled students will attend eight counseling sessions.	Counselor case files.	90% of all enrolled students will receive eight counseling sessions.
Outcome: short term	Enrolled student will show beginning use of skills to handle anger.	Student self-report on weekly reflection exercise completed during counseling session.	90% of students will accurately describe their use of anger management skills in counseling session each week.
Outcome: long term	Fewer fights at school.	Disciplinary records at school.	90% of students will have zero fights at school during the last 3 weeks of the program.

REFERENCES

Coley, S. M., & Scheinberg, C. A. (2016). *Proposal writing: Effective grantsmanship for funding* (5th ed.). Sage.

D'Brot, J., (2020). *Program evaluations under COVID-19.* Center for Assessment. https://www.nciea.org/blog/interim-assessment/program-evaluations-under-covid-19

Fischer, J., Corcoran, K., & Springer, D. (2020). *Measures for clinical practice and research: A sourcebook* (6th ed.). Oxford University Press.

Frechtling, J. (2007). *Logic modeling methods in program evaluation.* Jossey-Bass.

Lewis, J. A., Packard, T., & Lewis, M. D. (2011). *Management of human service programs* (5th ed.). Brooks/Cole.

Preskill, H., & Russ-Eft, D. (2015). *Building evaluation capacity: Activities for teaching and training* (2nd ed.). Sage.

Rossi, P. H., Lipsey, M. W., & Henry, G. T. (2019). *Evaluation: A systematic approach* (8th ed.). Sage.

Rubin, A., & Babbie, E. R. (2017). *Empowerment series: Research methods for social work* (9th ed.). Cengage.

Stith, S. M., & Hamby, S. L. (2002). The anger management scale: Development and preliminary psychometric properties. *Violence and Victims, 17*(4), 383–402.

Figure Credits

CHAPTER EIGHT

Budgeting and Finance

OVERVIEW

Once you complete this chapter, you will understand the basic reports used in budgeting and financial management and will be able to analyze each report. It is important to have a solid understanding of financial reports as the basis for developing a program budget. Additionally, you will be able to explain the budgeting process and describe the different budgeting systems. Finally, you will be able to develop the budget for your proposed program and incorporate it into the overall agency budget. In our real-life example, our budget requires matching funds that will come from our fundraising/development efforts.

Most human service administrators start their careers as direct service providers and come to human services with a desire to make a difference in people's lives through service, advocacy, and policy reform. Very few begin with the goal of becoming financial managers, and therefore, most have little formal education or training in financial management. However, new administrators learn very quickly, and sometimes painfully, that financial management is a major part of their job.

Human service administrators do not have to give up their natural inclination toward client services to adopt a financial management perspective. Financial management is a skill critical to assuring quality services for clients and is just as important as policy analysis, social planning, casework, and program evaluation (Martin, 2021). The phrase "Put your money where your mouth is" applies to a great extent to budgeting and financial management. If we say that we believe in diversity and in social and economic justice, we must be willing to apply our organization's financial resources to back up these words. This chapter provides you with information on how to apply resources to run programs in a responsible way. Without skillful application of such knowledge, an agency will not exist for long.

Human services administrators do not need to be accountants, but they must be able to prepare a budget and to read and understand financial reports. Budgets and **financial reports** are important management tools in assuring the financial health of the organization. Financial management is a critical skill needed to provide quality services for the clients of the organization.

This chapter will present the basic accounting terms you will need as an administrator and give you the tools you need to read and understand the key elements of a budget and financial statement. You will also learn the basic steps in preparing a budget, including identifying multiple funding sources, projecting income and expenses, and understanding concepts of program accounting.

THE FINANCIAL HEALTH OF THE NONPROFIT SECTOR

The health of the nonprofit sector is vital to our society, and you need a good understanding of the state of the sector as you consider developing a new program. Nonprofits play a critical social role in almost all areas of our lives. When nonprofits suffer financially, so do some of the most vulnerable in our society. The nonprofit sector is also the place of employment for many of our citizens, and the loss of a nonprofit means the loss of income or pensions for hardworking families.

An analysis from just a few years ago by Guidestar and Oliver Wyman (2018) showed just how fragile the nation's nonprofits were:

- 7%–8% are technically insolvent, with liabilities exceeding assets.
- 30% face potential liquidity issues, with minimal cash reserves and/or short-term assets less than short-term liabilities.
- 30% have lost money over the last 3 years.
- 50% have less than 1 month of operating reserves.

The situation had improved some by the beginning of 2020, but then COVID-19 hit, and many human service organizations had to endure crisis after crisis. For many, donations had to shift entirely online and via mail, situations they were not entirely prepared to handle. All in-person events (e.g., galas, casino nights, golf tournaments, auctions, etc.) were cancelled. (Recall information from Chapter 1 regarding current difficulties in dealing with unsteady funding.) Most human service agencies had to curtail implementing new programs unless they were directly tied to the pandemic. Many reported greater client needs and demands for services that were difficult to fulfill.

The financial stresses in the human services sector require that leaders be skillful financial managers. While the picture presented above is somewhat bleak, the reality is that there are many nonprofits that are financially sound, and a part of your job as a program developer may be to help create programs that bring in more revenue than they cost so that other programs can be supported. Whether your organization is one that is prosperous and flourishing or one that is struggling, you will need skills to navigate the financial waters of your particular situation.

UNDERSTANDING FINANCIAL STATEMENTS

Before you can develop a budget for your program, you need to have a foundational level of knowledge in budgeting and financial reporting. In developing your budget, you must consider the impact of the other programs of the agency.

Generally accepted accounting principles (GAAP) are a basic set of rules governing how the financial books and records of an organization are to be maintained, including how revenues, expenditures, and expenses are to be accounted for and how financial statements are to be prepared. The Financial Accounting Standards Board (FASB) establishes the GAAP for nonprofit and for-profit organizations. The FASB rules require all private nonprofit organizations to prepare general purpose external financial statements at

Human services leaders must be skillful financial managers.

least once each fiscal year and must be reflective of the overall financial activities in their entirety during that fiscal year. The rules change from time to time, and any accountant your organization uses should have recently been trained on the latest amendments to the rules (Nonprofit Accounting Basics, 2020).

The FASB requires that four types of financial statements be prepared annually by nonprofit human service organizations. The required reports are (a) a statement of activities, (b) a statement of financial position, (c) a statement of cash flows, and (d) a statement of functional expenses by functional and natural classifications. In most cases, these reports are prepared by an independent auditor hired by the organization to examine the financial records of the organization each year. These reports are based on the monthly statements prepared by the organization throughout the fiscal year.

Statement of Activities

In simple terms, the *statement of activities* is the profit and loss statement for the organization. It is essentially the same report that a business would use to report its profits and losses for the year. The report tells the reader that, for example, there was "excess of revenues over expenses" (a profit) or that the expenses exceeded the revenues (loss) during the fiscal year.

Can a nonprofit organization make a profit? Absolutely! They can and should. There is much confusion about this point, given the term "nonprofit." Many believe that a nonprofit human service agency is prohibited from making a profit; on the contrary, it is acceptable and desirable for the organization to bring in more revenue than it spends. The issue is what the organization does with the excess income. The revenues must be used to promote the mission of the organization. For example, the profits cannot be paid to the board members as dividends, but it is perfectly alright to develop a reserve fund, buy equipment, or establish an endowment—anything that furthers the mission of the organization.

To understand financial reports, it is necessary to understand the following terms.

Statement of Financial Position

A **balance sheet** is the term for a statement of the financial position of an organization that states the assets and liabilities at a particular point in time. The balance sheet illustrates the financial "worth" of the organization. Statements can be prepared as often as the administrator or the board of trustees wants but must be prepared at least annually, on the last day of the fiscal year. The annual audit will include a balance sheet and will, in most cases, compare the current year to the year before to see if there has been a change in the financial position of the organization. The sum of an organization's assets minus liabilities gives a picture of the organization's net assets or the "net worth" of the organization.

Statement of Cash Flows

The cash flow statement is used to analyze the cash inflows and outflows (i.e., where the money came from and where it went) during a designated time period. This is especially important for nonprofit agencies where donated funds come at specific times of the year rather than throughout. Many non-profits rely heavily on annual events that happen near the same time each year, as well as a substantial amount of end-of-year fundraising. From the monthly statement of activities report, you will find there are certain items that may not affect your statement of activities for some time, such as the following:

- substantial increase in inventory purchases
- increase in accounts receivable (money owed to you)
- purchase of equipment
- lump sum payment of debt

A cash flow statement will highlight these activities in a way that an income statement will not. Without the cash flow statement, you will have an incomplete picture of your organization.

Statement of Functional Expenses

All voluntary health and welfare organizations must provide a statement of functional expenses. FASB requires that the statement include the organization's total expenses for the fiscal year and that the expenses be separated out by functional categories, such as program, management, general, and fundraising, and by natural categories, such as salaries, and fringe and usual operating expenses. This report also presents revenue and expenses for each program of the organization.

The Independent Audit

The independent audit is an important part of the financial management of an organization. As a part of this process, the independent auditor examines the financial records for the fiscal year and makes a report to the board of trustees. If the report does not find any significant problems in the financial reporting of the organization, it is said to be a "clean" audit. Auditors will often make recommendations for changes in the financial procedures of an organization to strengthen the internal control processes. These recommendations assure checks and balances in the financial system of the organization. The report is made not to the administrator, but to the board of trustees. It is the board that has the ultimate responsibility to protect the financial health of the organization.

As mentioned earlier, the financial reports and the independent audit are based on the organization's fiscal year. A *fiscal year* is usually a 12-month period of time for which the financial records of the organization are maintained. The organization can decide on the fiscal year in which it will operate. Some organizations choose to use the calendar year, from January through December, as their fiscal year. Others choose to use the fiscal year of their primary funders. For example, the federal government's fiscal year is October through September. Some states operate on a July to June fiscal year, and others on a September to August fiscal year.

Cash and Accrual Accounting

Two major types of accounting are cash accounting and accrual accounting. For our purposes, we will be dealing with accrual accounting, since this is the method used by most human service organizations and most businesses. In cash accounting, transactions are recognized (recorded) only when cash is received and only when cash is paid out. This is an acceptable but simplistic method and has serious limitations as a planning tool for human services administrators.

Accrual accounting means that transactions are recognized (recorded) when revenues are earned and when expenses are incurred. Accrual accounting provides a more complete financial picture through the use of accounts receivable and accounts payable. Accrual is the preferred method of accounting in human services administration.

Examples of Cash and Accrual Accounting

Think of cash accounting as keeping the money in a shoebox. When the money comes in, you put it in the shoebox, and when you spend money, you take it out of the shoebox. In accrual accounting, you recognize the income when you earn it. So, for example, if you have a contract to provide counseling services, you recognize the income in the month you provide the services. For example, during the month of June, you provide 100 hours of counseling services and send a bill to the contract agency. Since you have provided the services, you record the income in June, not in August when the check finally comes. The same is true of expenses. If you receive $1,000 worth of office supplies in June, you recognize the $1,000 expense in June, not when you pay the bill in July.

Image 8.2

Invest the time to understand financial statements.

BOX 8.1	**Be Patient**

You will often hear people say, "I am just not mechanical," meaning that they are not good at making repairs or working on equipment. What they should say is, "I don't have the patience or take the time to see how things work." It is much the same when dealing with financial statements. Saying "I can't understand financial statements" is really saying "I don't have the patience or take the time to study financial statements." As you work on the exercises and assignments at the end of this chapter, make a commitment to be patient and invest the time in understanding the financial statements.

Financial Statement Examples

The following financial statements are examples of the statements prepared by organizations. For our purposes, we have presented the 12-month budget for Cornerstone Family Services and a balance sheet. Following these reports we present a series of reports based on 8-month financial performance of the agency. These are the basis of the financial reports prepared by the independent auditor. Take a few minutes to examine the following financial statements. Look at the heading of each column and the line items in each statement. Do not be intimidated by the numbers. Just look at each row and number and think about the purpose of the report and what information the report is giving you.

To understand the report, you will need to know the meaning of several terms used in the report. Here are a few you will need now. There is a more extensive list of terms at the end of this chapter.

Assets: Anything owned by an organization that has economic value. Assets may include cash, bank accounts, accounts receivable (see definition below), equipment, buildings, property, and automobiles.

Liabilities: Obligations to pay somebody something. All debts or amounts owed by an organization in the form of accounts payable (see below), loans, mortgages, and long-term debts are liabilities.

Net assets: What is left over when liabilities are subtracted from total assets.

Revenues: Usually in the form of cash and checks and may come from many sources, such as fees for service, contracts, grants, donations, third-party payments, insurance, managed-care firms, or investment income.

Revenue classifications: There are three classifications of revenues to human services:

1. **Permanently restricted funds**: Some funds may be permanently restricted to a specific use. Endowment funds are usually in this category. A donor may give a gift to the organization but requires that only the earnings from those funds be used by the organization. For example, a donor gives a $100,000 gift to the organization's endowment fund. Let's assume that the interest rates or earnings

rate on the $100,000 is 5%. This means that the organization can use $5,000 each year and still have the original $100,000 intact.

2. **Temporarily restricted funds**: These funds are given for a specific project. For example, a donor might give $50,000 to the organization to renovate a building owned by the organization. The donor might choose to give the entire $50,000 at one time and then the organization would pay the contractors for the work as the project progressed. The $50,000 would be temporarily restricted and could be used only to renovate the building.

3. **Unrestricted funds**: These are funds on which the donor has placed no restrictions. An example of these funds is operating funds raised in an annual campaign. A donor may respond to a direct mail solicitation by sending a $500 check. Unless the donor specifies that the gift is to be used by a specific program or for a specific purpose, the $500 is unrestricted and can be used by the organization as needed.

Expenses/expenditures: There is a difference in the meaning of the terms "expenditures" and "expenses." Expenditures are cash that goes out of the agency. For example, the salaries paid for staff are an expenditure to the organization. Expenses are resources consumed by an agency (e.g., insurance, computer equipment, etc.). To understand this concept, think about buying a new computer for the organization. You will pay for the computer with cash, but you will use the computer over several years. You have traded one asset (cash) for another asset (the computer). Assume the life of the new computer will be three years. If you paid $3,000 for the computer, you will have an "expense" of $1,000 per year for each of the 3 years.

While there is a difference between expenditures and expenses, you often hear the terms used interchangeably. The important concept to grasp from this discussion is the concept of depreciation (see next).

Depreciation: An estimate of the decrease in the value of an asset. Depreciation takes into account the reality that equipment, buildings, automobiles, and so on become obsolete or simply wear out over time. It is a method to show how much of the value of an asset remains.

Accounts receivable: Revenues earned by a human service agency but not yet received. For example, if services have been provided and a contract has been billed for that service, the amount of the bill is an account receivable. It remains as an account receivable until the cash is received by the organization.

Accounts payable: Money owed by the organization to someone else but not yet paid. For example, if office supplies are received but have not yet been paid for, that amount is an account payable for the organization. Employee vacation time that has accumulated but not been taken is carried on the financial statements as an account payable.

HOW ARE BUDGETS AND FINANCIAL STATEMENTS USED TO PLAN AND IMPLEMENT A PROGRAM?

The following reports are examples of reports used by executives and boards of directors to understand and monitor the financial health of the organization. The first report is the annual budget for the entire organization. Note that this is for the full 12 months of the program year. The balance sheet is also a 12-month report of the financial health of the agency. The following reports are based on 8 months of agency operation. This is to help you have a better understanding of how the budget and financial statements are used in the management of an agency.

TABLE 8.1   Sample Annual Budget

CORNERSTONE FAMILY SERVICES, INC FOR THE YEAR 20XX	
INCOME	
Fees for services—Dept. A: Foster Care	972,000
Fees for services—Dept. B: Independent Living	582,100
Church contributions	180,097
Individual contributions	112,404
Foundation/corp./board	325,000
Wills & estates—unrestricted	
Grants & contracts	76,999
Rental income	100,000
Investment income	42,000
Transfer from unrestricted endowment	158,507
TOTAL INCOME	2,549,107
OPERATING EXPENSES	
Salaries	1,424,289
Benefits	269,862
Advert./promo/printing/postage	135,072
Auto exp.	14,779
Computer exp.	
Contract services	72,808
Dues/memberships	16,323
Food	75,825
Insurance	48,298
Interest exp.	90,645
Legal & professional	13,449
Maintenance & repair	36,600
Office/other supplies	46,437
Recruiting exp.	2,244
Rent exp.	20,028
Staff development	15,550

(Continued)

TABLE 8.1 (Continued)

Travel	84,270
Telephone/communications	62,754
Utilities	93,300
Other	26,574
TOTAL OPERATING EXPENSES	2,549,107
NET INCOME (LOSS)	**0**

Spend some time looking at the following balance sheet. The two columns of numbers are a snapshot of the current year's financial picture compared to the prior year. Look at each of the line items in the report. The first section lists all the assets. The second section lists all the liabilities and the fund balances (also called the *equity*). The formula for the balance sheet is Assets = Liabilities + Fund Balances.

TABLE 8.2 Sample Balance Sheet

CORNERSTONE FAMILY SERVICES, INC COMPARATIVE BALANCE SHEET AUGUST 31, 20XX		
	YEAR TO DATE	
ASSETS	ACTUAL	PRIOR YEAR
CURRENT ASSETS		
Cash	507,058	156,314
Accounts receivable	329,561	342,035
Prepaid expenses	51,462	67,015
TOTAL CURRENT ASSETS	888,081	565,364
INVESTMENTS		
Permanent endowment assets	1,748,432	1,618,953
Investments	227,657	243,963
TOTAL INVESTMENTS	1,976,089	1,862,916
FIXED ASSETS		
Land & buildings	3,809,845	3,708,297
Equipment, vehicles, furniture	796,436	846,205
Less: accumulated depreciation	(1,966,301)	(1,822,562)
TOTAL FIXED ASSETS	2,639,980	2,731,940
TOTAL ASSETS	5,504,150	5,160,220
LIABILITIES AND FUND BALANCES		
CURRENT LIABILITIES		
Accounts payable	55,801	55,293
Accrued expenses & payroll	110,773	106,471
Notes payable	1,095,531	

(Continued)

TABLE 8.2   (Continued)

Interagency transfers	70,000	821,540
Designated funds	117,412	74,517
TOTAL CURRENT LIABILITIES	1,449,517	1,057,821
FUND BALANCES		
Unrestricted	2,242,049	2,723,851
Retained earnings—current year	57	(317,345)
Temporarily restricted	73,293	81,659
Permanently restricted endow	1,739,234	1,614,234
TOTAL FUND BALANCES	4,054,633	4,102,399
TOTAL LIABILITIES AND FUND BALANCES	5,504,150	5,160,220
UNAUDITED FINANCIAL STATEMENTS FOR INTERNAL USE ONLY		

What assets does this organization have (own), and in what form? What are the liabilities of the agency? How does the financial picture for the current year compare to the previous fiscal year?

Now look at the monthly statement of revenue and expenses reports (Table 8.3, All Departments; Table 8.4, Administration; Table 8.5 Department A; and Table 8.6, Department B). This imaginary organization, Cornerstone Family Services, has two major program components, plus the administrative structure. The first report (Table 8.3) is the combined report of the two programs and the administration. The columns give information about the current period (last month) and then compare the actual figures to the budgeted amounts. For now, look only at the current period. Which of the income categories exceed the budgeted amount? Which income items are falling short of the budgeted amounts? Next look at the "year to date" columns. Are the same items that were under or over budget for the month also over or under for the year?

TABLE 8.3   Sample Monthly Statement of Revenue and Expenses: All Departments

CORNERSTONE FAMILY SERVICES, INC MONTHLY STATEMENT OF REVENUE AND EXPENSES—ALL DEPARTMENTS COMBINED FOR THE EIGHT PERIODS ENDING AUGUST 31, 20XX				
	PERIOD TO DATE		YEAR TO DATE	
	ACTUAL	CURR BUDGET	ACTUAL	CURR BUDGET
INCOME				
Fees for services—Dept. A: Foster Care	98,343	81,000	808,068	648,000
Fees for services—Dept. B: Independent Living	30,965	48,508	422,075	388,067
Church contributions	3,155	6,390	126,958	120,065
Individual contributions	13,501	3,690	124,589	74,936
Foundation/corp./board	7,900	8,333	197,018	216,667

(Continued)

TABLE 8.3 (Continued)

Wills & estates—unrestricted	3,750		48,950	
Grants & contracts	7,452	6,417	58,526	51,333
Rental income	2,935	8,333	71,260	66,667
Investment income	2,816	3,500	31,437	28,000
TOTAL INCOME	170,817	166,171	1,888,881	1,593,735
OPERATING EXPENSES				
Salaries	132,005	118,691	1,021,329	949,526
Benefits	20,366	21,988	167,367	179,908
Advert./promo/printing/postage	7,713	17,657	62,966	90,072
Auto exp.	2,158	1,231	16,189	9,853
Computer exp.	30		13,435	
Contract services	11,021	5,998	90,941	48,539
Dues/memberships	382	1,156	4,752	10,882
Food	9,499	6,250	99,110	50,550
Insurance	3,937	4,025	31,061	32,199
Interest exp.	6,121	7,554	57,491	60,430
Legal & professional	780	871	7,399	8,966
Maintenance & repair	6,125	2,849	35,472	24,400
Office/other supplies	3,991	3,781	37,305	30,958
Recruiting exp.		106	12,057	1,496
Rent exp.	2,894	1,694	15,154	13,352
Staff development	80	1,133	8,380	10,367
Travel	2,546	7,023	30,641	56,180
Telephone/communications	3,654	5,180	35,588	41,836
Utilities	8,475	9,500	73,525	62,200
Other	322	1,533	46,003	17,716
TOTAL OPERATING EXPENSES	222,099	218,220	1,866,165	1,699,430
NET INCOME (LOSS)	(51,282)	(52,049)	22,716	(105,695)
	UNAUDITED FINANCIAL STATEMENTS FOR INTERNAL USE ONLY			

TABLE 8.4   Sample Monthly Statement of Revenue and Expenses: Administration

CORNERSTONE FAMILY SERVICES, INC MONTHLY STATEMENT OF REVENUE AND EXPENSES—ADMINISTRATION FOR THE EIGHT PERIODS ENDING AUGUST 31, 20XX				
	PERIOD TO DATE		YEAR TO DATE	
	ACTUAL	CURR BUDGET	ACTUAL	CURR BUDGET
INCOME				
Fees for services—Dept A: Foster Care				
Fees for services—Dept B: Independent Living				
Church contributions	3,155	6,390	126,958	120,065
Individual contributions	8,186	3,690	118,574	74,936
Foundation/corp./board			173,318	95,000
Wills & estates—unrestricted	3,750		48,951	
Grants & contracts	7,452	6,417	58,526	51,333
Rental income	2,935	8,333	70,960	66,667
Investment income	2,815	3,500	31,336	28,000
TOTAL INCOME	28,293	28,330	628,623	436,001
OPERATING EXPENSES				
Salaries	41,830	49,065	356,901	392,519
Benefits	6,693	9,333	63,306	75,665
Advert./promo/printing/postage	2,480	11,342	19,652	39,690
Auto exp.	2,158	1,190	16,189	9,520
Computer exp.			12,134	
Contract services	5,103	4,517	44,890	36,133
Dues/memberships	175	346	1,875	3,117
Food	9,451	6,250	98,270	50,000
Insurance	3,137	3,258	24,617	26,067
Interest exp.	6,085	7,554	57,137	60,429
Legal & professional	780	700	6,910	7,600
Maintenance & repair	6,125	2,083	34,918	18,267
Office/other supplies	3,786	2,592	31,943	20,733
Recruiting exp.		10	11,115	330
Rent exp.	1,561	1,089	14,378	8,512
Staff development	80	263	3,767	4,500
Travel	784	2,188	5,386	17,500
Telephone/communications	2,206	2,005	20,958	16,439

(Continued)

TABLE 8.4 (Continued)

Utilities	8,475	9,500	73,526	62,200
Other	(79)	397	30,490	8,523
Allocation of indirect o/h	63,937	(18,214)	(300,173)	(145,709)
TOTAL OPERATING EXPENSES	164,767	95,468	628,189	712,035
NET INCOME (LOSS)	(136,474)	(67,138)	434	(276,034)
	UNAUDITED FINANCIAL STATEMENTS FOR INTERNAL USE ONLY			

TABLE 8.5 Sample Monthly Statement of Revenue and Expenses: Department A—Foster Care

CORNERSTONE FAMILY SERVICES, INC
MONTHLY STATEMENT OF REVENUE AND EXPENSES—DEPT A Foster Care
FOR THE EIGHT PERIODS ENDING AUGUST 31, 20XX

	PERIOD TO DATE		YEAR TO DATE	
	ACTUAL	CURR BUDGET	ACTUAL	CURR BUDGET
INCOME				
Fees for services—Dept A: Foster Care	98,343	81,000	808,068	648,000
Fees for services—Dept B: Independent Living				
Church contributions				
Individual contributions	5,290		5,290	
Foundation/corp./board	7,900	8,333	23,700	121,667
Wills & estates—unrestricted				
Grants & contracts				
Rental income				
Investment income				
TOTAL INCOME	111,533	89,333	837,058	769,667
OPERATING EXPENSES				
Salaries	64,563	42,494	439,360	339,951
Benefits	9,090	8,139	65,176	65,116
Advert./promo/printing/postage	520	1,114	4,203	8,675
Auto exp.				
Computer exp.	30		1,070	
Contract services	4,065	1,122	39,240	9,539
Dues/memberships	167	120	925	1,645
Food	10		565	350

(Continued)

TABLE 8.5 (Continued)

Insurance	400	384	3,222	3,066
Interest exp.	36		354	
Legal & professional		25		200
Maintenance & repair		666	516	5,334
Office/other supplies	66	530	3,728	4,350
Recruiting exp.		63	82	500
Rent exp.		605	(2,206)	4,840
Staff development		450	3,657	3,250
Travel	409	1,735	7,313	13,880
Telephone/communications	573	1,015	5,156	8,118
Utilities				
Other	103	176	4,039	1,413
Allocation of indirect o/h	51,517	13,733	239,671	109,861
TOTAL OPERATING EXPENSES	131,549	72,371	816,071	580,088
NET INCOME (LOSS)	(20,016)	16,962	20,987	189,579
	UNAUDITED FINANCIAL STATEMENTS FOR INTERNAL USE ONLY			

TABLE 8.6 Sample Monthly Statement of Revenue and Expenses: Department B—Independent Living

CORNERSTONE FAMILY SERVICES, INC MONTHLY STATEMENT OF REVENUE AND EXPENSES—DEPT B: Independent Living FOR THE EIGHT PERIODS ENDING AUGUST 31, 20XX				
	PERIOD TO DATE		YEAR TO DATE	
	ACTUAL	CURR BUDGET	ACTUAL	CURR BUDGET
INCOME				
Fees for services—Dept A: Foster Care				
Fees for services—Dept B: Independent Living	30,965	48,508	422,075	388,067
Church contributions				
Individual contributions	25		725	
Foundation/corp./board				
Wills & estates—unrestricted				
Grants & contracts				
Rental income			300	
Investment income			100	

(Continued)

TABLE 8.6 (Continued)

TOTAL INCOME	30,990	48,508	423.200	388,067
OPERATING EXPENSES				
Salaries	25,612	27,132	225,069	217,056
Benefits	4,583	4,516	38,885	39,127
Advert./promo/printing/postage	4,713	5,201	39,111	41,707
Auto exp.		41		333
Computer exp.			231	
Contract services	1,853	359	6,811	2,867
Dues/memberships	40	690	1,953	6,120
Food	38		275	200
Insurance	400	383	3,222	3,067
Interest exp.				
Legal & professional		146	489	1,166
Maintenance & repair		100	38	800
Office/other supplies	139	659	1,634	5,874
Recruiting exp.		33	860	666
Rent exp.	1,333		2,982	
Staff development		421	957	2,617
Travel	1,353	3,100	17,942	24,800
Telephone/communications	875	2,160	9,473	17,280
Utilities				
Other	298	960	11,474	7,780
Allocation of indirect o/h	12,421	4,481	60,502	35,847
TOTAL OPERATING EXPENSES	53,658	50,382	421,908	407,307
NET INCOME (LOSS)	(22,668)	(1,874)	1,292	(19,240)
	UNAUDITED FINANCIAL STATEMENTS FOR INTERNAL USE ONLY			

WHAT ARE THE DIFFERENT TYPES OF BUDGETS?

A **budget** is a plan for anticipating income and expenses to achieve specific objectives within a certain time frame (Brody & Nair, 2013). Some view budgeting as a planning process, while others see budgeting more as a political process. As a planning process, budgeting can be seen as a process to make rational decisions about the allocation of resources. Those who view budgeting more as a political process see competition between different factions for scarce financial resources. In this chapter, we will focus on the mechanics and planning aspects of budgeting, but it is important to always remember that there is a political element to the process.

There are many different types of budget systems, but there are three major types that you will need to understand.

Line-Item Budget

The line-item budget is the simplest and most common form of budgeting and the form used by most human service organizations. This budget type is concerned with expenditures and revenues related to commodities. The question is, "How much do things cost, and how much of each thing do we need?" This question relates to everything from number of employees to amounts of office supplies. The major purpose of this approach is economy and control of costs. A major purpose of the line-item budget is to identify all sources of anticipated funding and then allocate that funding to the different units of the agency for the next fiscal year.

Performance Budget

Performance budgeting is based on the output of each department of the agency. The typical measure is based on a unit of service. *Unit of service* can be defined in many ways. Some examples are counseling hours, foster placements, housing units developed, or however the product of the agency is defined. To develop a performance budget, it is necessary to determine the total program costs for a fiscal year and divide the total cost by the units of service to be provided for the fiscal year. If a department's total budget is $1,000,000 and they provide 10,000 counseling hours, the unit cost for this service is $100. Performance budgeting helps evaluate the productivity of an agency. In our example, if the department provided only 2,500 counseling sessions for the year and the budget remained at $1,000,000, then the unit cost would be $400 per counseling hour. As the administrator, this would likely raise concerns for you, which would lead you to reduce expenses or increase productivity. The counseling hour example is a simple and straightforward unit of service. Unfortunately, most units of service are not as easily defined. Even if an agency does not adopt a true performance budget, it is essential that the administrator have a method to monitor the unit costs for each department of the agency.

Program Budget

A program system budget is built by examining the expenses of each program in the organization, defining the measures of program outcomes, and calculating the cost to the program to achieve the desired outcomes. The program budget computes the total program cost for the fiscal year and divides that cost by the number of outcomes to establish a cost per outcome. Much like performance budgeting, program budgeting is effectiveness budgeting. The primary difference is that performance budgeting is based on outputs, whereas program budgeting is based on outcomes (Martin, 2021).

A Comprehensive Budgeting System

Line-item budgeting, performance budgeting, and program budgeting are all important tools for the human services administrator. Each provides important information essential to the management of a human service organization. Each provides data and information from a different perspective. The line-item budget emphasizes financial control, whereas the performance budget focuses on productivity, and the program budget stresses effectiveness. The competent administrator will use elements from all three of the major budgeting systems (Martin, 2021).

HOW DO YOU CREATE A BUDGET?

As stated earlier, budgeting has both a planning and a political component. When we think of the politics of budgeting, we often think of the budget battles in Congress or in the state legislatures, but we should also remember that there is a political component to the decisions made about how much one unit of an organization will get compared to another unit. The complex interplay between budget planning and budget politics makes it difficult to reduce the budgeting process to a few simple steps, but it is important to have a framework when engaging the process of developing a budget.

In this section, we will concentrate on developing a line-item budget since it is the most common budget system in human service organizations and is the base from which you as an administrator can build measures of performance using program and performance budgeting techniques. There are several steps in the budget process. For our purposes, we will use the steps outlined by Brody and Nair in *Effectively Managing and Leading Human Service Organizations* (2013).

Image 8.3

Creating budgets requires balancing many elements and may take more than one try to be successful.

Step 1: Set Organizational Objectives

The budget is one of the tools used to help an organization carry out its mission and achieve its objectives. Building the budget is a process of setting priorities and defining what is important to the organization. The old saying "Follow the money" is good advice when developing a budget. To allocate resources of one activity over another is to declare that activity to be a higher priority than the other. For example, leasing an additional van for client transportation rather than buying new computers for staff members prioritizes one stakeholder group over another, and good arguments can be made for both. The selection of one over the other, which is a budgeting decision, clearly also has value elements embedded in it. It is critical to be clear on the mission, goals, and objectives of the organization before engaging in the budget-building process.

Step 2: Establish Budget Policies and Procedures

Budget building is a complex task and requires the same level of organization and planning as other major projects. As the administrator, you should develop a budget time line so that all the parties involved in the process can coordinate their efforts. You, the program directors, the finance committee, and the board of trustees all have a role in the budget process. As the leader of the budget-building process, you will assign responsibilities for gathering the needed information. There will be many questions to be answered: What are the staffing needs for the next year? Will the cost of medical insurance be going up? How accurate were our predictions in the last budget year? In which line items did we overspend or underspend? Were our income projections realistic, and what is the outlook for the coming year?

Finally, you will need to develop the budget format to be used by each person involved in the process. In most cases, you will provide each person working on the budget with a report that compares the actual income and expenses to date in the current year to the current year's budgets. From this information, program directors are asked to project their needs for the next fiscal year. You may also set guidelines for preparing the budget. For example, you may set a guideline that budget increases may not exceed 3% (or whatever is appropriate).

Step 3: Set Annual Income and Expense Targets

The arithmetic of developing a budget is very simple:

Projected income – projected operation expenses = projected operating surplus or deficit.

Remember that it is perfectly acceptable for nonprofit organizations to have a surplus at the end of the year. In most cases, the budget presented to the board is a balanced budget in which the projected income and projected expenses are equal, but there are times when an agency may adopt a deficit budget. It is also very common for organizations to budget a surplus to build cash reserves for the organization.

The first section of the budget deals with the projected income for the coming fiscal year. Sources of income can include donations, corporate gifts, foundation grants, government contracts or grants, fees for service, and third-party payments. Any money anticipated to come into the agency should be included in the income budget. Remember that the expenses you budget are dependent on meeting the income goals in the budget. You can budget all the expenses you want, but if the income is not available, you will be forced to cut budget expenses to be within the projected net income.

The next section of the budget is the expense side, which includes all of the cash operation expenses of the organization. Salaries, fringe benefits, office supplies, rent, utilities, advertising, liability insurance, and any other expenses are to be categorized and included in the expense side of the budget.

Once the administrator has examined the income and expenses to date and made preliminary projections about the following year, the individual departments or units are given the information so they can propose their departmental budget. Your work will be the basis on which they will make their recommendations for their departmental budgets.

Step 4: Each Unit Proposes Its Budget

Each unit head will go through the same process in projecting income and expenses for the department and must justify increases in expenses. If new expenses are proposed, the program director must specify what new income will be generated to support the expenses. When this process is completed, the management team meets to develop the final draft of the overall budget document.

Step 5: Management Team Proposes Budget to Board

It is the responsibility of the administrator to develop the final budget proposal for the board. While there is a great deal of work from many parts of the organization to develop the budget, it is ultimately the responsibility of the administrator to present a budget to the board. The administrator will also be held accountable for carrying out the budget plan.

In this step, the administrator presents the budget proposal to the finance committee of the board. This is the place for the representatives of the board to take a hard look at the budget proposal. The finance committee should be asking certain questions: Are the income projections realistic? Are the expenses reasonable? Does this budget advance the mission of the organization? Any adjustments required by the finance committee are made, and then the finance committee presents the budget to the full board with a recommendation. Finally, the board adopts the budget for the next fiscal year.

 SPOTLIGHT ON DIVERSITY

According to *Forbes*, "The new trend is for companies to shout from the rooftops their pledges and promises to foster an equitable and inclusive environment. Although it can sometimes be challenging to decipher which companies are really walking the walk and talking the talk, a strong indication of a company's commitment to diversity, equity, and inclusion (DEI) can be found in the money that is apportioned for diversity, equity and inclusion (DEI) initiatives efforts. No budget at all or a minuscule budget sends the message to the world that DEI is not a priority for your organization" (Asare, 2020, Section 3).

DIFFICULTIES AND JOYS

This chapter examines one of the most challenging tasks for administrators of human service organizations. There are great needs to be addressed by a human service organization, but there are always limited resources. Budgeting and financial management are the tools used to plan and use the resources of the organization in the most effective way. The administrator must manage many tasks at the same time, but financial management must be a priority, or the organization will have little chance to live up to the challenges of its mission.

The joy in budgeting and financial management comes from the satisfaction of using limited resources to provide the best quality services to the most people possible. There is joy in knowing that the resources available to the agency are used to promote equality and social justice. It is a joy to know that you have done your best to manage the financial resources of the agency in a way that is equitable and fair to the clients, the funders, the staff, and the larger community. There are times when people will leave their estates to the organization with the desire that their lifetime of work will live on to help others. It is a joy to be the person that makes that hope become a reality by being a good steward of the money given to the agency.

LESSONS FROM THE PANDEMIC

The COVID-19 pandemic threw budgeters into a spin. Revenues were cut, if not slashed. The stock market crashed, as did the job market, with job losses in the millions, so donations from individuals were uncertain. Expenses hardly budged, with so much of any human service organizations' funding used to pay salaries. Layoffs from human service organizations happened, as with almost all other organizational types. Deep discussions have been held to see which programs could be operated with the least amount of disruption. As the crisis continued, these discussions had to be held again, and again.

Organizations that had significant endowments or access to loans used them up as well as other reserves. Because no one knew how long lockdowns were going to last, planning was next to impossible. Organizations with government grants or contracts had a somewhat easier time, but it was not easy for them either.

Some nonprofits were saved when stimulus funds became available to continue paying salaries. This process was not an easy one to follow, but for those who received support in this way, the program was a lifesaver.

Are there any lessons to be learned from such a catastrophic circumstance? Perhaps it is that you can never be too prepared with contingency plans. COVID-19 or other viral outbreaks are not the only disaster that can occur. With climate change leading to more severe weather events, flooding or wind damage can occur.

In this situation, individual agencies should not be blamed any more than individuals who lose their jobs in an economic crisis. The actions of the individual actor can hardly impact, much less overcome, the negative situation. In this case, it would be helpful if the funding and budgeting situation became more cognizant of the possibility of crises and more flexible in the way foundations, philanthropic individuals, and government funders react. Foundations can choose to spend more, even going into their corpus. Individuals of high net worth can open their purse strings wider and encourage their compatriots to do the same. The federal government can overlook partisan differences and act more quickly and more generously. Individual program developers and other employees can return to Chapter 3 and practice becoming advocates and policy entrepreneurs to increase the possibilities of keeping human service programs operating.

CONCLUSION

This chapter will surely not make you an accountant, but it will give you the basic tools to learn the art of financial management and give you the tools needed to prepare a program budget within the context of a larger agency budget. As the program developer, you will depend on the expertise of the chief financial officer of the organization, who is an important member of the management team. In addition to a strong in-house financial person, every organization should have a contract agreement with a certified public accountant (CPA). Any knowledge you can bring to the table in your program development role is helpful so that you can make stronger arguments for the budget you believe is needed for your carefully crafted program.

 ## SUMMARY/KEY POINTS

- Human service administrators do not have to give up their natural inclination toward client services to adopt a financial management perspective.
- A budget is a plan for anticipating income and expenses to achieve specific objectives within a certain time frame (Brody & Nair, 2013).
- As a planning process, budgeting can be seen as a process to make rational decisions about the allocation of resources.
- Those who view budgeting more as a political process see competition between different parts of the organization.
- The budgeting process outlined by Brody and Nair in *Effectively Managing and Leading Human Service Organizations* (2013) is:
    - Step 1: Set organizational objectives.
    - Step 2: Establish budget policies and procedures.
    - Step 3: Set annual income and expense targets.
    - Step 4: Each unit proposes its budget.
    - Step 5: Management team proposes budget to board.

KEY TERMS

Accounts payable: Money owed by the organization to someone else but not yet paid. For example, if office supplies are received but have not yet been paid for, that amount is an account payable for the organization. Employee vacation time that has accumulated but not been taken is carried on the financial statements as an account payable.

Accounts receivable: Revenues earned but not yet received. For example, if services have been provided and a contract has been billed for that service, the amount of the bill is an account receivable. It remains as an account receivable until the cash is received by the organization.

Accrual accounting: Transactions are recognized (recorded) when revenues are earned and when expenses are incurred. Accrual accounting provides a more complete financial picture through the use of accounts receivable and accounts payable.

Assets: Anything owned by an organization that has economic value. Assets may include cash, bank accounts, accounts receivable (see definition above), equipment, buildings, property, and automobiles.

Balance sheets: A snapshot in time of an organization's assets and liabilities, produced monthly, quarterly, or annually. These reports subtract liabilities from assets to show the organization's worth.

Budget: A plan for anticipating income and expenses to achieve specific objectives within a certain time line.

Depreciation: An estimate of the decrease in the value of an asset. Depreciation takes into account the reality that equipment, buildings, automobiles, and so on become obsolete or simply worn out over time. It is a method to show how much of the value of an asset remains.

Expenses/Expenditures: Expenditures are cash that goes out of the agency, and expenses are resources consumed by an agency (insurance, computer equipment, etc.).

Financial reports/Financial statements: Reports on historical financial transactions. Examples include budget reports, activity reports, and balance sheets.

Generally accepted accounting principles (GAAP): Basic sets of rules governing how the financial books and records of an organization are to be maintained, including how revenues, expenditures, and expenses are to be accounted for and how financial statements are to be prepared.

Liabilities: Obligations to pay somebody something. All debts or amounts owed by an organization in the form of accounts payable (see above), loans, mortgages, and long-term debts are liabilities.

Net assets: What is left over when liabilities are subtracted from assets.

Permanently restricted funds: Funds permanently restricted to a specific use. Endowment funds are usually in this category. For example, a donor may give a gift to the organization but require that only the earnings from those funds be used by the organization.

Revenues: Usually in the form of cash and checks and may come from many sources, such as fees for service, contracts, grants, donations, third-party payments, insurance, managed-care firms, or investment income.

Temporarily restricted funds: Funds given for a specific project.

Unrestricted funds: Funds on which the donor has placed no restrictions.

ADDITIONAL RESOURCES

Capital Business Solutions. (2018). *3 major differences between government & nonprofit accounting.* https://www.capitalbusiness.net/resources/3-major-differences-government-nonprofit-accounting/

McCarthy, J. H., Shelmon, N. E., & Mattie, J. A. (2012). *Financial and accounting guide for not-for-profit organizations* (8th ed., Vol. 6). John Wiley & Sons.

Mitchell, G. E., & Calabrese, T. D. (2018). Proverbs of nonprofit financial management. *The American Review of Public Administration*, *49*(6), 649–661. https://doi.org/10.1177/0275074018770458

Wallace Foundation. (2015). *5 step guide to budget development: Resources for nonprofit financial management* [Video]. YouTube. https://www.youtube.com/watch?v=edC7v81Fmj8

Zietlow, J., Hankin, J. A., Seidner, A., & O'Brien, T. (2018). *Financial management for nonprofit organizations: Policies and practices.* John Wiley & Sons.

DISCUSSION QUESTIONS

1. Budgeting has both a planning and a political component. There is a political component to the decisions made about how much one unit of an organization will get compared to another unit. As an administrator, how would you deal with this reality in the budgeting process? What precautions would you take as you bring in a third program to Cornerstone Family Services?

2. Working in a small group in class, discuss your personal strengths and weaknesses related to financial management and budgeting. Report to the class how you plan to better prepare yourself for the financial functions you will need to perform as a human service administrator.

REAL-LIFE EXAMPLE

Our real-life example budget is presented to give you an overview of the complexity of budgeting for a federal grant. In this example, federal resources is the amount of funds being requested from the federal program. The nonfederal resources (CFS match amount) are the matching funds required for the grant. Nonfederal resources (other sources) are the additional funds provided to support the program. Total RHY (Runaway and Homeless Youth Program) budget is the budget from all sources.

Line-Item Budget

Funding Source (Estimates)	Federal Resources (Basic Center Funded Amount)	Nonfederal Resources (CFS Match Amount)	Nonfederal Resources (Other Sources Amount)	Total RHY Program Budget
United Way			$127,250	$127,250
Church Contributions			$9,407	$9,407
Basic Center Grant	$198,000			$198,000
Community Foundation			$15,000	$15,000
Individual Donations		$23,000		$23,000
Total Estimated Funding	$198,000	$23,000	$151,657	$372,657

	# of Staff	Shelter Program FTEs	Shelter % of Time	RHY Program % of Shelter Service Days	Average Annual Wages	% of Shelter Cost Charged to Basic Center	Federal Resources (Basic Center Funded Amount)	Nonfederal Resources (CFS Match Amount)	Nonfederal Resources (Other Sources Amount)	Total RHY Program Budget
A. Personnel										
Shelter Team Supervisor (FT)	2	2	100%	44%	$30,050	35%	$21,035	$0	$5,409	$26,444
2 staff x $30,050 x .44=RHY allocation										
2 staff x $30,050 x .35=Basic Center allocation										
Shelter Team Supervisor (PT)	1	.5	100%	44%	$14,850	35%	$5,197	$0	$1,337	$6,534
1 staff x $14,850 x .44=RHY allocation										
1 staff x $14,850 x .35=Basic Center allocation										

Shelter Youth Care Specialist (FT)	9	9	100%	44%	$22,800	35%	$71,820	$0	$18,468	$90,288
9 staff x $22,800 x .44 = RHY allocation										
9 staff x $22,800 x .35 = Basic Center allocation										
Shelter Youth Care Specialist (PT)	13	3	100%	44%	$5,200	35%	$23,660	$0	$6,084	$29,744
13 staff x $5,200 x .44 = RHY allocation										
13 staff x $5,200 x .35 = Basic Center allocation										
Shelter Case Manager	1	1	100%	44%	$35,525	35%	$12,434	$0	$3,197	$15,631
1 staff x $35,525 x .44=RHY allocation										
1 staff x $35,525 x .35=Basic Center allocation										
Residential Assessment Counselor	1	0.85	85%	44%	$45,895	35%	$13,654	$0	$3,511	$17,165
1 staff x $45,895 x .85 x .44=RHY allocation										
1 staff x $45,895 x .85 x .35=Basic Center allocation										
Shelter Supervisor	1	1	100%	44%	$60,000	35%	$21,000	$0	$5,400	$26,400
1 staff x $60,000 x .44=RHY allocation										
1 staff x $60,000 x .35=Basic Center allocation										
RHY Program Manager	1	.80	80%	44%	$51,240	35%	$14,347	$0	$3,689	$18,036
1 staff x $51,240 x .80 x .44=RHY allocation										
1 staff x $51,240 x .80 x .35=Basic Center allocation										
Senior Director of Residential Services	1	.20	20%	44%	$77,000	0%	$0	$0	$6,776	$6,776
1 staff x $77,000 x .20 x .44=RHY allocation										
Personnel Subtotals	**30**	**18.35**					**$183,147**	**$0**	**$53,871**	**$237,018**

	RHY Program % of Shelter Service Days	% of Shelter Cost Charged to Basic Center	Federal Resources—Basic Center Funded Amount	Nonfederal Resources—ACH Match Amount	Nonfederal Resources—Other Sources Amount	Total RHY Program Budget
B. Fringe Benefits						
FICA Employer Taxes	N/A	N/A	$11,355	$0	$3,340	$14,695
6.2% of wages						
Medicare Employer Taxes	N/A	N/A	$2,656	$0	$781	$3,437
1.45% of wages						
Worker's Comp Insurance	N/A	0%	$0	$0	$2,370	$2,370
1.0% of wages						
401k Retirement Match	44%	0%	$0	$0	$4,752	$4,752
Average $900/mo. x 12 mos. x .44=RHY allocation						
Health Insurance	44%	9.64%	$842	$23,000	$14,596	$38,438
$520/mo. x 12 mos. x 14 eligible FT staff x .44=RHY allocation						
$520/mo. x 12 mos. x 14 eligible FT staff x .0964=Basic Center allocation						
Fringe Subtotal			$14,853	$23,000	$25,839	$63,692
C. Travel						
Travel Subtotal						$0
D. Equipment						
Equipment Subtotal						$0
E. Supplies						
Household Supplies	44%	0%	$0	$0	$1,478	$1,478
$280/mo. x 12 x .44=RHY allocation						
Office Supplies	44%	0%	$0	$0	$396	$396
$75/mo. x 12 x .44=RHY allocation						
Dietary Expenses	44%	0%	$0	$0	$9,662	$9,662
$1,830/mo. x 12 x .44=RHY allocation						
Clothing and Personal Care	44%	0%	$0	$0	$660	$660
$125/mo. X 12 x .44=RHY allocation						

	RHY Program % of Shelter Service Days	% of Shelter Cost Charged to Basic Center	Federal Resources—Basic Center Funded Amount	Nonfederal Resources—ACH Match Amount	Nonfederal Resources—Other Sources Amount	Total RHY Program Budget
Supplies Subtotal			$0	$0	$12,196	$12,196
F. Contractual						$0
Contractual Subtotal						$0
G. Construction						$0
Construction Subtotal						$0
H. Other						
Medical	44%	0%	$0	$0	$3,696	$3,696
$700/mo. x 12 x .44=RHY allocation						
Youth Activities	44%	0%	$0	$0	$1,980	$1,980
$375/mo. x 12 x .44=RHY allocation						
Education & Tutoring	44%	0%	$0	$0	$132	$132
$25/mo. x 12 x .44=RHY allocation						
Interpreter Services	44%	0%	$0	$0	$264	$264
$60/call x 10 calls/yr. x .44=RHY allocation						
Utilities (gas, electric, water, garbage, sewer)	N/A	0%	$0	$0	$27,000	$27,000
$2,250/mo. x12=RHY allocation						
Telephone (Local, Long Distance, Cell)	N/A	0%	$0	$0	$3,600	$3,600
$300/mo. x 12=RHY allocation						
Cleaning/Janitorial	44%	0%	$0	$0	$3,696	$3,696
$700/mo. x 12 x .44=RHY allocation						
Maintenance and Repairs	44%	0%	$0	$0	$396	$396
$75/mo. x 12 x .44=RHY allocation						
Vehicles—Fuel	44%	0%	$0	$0	$1,848	$1,848
$350/mo. x 12 x .44 = RHY allocation						
Vehicles—Maintenance and Repairs	N/A	0%	$0	$0	$1,200	$1,200
$100/mo. x 12=RHY allocation						

	RHY Program % of Shelter Service Days	% of Shelter Cost Charged to Basic Center	Federal Resources—Basic Center Funded Amount	Nonfederal Resources—ACH Match Amount	Nonfederal Resources—Other Sources Amount	Total RHY Program Budget
Vehicles–Licenses	N/A	0%	$0	$0	$76	$76
$78 x 1 van=RHY allocation						
Vehicles–Insurance	N/A	0%	$0	$0	$1,740	$1,740
$145/month x 12=RHY allocation						
IT Support/Data Systems	44%	0%	$0	$0	$5,280	$5,280
$1,000/mo. x 12 x .44=RHY allocation						
Printing and Copying	44%	0%	$0	$0	$660	$660
$125/mo. x 12 x .44=RHY allocation						
Conferences and Training	44%	0%	$0	$0	$550	$550
25 direct staff x $50/ea. x .44=RHY allocation						
Travel for Conferences and Training	N/A	0%	$0	$0	$625	$625
25 direct care staff x $25/ea.=RHY allocation						
Mileage	N/A	0%	$0	$0	$672	$672
100 miles/mo. x $.56/mile x 12 mos.=RHY allocation						
General Insurance (property, liability, umbrella)	44%	0%	$0	$0	$6,336	$6,336
$1,200/mo. x 12 x.44 = RHY allocation						
Other Subtotal			$0	$0	$59,751	$59,751
Total RHY Shelter Program			$198,000	$23,000	$151,657	$372,657

Budget Justification: General Information

CFS operates an Emergency Youth Shelter (referred to as the Shelter) that serves several different client populations: (a) RHY, (b) youth placed by the Department of Family and Protective Services, and (c) youth referred by MHMR. Some costs that are directly related to the care of youth are allocated according to the days of service by population group for 2013. In 2013, RHY accounted for approximately 44% of the days of service. The overall RHY program budget is based on costs associated with the physical building that houses the program and the allocation of direct care costs, including staff time, based on the population group calculation (44%). A portion of the RHY program budget will be charged to the Basic Center grant.

Personnel

Shelter Team Supervisor (full-time): Provides supervision of youth, implements crisis intervention, and assists youth in achieving goals. There are two staff in this position, 2.0 FTEs; each works 40 hrs./week at an average annual wage of $30,050. 100% of the staff time is devoted to the Shelter, 44% of the time working with RHY program youth. 35% of actual wages for this position will be paid from Basic Center grant funds.

Shelter Team Supervisor (part-time): Provides supervision of youth, implements crisis intervention, and assists youth in achieving goals. There is one staff in this position, .5 FTE; this staff person works 16–20 hrs./week at an average annual wage of $14,850. 100% of the staff time is devoted to the Shelter, 44% of the time working with RHY program youth. 35% of actual wages for this position will be paid from Basic Center grant funds.

Shelter Youth Care Specialist (full-time): Provides basic care for youth, adult guidance, and a supportive learning experience. There are nine staff in this position, 9.0 FTEs; each works 40 hrs./week at an average annual wage of $22,800. 100% of the staff time is devoted to the Shelter, 44% of the time working with RHY program youth. 35% of actual wages for this position will be paid from Basic Center grant funds.

Shelter Youth Care Specialist (part-time): Provides basic care for youth and a supportive learning experience with adult guidance. There are 13 staff in this position, 3.0 FTEs; most of these staff work 16–20 hrs./week while others work on an as-needed basis, at an average annual wage of $5,200. 100% of the staff time is devoted to the Shelter, 44% of the time working with RHY program youth. 35% of actual wages for this position will be paid from Basic Center grant funds.

Shelter Case Manager (full-time): Provides and coordinates crisis intervention, case management, and transition planning for youth. There is one staff in this position, 1.0 FTE; this staff person works 40 hrs./week at an average annual wage of $35,525. 100% of the staff time is devoted to the Shelter, 44% of the time working with RHY program youth. 35% of actual wages for this position will be paid from Basic Center grant funds.

Residential Assessment Counselor (full-time): Performs assessment of client needs, assists with client intake, and provides counseling for current and discharged clients. There is one staff in this position, 1.0

FTE; this staff person works 40 hrs./week at an average annual wage of $45,895. Approximately 85% of the staff time is devoted to the Shelter, 44% of the time working with RHY program youth. 35% of the 85% of actual wages allocated to the Shelter for this position will be paid from Basic Center grant funds.

Shelter Supervisor (full-time): Manages shelter operations, ensures compliance with licensing standards, and supervises staff training and scheduling. There is one staff in this position, 1.0 FTE; this staff person works 40 hrs./week at an average annual wage of $60,000. 100% of the staff time is devoted to the Shelter, 44% of the time working with RHY program youth. 35% of actual wages for this position will be paid from Basic Center grant funds.

RHY Program Manager (full-time): Supervises and manages all program activities and staff for several programs, including the Shelter. There is one staff in this position, 1.0 FTE; this staff person works 40 hrs./week at an average annual wage of $51,240. Approximately 80% of the staff time is devoted to the Shelter, 44% of the time working with RHY program youth. 35% of the 80% of actual wages allocated to the Shelter for this position will be paid from Basic Center grant funds.

Senior Director of Residential Services (full-time): Develops, maintains, and evaluates residential programs and support services for several residential programs, including the Shelter. There is one staff in this position, 1.0 FTE; this staff person works 40 hrs./week at an average annual wage of $77,000. Approximately 20% of the staff time is devoted to the Shelter, 44% of the time supervising the Shelter Supervisor in efforts for RHY program youth. No wages for this position will be paid from Basic Center grant funds.

Fringe Benefits

FICA taxes: As required by law, taxes are paid by the employer on taxable employee wages at a rate of 6.2%. These taxes will be paid from Basic Center grant funds in proportion to the wages paid from Basic Center grant funds.

Medicare taxes: As required by law, taxes are paid by the employer on taxable employee wages at a rate of 1.45%. These taxes will be paid from Basic Center grant funds in proportion to the wages paid from Basic Center grant funds.

Worker's compensation insurance: Employees are covered by worker's compensation insurance. Premiums for this insurance are based on the type of work that is done at an average rate of 1.0% of total wages. The costs are allocated to the Basic Center Program in proportion to the wages paid. None of these costs will be paid from Basic Center grant funds.

401k retirement match: Employees are eligible to participate in an employer-sponsored 401k plan with a discretionary match component. Average match amounts for participating employees amount to approximately $900 per month. The costs are allocated to the Basic Center Program in proportion to the wages paid. None of these costs will be paid from Basic Center grant funds.

Health insurance coverage: Full-time employees are eligible for medical, dental, vision, and life insurance. Premium costs for the employee only average $520/month. There are 14 eligible full-time direct care staff. 44% of these premium costs are allocated to the Basic Center Program. 9.64% of premium costs will be paid from Basic Center grant funds.

Travel

No costs for out-of-town or out-of-state travel are anticipated at this time. If costs are incurred, they will not be paid from Basic Center grant funds.

Equipment

The Emergency Youth Shelter has the equipment required for providing care to youth and for meeting requirements for data collection, reporting, and analysis. Computer equipment is already in place. No costs are anticipated at this time for equipment.

Supplies

Household supplies: Includes supplies for the kitchen, laundry, and bathrooms; general bedding supplies; and light general maintenance supplies. These supplies are necessary to provide a clean, safe, and comfortable environment for youth in the Shelter. Annual household supplies costs for the Shelter are estimated based on historical spending at a rate of $280/month. 44% of these costs are allocated to the Basic Center Program. No costs will be paid from Basic Center grant funds.

Office supplies: Includes general office supplies necessary for staff to maintain files, organize scheduling and employee supervision, and to plan and prepare for youth training and activities. Office supplies costs for the Shelter are estimated based on historical spending at a rate of $75/month. 44% of these costs are allocated to the Basic Center Program. No costs will be paid from Basic Center grant fund.

Dietary expenses: Includes food for meals and snacks necessary for the health and well-being of youth. Food costs for the Shelter are estimated based on historical spending at a rate of $1,830/month. 44% of these expenses are allocated to the Basic Center Program. No costs will be paid from Basic Center grant funds.

Clothing and personal care: Includes adequate clothing and personal care items needed by youth, such as shampoo, toothpaste, and other toiletries. Clothing and personal care costs for the Shelter are estimated based on historical spending at a rate of $125/month. 44% of these expenses are allocated to the Basic Center Program. No costs will be paid from Basic Center grant funds.

Contractual: N/A
Construction: N/A
Other

Medical care: Includes general medical care, first-aid supplies, medication and optical supplies for youth to promote wellness and healing. Medical care costs for the Shelter are estimated based on historical spending at a rate of $700/month. 44% of these expenses are allocated to the Basic Center Program. No costs will be paid from Basic Center grant funds.

Youth activities: Includes outings and field trips for youth to area attractions for entertainment, recreation, and educational purposes. Youth activities costs for the Shelter are estimated based on historical spending at a rate of $375/month. 44% of these expenses are allocated to the Basic Center Program. No costs will be paid from Basic Center grant funds.

Education and tutoring: Includes materials and supplies for educational support of RHY to enhance learning. The Fort Worth Independent School District, the largest public ISD in Tarrant County, provides an onsite school for Shelter youth. These supplies are for education-related materials but not for classroom costs. Education and tutoring costs for the Shelter are estimated based on historical spending at a rate of $25/month. 44% of these expenses are allocated to the Basic Center Program. No costs will be paid from Basic Center grant funds.

Interpreter services: Interpretation services are available through the Language Line telephone translation service when needed to communicate with youth or a family member. Other interpretation services are available for cases when the interpreter's presence is required. These costs are not routine but are budgeted based on historical experience with frequency of use and costs of services. It is estimated that there may be approximately 10 occurrences at a cost of approximately $60 each, with 44% allocated for Basic Center Program youth. No costs will be paid from Basic Center grant funds.

Utilities: Includes gas, electricity, water, garbage, and sewage costs necessary to provide a safe, clean, healthy, and comfortable environment for Shelter youth. These costs are estimated based on historical experience and present utility pricing at a rate of $2,250/month. No costs will be paid from Basic Center grant funds.

Telephone: Includes local and long-distance calling from a land line and cell phone coverage for Shelter on-call and supervisory staff. Costs are estimated based on historical experience at a rate of $300/month. No costs will be paid from Basic Center grant funds.

Cleaning/Janitorial services: Includes contracted cleaning services used to keep the Shelter clean, safe, and hygienic. Costs allocated based on square footage of the Shelter building relative to the total square footage served by the contract at a rate of $700/month. 44% of these costs are allocated to the Basic Center Program. No costs will be paid from Basic Center grant funds.

Maintenance and repairs: Includes general maintenance of the Emergency Youth Shelter building and equipment to provide a safe, healthy environment. These costs are directly charged and are estimated based on historical experience at a rate of $75/month. 44% of these costs are allocated to the Basic Center Program. No costs will be paid from Basic Center grant funds.

Vehicles: The Shelter operates a van to transport youth to appointments, recreation, and educational outings. Van requires an annual vehicle registration renewal, repairs, maintenance, fuel, and insurance. None of these costs will be paid from Basic Center grant funds.

Fuel: Fuel costs are directly charged for the Shelter van and are estimated based on historical experience and current costs at a rate of $350/month. 44% of these costs are allocated to Basic Center. No costs will be paid from Basic Center grant funds.

Repairs and Maintenance: Costs of oil changes, tire repairs, mechanical repairs, washing, and routine upkeep. Costs are directly charged and estimated based on historical experience at a rate of $100/month. No costs will be paid from Basic Center grant funds.

Licenses: The annual registration renewal is projected at $76 for the year. No costs will be paid from Basic Center grant funds.

Insurance: Coverage for the Shelter van is projected at $145/month, based on the premium charged specifically for this vehicle. No costs will be paid from Basic Center grant funds.

IT support/Data systems: Includes technical support of computer hardware, software, and related peripheral equipment as well as the training of users and modifications or enhancements to technology tools, at a cost allocated by workstation. A client data management system is utilized by Shelter staff to maintain electronic client files and to prepare reporting. Estimated costs for the Shelter are $1,000/month. 44% of these costs are allocated to the Basic Center Program. No costs will be paid from Basic Center grant funds.

Printing and copying: Includes allocations for copier usage as well as printing costs for brochures, business cards, and information handouts for staff and youth. Costs are allocated based on historical usage at a rate of $125/month. 44% of these costs are allocated to the Basic Center Program. No costs will be paid from Basic Center grant funds.

Conferences and training: Staff may attend local, in-state trainings relevant to their work with youth in the Shelter. Specific trainings have not been identified, but estimated costs are based on approximately $50/staff person for 25 staff. (Please note: Although there are 31 total staff, only the training costs for direct care staff are allocated to this budget.) 44% of these costs are allocated to the Basic Center Program. No costs will be paid from Basic Center grant funds.

Travel for conferences and training: Travel expenses related to the aforementioned conferences and trainings are estimated to be $25/staff person for 25 staff. (Please note: Although there are 31 total staff, only the training costs for the direct care staff are allocated to this budget.) No costs will be paid from Basic Center grant funds.

Mileage: Staff may incur mileage expenses when using personal vehicles to attend meetings, conferences, or trainings in the local area. Mileage is paid at the prevailing federal rate, currently $.56/mile. Mileage logs are required that indicate date, purpose of travel, beginning odometer, and ending odometer and are signed by the employee and the supervisor. Estimated costs based on historical experience are approximately 100 miles/month. No costs will be paid from Basic Center grant funds.

General insurance: Includes coverage for property, liability, umbrella, and professional conduct. These costs are estimated based on historical experience at a rate of $1,200/month. 44% of these costs are allocated to the Basic Center Program. No costs will be paid from Basic Center grant funds.

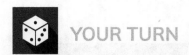 YOUR TURN

Developing the Project Budget

Now that you understand the budget process and the use of the budget in financial management, you are ready to prepare the budget for project. You will develop a line-item budget for the project. The first step will be to develop all the projected expenses for the proposed project. Use the following templet to help you develop your budget. You may not need every line item for your project. If so, simply delete the line item. Also, there may be other expenses that are not listed in the agency's overall budget. If so, add these items to the budget line items.

Personnel costs: In most cases the largest budget item in your program budget will be the salaries and benefits. These items will need a bit more explanation than some of the other line items. The potential funder will want to know exactly who will be delivering the proposed services, how much they will be paid, and how much time they will spend on the project. The common method to outline personnel cost is to present information in terms of FTEs, which stands for full-time equivalents. If a counselor is to work 100% of the time on the project, they would be presented as an FTE = 1. It may be that not every position will work 100% time on the project. For example, if an administrative assistant will work 25% time on the project and 75% time on the other two agency programs, the FTE would be .25. See the examples provided in the templet below.

Benefits is also a large budget item and is often as much as 25% of the total amount for salaries. Your program budget will need to include the same benefits that all employees receive in your agency. This amount will include the employer contributions to FICA, Medicare, and Social Security. Benefits also includes employer-provided health insurance and contributions to the employee's retirement plan. Cornerstone's benefits package is just over 19%, so you can use 20% of salary as benefits amount in your project budget.

Indirect costs rates refer to the organization's overhead cost that are charges to all grants and contracts. Such cost includes administrative cost not covered directly by each program. Some funders will limit the amount of indirect costs they are willing to pay (if any). Many organizations, such as universities, have negotiated indirect cost rates that may be 50% or more of the total grant. In our example the two programs pay an indirect cost. In most cases this is determined by an internal formula that may include the square footage of space used by each program, the number of employees, or the percentage of income generated by the program. The indirect cost is generally developed by the agency accountant. For the purposes of your project, use an indirect rate of 15%.

TABLE 8.7 **Sample Project Budget Template**

CORNERSTONE FAMILY SERVICES, INC PROJECT BUDGET FOR THE YEAR 20XX		
Item	Salary	Total
Salaries		
Benefits @ 20%		
Advert./promo/printing/postage		

(Continued)

TABLE 8.7   **Sample Project Budget Template (Continued)**

Item	Salary	Total
Auto exp.		
Computer exp.		
Contract services		
Dues/memberships		
Food		
Insurance		
Interest exp.		
Legal & professional		
Maintenance & repair		
Office/other supplies		
Recruiting exp.		
Rent exp.		
Staff development		
Travel		
Telephone/communications		
Utilities		
Other		
TOTAL OPERATING EXPENSES		

REFERENCES

Asare, J. G. (2020). If you really care about equity and inclusion, stop cutting your diversity budget. *Forbes.* https://www.forbes.com/sites/janicegassam/2020/08/30/if-you-really-care-about-equity-and-inclusion-stop-cutting-your-diversity-budget/#1fad6ab14549

Brody, R., & Nair, M. (2013). *Effectively managing and leading human service organizations.* Sage.

Martin, L. L. (2021). *Financial management for human service administrators* (2nd ed.). Waveland Press.

Nonprofit Accounting Basics. (2020). *Accounting and bookkeeping: Generally accepted accounting principles (GAAP).* https://www.nonprofitaccountingbasics.org/accounting-bookkeeping/generally-accepted-accounting-principles

Women's Economic Self-Sufficiency Team. (2001). *Preparing your cash flow statement.* http://www.onlinewbc.gov/docs/finance/cashflow.html

Wyman, O. (2018). The financial health of the United States nonprofit sector: Facts and observations. *Guidestar.* https://learn.guidestar.org/products/us-nonprofits-financial-health

Figure Credits

CHAPTER NINE

Organizational Capacity

OVERVIEW

This chapter addresses the section of a program proposal that requires you to build a case for your organization's ability to deliver the program you propose. For every person who is enthusiastic about your idea, you may find that someone else will be skeptical that the agency can carry it off. While this topic is essential when you write a grant proposal because you are dealing with an outside funder, you need to realize that your board may be almost as skeptical because they have responsibility for the entire agency. It is up to them to protect the organization from moving forward with what they may see as an unwise idea. This chapter will show you how to make a strong case for the ability of your organization to create and run the program you have in mind.

If you intend to submit a grant proposal to the federal or your state's government, you will likely have to answer many questions about your organization's capacity and capabilities. (See Box 9.1 for examples from one federal agency's request for proposals). Most of the questions relate to various policies that the organization has in place in order to protect clients, and to protect the funds that are being asked for. Even if you are not planning to submit a grant proposal at this time, it is good to have this list of questions so that you can assure yourself that your organization is prepared in the future.

All program developers are likely optimistic people—people who see what could be and focus on the ways that the community could be a better place. In this regard, they are like Robert Kennedy, brother of President John F. Kennedy, who is quoted as saying, "Some men see things as they are and ask 'Why?' I dream of things that never were and ask 'Why not?'" (Kennedy, n.d.). While this is an admirable quality, and an essential one for developing programs, the world is full of people who are quite willing to provide a list of reasons "why not"—it costs too much, the people brought the problem on themselves, it is politically unwise, no one knows if it will work, our donors will not like it, and so on. This chapter will help you know how to set forth your ideas so that many of the objections are overcome. In short, your aim is to show that your organization truly has the capacity and capabilities to achieve what the program proposal promises.

Because the topic of organizational capacity has several subtopics, we cover a number of things that may seem at least slightly unconnected. The concept that ties them together, however, is that you are

BOX 9.1	**Parts of a Request for Proposals Related to Organizational Capacity**

Below are some of the aspects of the federal grant request for proposals that relate to organizational capacity.

1. The applicant clearly demonstrates the organizational capacity necessary to oversee federal grants through a description of the organization's fiscal controls or procedures and an explanation of the organization's governing structure.
2. The applicant describes the organization's policies prohibiting harassment based on race, sexual orientation, gender, gender identity (or expression), religion, and national origin.
3. The applicant describes procedures established to monitor harassment claims, address them seriously, and document their corrective action(s) so all participants are assured that programs are safe, inclusive, and nonstigmatizing by design and in operation.
4. The applicant describes policies and procedures that protect the rights of youth with respect to their confidentiality and personal information.
5. The applicant describes the activities or strategies that will be utilized to assess and improve project performance in the areas of safety, well-being, self-sufficiency, and permanent connections, including the methodology and frequency of the data collection and how the methodology and frequency will provide the desired outcomes.
6. The applicant describes policies and procedures for addressing the most likely local and national crises that might pose a risk to the health and safety of staff and youth.
7. Disaster policies and procedures include a plan for how FYSB will be immediately notified in the event of a disaster.
8. The applicant sufficiently demonstrates and substantiates their experience and previous accomplishments in providing shelter and services to runaway, homeless, and street youth.
9. The applicant includes an organizational chart for the BCP that demonstrates the relationship between all positions (including consultants and subcontractors) to be funded through this grant.
10. The applicant provides the name of the person employed in each position on the organizational chart or notes if the position is vacant.
11. The applicant clearly describes the relationship between staff's responsibilities and the educational and professional experience required for staff positions.
12. The applicant provides position descriptions and résumés for all key staff.
13. The applicant includes the agency's policy for conducting criminal history and child abuse registry checks on staff and volunteers who come into contact with children and youth served or proposed to be served by the agency and describes how that policy is in compliance with state, local, or other applicable laws.
14. The applicant describes a plan to train staff on all required training topics listed in "administrative activities" under "program requirements." (See Section IV.2., Project Description.)
15. The applicant describes a supervision plan that ensures the safety of staff both in the shelter facility and nonresidentially, as applicable.
16. The applicant describes a safety protocol that addresses the safety of the youth both in the shelter facility and nonresidentially, including host homes, and meets state and/or local licensing requirements for staff-to-youth ratio.

working to convince decision makers that you (and your organization) are capable of using the requested resources in a way that will achieve the goals set forth. After providing an overview of organizational capacity, the chapter will describe the critical elements for demonstrating organizational capacity.

WHAT IS ORGANIZATIONAL CAPACITY?

Program developers must demonstrate that their agency has the organizational capacity to begin and run a new program (and hopefully to sustain it, but that is covered elsewhere). But what is meant when using the term **organizational capacity**? According to the Child Welfare Capacity Building Collaborative (The Collaborative, n.d.; connected with the Children's Bureau of the U.S. Department of Health and Human Services' Administration for Children and Families), "organizational capacity refers to the potential of a child welfare system to be productive and effective" (What Is Organizational Capacity? section).

Image 9.1

Many elements are important to building an organization's capacity for acting effectively and efficiently.

This basic definition can be adapted to fit any area of social services—the key element is that an organization has the potential to be productive and effective. What that looks like may differ from one area to another, but The Collaborative believes that five dimensions cover what is involved in organizational capacity. Each dimension has two or more subdimensions. Box 9.2 presents the dimensions and subdimensions and has a link to detailed information on each.

All of the dimensions and subdimensions are vitally important for the type of in-depth analysis envisioned by the Child Welfare Capacity Building Collaborative. For the purposes of a program proposal, we believe that the most important elements to cover include Dimension 1's subdimensions of staffing and fiscal resources (which can be used to purchase necessary supplies and training), which then generate activities and outputs; Dimension 3's cultural competence and humility, which allow for meaningful connection with all stakeholders; Dimension 4's leadership vision and commitment; and all of the subdimensions of Dimension 5: internal and external organizational relationships and collaboration and client and community engagement, participation, and buy-in. If you can have clear and compelling information addressing this smaller group of elements, you will be able to provide a skeptic with a well-rounded statement of how the agency will be able to be productive in implementing the program and effective in assisting clients. (Of course, different situations may need to have a different set of organizational capacity statement elements, so be sure to review the list with each proposal.) Let's look at each of these, in turn.

BOX 9.2	**The Five Key Dimensions of Organizational Capacity**

Dimension 1: Organizational resources

Subdimensions are staffing; fiscal resources; facilities, equipment, and technology; and informational resources and materials.

Resources for this examining and strengthening this dimension are available online (https://capacity.childwelfare.gov/states/focus-areas/cqi/organizational-capacity-guide/organizational-resources/resources/).

Dimension 2: Organizational infrastructure

Subdimensions are governance and decision-making structures; administrative structures; policies, operating procedures, and protocols; human resources, recruitment, and staff selection; training system; supervisory and coaching system; service array and service delivery system; information system and data supports; evaluation, quality assurance, and continuous quality improvement systems; communication systems (internal); and communication systems (external).

Resources for this examining and strengthening this dimension are available online (https://capacity.childwelfare.gov/states/focus-areas/cqi/organizational-capacity-guide/organizational-infrastructure/resources/).

Dimension 3: Organizational knowledge and skills

Subdimensions are skills and knowledge in and of practice in the policy area; analysis and evaluation; leadership and management; policymaking and administration; workforce development and supervision; cultural competence and humility; and change management and implementation.

Resources for this examining and strengthening this dimension are available online (https://capacity.childwelfare.gov/states/focus-areas/cqi/organizational-capacity-guide/organizational-knowledge-and-skills/resources/).

Dimension 4: Organizational culture and climate

Subdimensions are organizational norms, values, and purpose; workforce attitudes, morale, motivation, and buy-in; and leadership vision and commitment.

Resources for this examining and strengthening this dimension are available online (https://capacity.childwelfare.gov/states/focus-areas/cqi/organizational-capacity-guide/organizational-culture-and-climate/resources/).

Dimension 5: Organizational engagement and partnership

Subdimensions are internal organizational relationships and collaboration; external organizational relationships and collaboration; client engagement, participation, and buy-in; and community and cultural group engagement, participation, and buy-in.

Resources for this examining and strengthening this dimension are available online (https://capacity.childwelfare.gov/states/focus-areas/cqi/organizational-capacity-guide/organizational-engagement-and-partnership/resources/).

Source: The Child Welfare Capacity Building Collaborative. (n.d..) A guide to five dimensions of organizational capacity. https://capacity.childwelfare.gov/states/focus-areas/cqi/organizational-capacity-guide/

TABLE 9.1   Selected Dimensions and Subdimensions for Organizational Capacity

Dimension	Subdimension	Details	Key issues
#1. Organizational resources	Staffing	The right number of people with the capabilities and time to apply desired practices and deliver services	Worker caseload, workload management, keeping enough workers
#1. Organizational resources	Fiscal resources	Adequate funding to implement and sustain practices and innovation	Funding streams, budget allocations
#3. Organizational knowledge and skills	Cultural competence and humility	Understanding of cultural issues and cultural groups and the skills and techniques that reflect worker knowledge and respect of cultural groups. Cultural humility reflects the recognition of the uniqueness of individuals and their cultural expertise.	Everyday worker and client interactions, selection of approaches and practice innovations, efforts to address racial disproportionality and disparity
#4. Organizational culture and climate	Leadership vision and commitment	Agency leaders' commitment to a new practice or program and their communication of intended change to stakeholders	How leaders prioritize a program and align it with other initiatives and the extent to which resources are dedicated to support it
#5. Organizational engagement and partnership	Internal organizational relationships and collaboration	Connections and results of partnerships within the agency	Engagement of staff across multiple levels within the agency; Engagement of staff across program areas
#5. Organizational engagement and partnership	External organizational relationships and collaboration	Connections and results of partnerships outside the agency	Engagement of diverse partners to support program implementation and service deliver to clients
#5. Organizational engagement and partnership	Client engagement, participation, and buy-in	Partnership with clients and former clients	Seeking input from clients and involving them in selecting, designing, and/or assessing program
#5. Organizational engagement and partnership	Cultural group engagement, participation, and buy-in	Partnerships between agency and community	Building trust; identifying shared vision; developing working relationships through connection with cultural groups in community

SOURCE: Adapted from Child Welfare Capacity Building Collaborative, 2020.

Dimension 1: Organizational Resources—Staffing

This subdimension examines whether the right number of staff members are posted to the new program (or could be) and the amount of their time that is allocated to the program. This is important so that the staff members have the training and time to apply and implement the new program. Without having the correct staff members, the program will be unlikely to work well in practice. That is why the program proposal must show that staffing will be adequate if the requested levels of funding are provided. Training is also vital for the staff, particularly if you are choosing a new evidence-based program to implement. This training will usually include the theory and practices behind the EBP as well as fidelity assessment and monitoring tools. Managers in charge of the program will need to pay attention to worker caseloads so they do not grow too large. This entails workload management to distribute cases appropriately amongst trained workers and keeping enough trained workers on staff. Turnover is natural, but be sure to calculate the need to train any new staff members in the EBP before assigning cases. Retraining for workers is also frequently needed because workers sometimes lose sight of the EBP practices and do other things. In your capacity statement, you will want to address each of these issues.

Dimension 1: Organizational Resources—Fiscal Resources

Fiscal resources (otherwise known as "money") are needed to pay staff, of course, and also for training, supplies, and other elements of the program. This is no mystery and can be explained in the budget section of any proposal. One aspect that is not always considered, however, is cash flow. Funding can be promised but not actually available at the time it is needed. Starting a new program, including hiring staff members, often has up-front costs to consider. If the funding comes to your organization only quarterly, are enough cash reserves available until the payment arrives to the agency's bank account? Similarly, some sources of funding reimburse expenses and do not provide up-front funds. Agencies without substantial cash reserves or credit can be seriously hurt in these situations. While this may be beyond most program developers' usual knowledge, such information can be gathered if you know to ask for it.

Another aspect of fiscal resources to understand is to project how budget allocations may change over time. No program is forever, and ones funded by a fixed term (3 years is common) will need to be cognizant of what may occur at the end of the established period. Sustainability planning should be considered even before the first funding is received.

Dimension 3: Organizational Knowledge and Skills—Cultural Competence and Humility

As we have stressed thus far in this book, the best program developers and designers are deeply invested in understanding cultural issues and the cultures of the program's potential clients. Cultural humility requires all staff members to check in with representatives of the community during all steps of the design process. If designers are not part of (or at least intimately knowledgeable about) the groups that are targets for the program, errors are likely to creep in, jeopardizing the success of the new program in many ways. It could even be that a backlash develops as news spreads about the program being developed. Much work and effort can be wasted if relationships are not built first.

Addressing in your proposal how workers will interact with clients as well as how community input has been sought during the selection and development of the program (evidence based or not) are important aspects of this part of organizational capacity development and should be noted. Efforts to address past and/or current racial disproportionality and disparity can be part of a section detailing organizational capacity. These elements contribute greatly to the ability of the organization to be productive and effective in its work.

Dimension 4: Organizational Culture and Climate—Leadership Vision and Commitment

Program designers are sometimes eager to address a problem that they have heard about from community contacts and stakeholders. When the topic is raised with organizational leaders, the designers are given the go-ahead to begin work. In some cases, developers later feel that their work is cut off or undermined by those same agency leaders without consultation. While you may not want to put this in writing, as you analyze the capacity situation for yourself, be sure to rate the level of support you believe exists among the most important decision makers for the program you are developing. If you are unsure, it may be valuable to check in to ensure backing before you expend too much effort. It can also be worthwhile to think about how long the current leaders are expected to be in their positions because new leadership may not be as enthusiastic as the current one. If everything seems positive in terms of backing, you may wish to provide updates and assist in conceptualizing how your new program aligns with other initiatives and fits with community needs and preferences.

Dimension 5: Organizational Engagement and Partnership— Internal Organizational Relationships and Collaboration

This dimension has the most subdimensions that we consider vital for all programs. The four are really two elements, but each of the two has an inward and outward face to it. For example, internal organizational relationships and collaboration focuses on how different levels of the organization (executives, middle managers, and line and support staff) get along to support services. If conflict is intense, that is a negative in the capacity arena. For example, orders may come down from executives to implement a new program, but if front-line staff disagree with the program, actual capacity will not meet theoretical capacity. Similarly, if two departments need to work together to ensure a smoothly running program and there is conflict between them, effectiveness will suffer. In such cases, a wise program designer will minimize conflict beforehand and work to resolve the issues for the greater good.

Dimension 5: Organizational Engagement and Partnership— External Organizational Relationships and Collaboration

Just as the agency's capacity to be effective relies on internal dynamics, positive connections with the community outside the organization can make or break any programmatic initiative you develop. If your agency has diverse partners to support the program's development and implementation, it has in place an important aspect of organizational capacity. Likewise, having community-based sources for client referral and other forms of showing legitimacy is a big plus for the new program. Community partners' assistance may include fundraising efforts and statements of programmatic validity to bring widespread support for the program.

Dimension 5: Organizational Engagement and Partnership—Client Engagement, Participation, and Buy-in

Although the Child Welfare Capacity Building Collaborative refers only to people involved or formerly involved with the child welfare system, we extend the idea to any field of practice's participants and supporters. These diverse partners (including current program participants for other programs) are an important aspect of organizational capacity. Involving them in the program design and development is important to assure a culturally sensitive and thus successful program. If the organization is moving into a very different type of program than before, reaching out to people in similar programs and from similar cultures is especially important in making a case that your agency can be successful in the effort.

Dimension 5: Organizational Engagement and Partnership—Cultural Group Engagement, Participation, and Buy-in

The last element to discuss is the engagement, participation, and buy-in of community and cultural groups. This entails creating real partnership with clients and former clients. This involves building trust by being open and authentic, even when disagreements exist. The ideal outcome of this aspect of organizational capacity is a shared vision between the organization and outside groups. This is likely to lead to culturally sensitive and responsive services for the community.

INFORMATION FROM FEDERAL REQUESTS FOR PROPOSALS

Another set of criteria to determine whether your organization has the capacity to conduct a new program can be gleaned from looking over federal requests for proposals where they explain what is to be included in a funding request. While the exact criteria are different for each funding opportunity, several qualifications are common, and you can use this list as a rough guide for your organization's capacity assessment.

Five elements are typically in the section regarding organizational capacity in federal grant proposal requests. We explore these five elements one-by-one throughout the rest of this chapter:

- experience with this or similar programs and/or populations
- sufficient administrative and financial capacity and oversight to run a federal program
- if a collaborative program, experience in leading or being a part of a collaborative system
- description of how program will be staffed and managed, including an organizational chart and/or information on the roles and responsibilities of key staff and the extent of time devoted by key staff members to this proposed project
- qualifications of current staff for working with this population and job descriptions of staff members

We also cover one final topic that helps build a case for your organization's capacity to fulfill the grant requirements: memoranda of understanding (MOUs) and letters of support.

Experience with Similar Programs and/or Populations

The key element here is to show that your organization has a history of doing what is needed to be done with people who are similar to those who will be assisted in the proposal you are writing. History can best be shown by laying out in chronological order, starting with the present, the program(s) and populations being discussed in your grant application. Nonprofits usually tend to specialize in one type of treatment or population so this should not be too difficult. If this is a new venture for the organization, grantwriters can sometimes feel that it is very difficult to get funding because it seems you must already have provided the services you are requesting resources for. One way around the issue of needing to "have a grant" before you can "get a grant" is to enlist and collaborate with well-qualified partners with a strong history of funding in this area. They become your mentor and thus the sponsor of your organization to help you acquire related expertise. In a sense, the experienced organization is lending its experience to you so that both organizations may have a better chance of securing the funding that is needed.

Another approach is to try to receive smaller grants from other sources (e.g., foundations) that can get you started building a track record in this programmatic area. This is likely to be a risky effort unless you can access foundation grant officers who support your organization and strongly believe in your capacity to create and implement new ideas.

It may be that you have experience with a population (e.g., people who are homeless), but not the precise services being proposed (e.g., substance abuse treatment services within a housing first model). Or it may be that you have considerable experience with the type of programmatic approach (e.g., motivational interviewing/stages of change) but with a different population (e.g., you are used to dealing with people who chronically abuse substances but now want to expand your agency's work to people with a high risk of contracting HIV/AIDS through unprotected sex). Ideally, you can show that your organization has a record with the type of service you are proposing and has worked with the population in question so you can overcome any skepticism about your capacity. Because you may not be in this ideal situation, your job in this section of the proposal is to make the best possible case for your ability to implement and run the proposed program based on what you have done successfully in the past.

As part of indicating that your organization has the needed capacity, it is mandatory to already have highly qualified people working for you as well as having clear, up-to-date job descriptions for any new positions that will be created after the grant is awarded. Reviewers will look for evidence that your organization can hire and retain employees with the skills and experience needed to be successful in the proposed program. (See Box 9.3 for information regarding how to write any job descriptions you develop to be included in your organizational capacity statement.)

Having Sufficient Administrative and Financial Capacity to Run a Federal Program

Receiving a federal grant for the first time is a wonderful infusion of funds. It is, however, also a demanding and somewhat overwhelming process. After the grant proposal has been deemed worthy, but before the agency receives any money, the agency must meet a variety of standards that indicate a well-functioning organization. Of primary importance are internal controls and procedures that ensure that the funds will be well accounted for and used only for the purposes of the grant. Before you decide to write the proposal, be sure that you have adequate staff in the accounting department, with proper procedures in place to be able to handle high-level demands for tracking and segregating the funds. Be prepared to describe and articulate these procedures with a level of detail that communicates your commitment to responsibly administering grant funds, whether from government or foundation sources.

Collaborative Program Experience

In recent years, many funders have moved to a community- or sector-wide approach to solving problems (Friedman et al., n.d.). These grantors believe that individual organizations, no matter how capable, cannot adequately address deep-seated issues, such as homelessness, poverty, or substance abuse, on their own. Agencies applying for grants in these cases must be prepared to work collaboratively with other organizations in a comprehensive effort to address the underlying issues.

A human service program working collaboratively together with one or more other organizations may increase the capacity of all.

Because this type of programmatic structure is challenging, funders want to know the likelihood of success in establishing and maintaining collaborations. Previous experience is helpful in learning how to use this approach for better client outcomes. One of the most important lessons from studies on collaborations is that there must be clear processes for running the project. Four areas that have been identified by Friedman and colleagues (2003) as particularly crucial for collaborations to flourish include determining:

- **Distribution of funds within the collaboration**: How will resources within the collaboration be divided and reallocated, if needed?
- **Recruitment and enrollment of clients**: How will clients be brought into the collaborative system? Who gets "credit" for helping achieve collaboration goals?
- **Access to client records**: How will client records be accessible appropriately to all involved organizations? Who is in charge of client data management?
- **Collecting evaluation data**: How will data collection and entry regarding project outcomes be handled?

If you are proposing a collaboration to address a problem in your community, your experience in handling these topics is of considerable interest to the potential funder. Evidence that you have encountered and overcome challenges should be highlighted in your organizational capacity statement. If you do not have any experience with collaborations, it may be better to acquire some before taking the lead role in such a proposal.

Description of Program Staffing and Management, Including Organizational Chart

You are expected to be able to describe how the proposed program will be staffed and managed and to include an organizational chart to demonstrate organizational capacity. An organizational chart is a snapshot of your agency's structure that illustrates staffing and reporting responsibilities. A lot of information can be packed into a small amount of space in your statement by using a chart.

In very small organizations, there is little structure and the staff members may be called upon to do any and all tasks. Founders of organizations, for example, may write grants, develop marketing plans, solicit donors, work with clients, get the mail, buy supplies, answer the phone, provide their own IT support, and everything else. This is not really a sustainable approach to running an organization, however. Once sufficient funds come in, one or more other people are hired to do some of these tasks.

Organizations that are capable of handling the demands of a federal grant, or any but the smallest foundation grants, will have more structure than just a CEO. An organizational chart allows you to show that the agency is put together in a logical way. You can also give a sense of how many people are in the organization. Very importantly, you show how the initiative being proposed fits into the existing organization.

Image 9.3

An organizational chart shows how positions relate to each other regardless of who is filling each position.

Organizational charts also show who reports to whom, which is important to illustrate the chain of command and who is directly supervising the program and its workers. Just as with a logic model, a well-done organizational chart can convey a great deal of information to someone who understands their power. Charts like this can be made easily using Microsoft Word. Here is a link for a YouTube video showing the process of developing an organizational chart in MS Word, once you know what positions and individuals go where in the chart (http://www.youtube.com/watch?v=mDZrBxzfmOg). Microsoft Excel can also be used.

Here are three tips from the literature for developing an organizational chart for your proposal, if one does not already exist:

- **Unless your organization is unusual, create an organizational chart that is hierarchical**: In such charts, the chief executive officer (CEO) is at the top of a pyramid. The row below the CEO shows the positions that report directly to the CEO, a relationship that is denoted by a solid line. The next row shows the people who report to the CEO's direct reports, and so on. Organizational charts can show more or less detail, depending on the size of the organization. The International Red Cross, for example, would have much less detail in its organizational chart than would a local domestic violence shelter. There are other organizational chart styles that show different types of organizations, but the hierarchical model fits almost all human service agencies.
- **Know the difference between line and staff positions and show them appropriately**: A line position is directly working to accomplish program goals, while a staff position is supporting program goals indirectly. For example, a caseworker and a casework supervisor would be line positions, whereas an evaluator, a grantwriter, a human resource manager, or an accountant would be in a staff position. This difference is important because funders generally want to see their resources going to support line positions and their supervisors, even while knowing that staff positions are essential for organizations to function.
- **Remember that "size matters"**: The boxes for people higher in the organization are typically larger than are the boxes for people lower in the hierarchy. People who are considered peers in the organization have boxes of the same size.

To draw an organizational chart for a program that does not yet exist (as is appropriate for any new program), one could follow these steps using pen and paper or software such as Microsoft Word (see Figure 9.1 for an example made using SmartArt in Microsoft Word).

1. Begin by drawing a box for the program director.
2. On a row below that box, draw a smaller box for each of the positions that will report to the program director (i.e., for each person who the director will supervise).
3. Draw a horizontal line between each person at this level.
4. Draw a vertical line from the horizontal line to the program director box.
5. Repeat for each level in the hierarchy, showing which positions report to which positions already on the chart. Each level's boxes should be smaller than the one above.
6. To position this program in the larger agency, draw a vertical line from the program director. At the top of this line, place a box that is the position that the program director reports to. This new box should be larger than the program director's box.

In Figure 9.1, we have the proposed program (the Triple A Project) illustrated. Five line positions and one staff position will be created. The program director will directly supervise two positions, the case manager supervisor and the client recruitment and follow-up specialist. The case manager supervisor has two case managers to supervise. None of these people have yet been hired. The organization will need to create job descriptions for these positions so that it is clear what their jobs entail. The Triple A Project program director reports to an existing position, the vice president for clinical services, Rhonda Jones. You should be able to provide her qualifications to be the overseer of the new program.

In addition, a contract program evaluator position is created, and Dr. Richard Hoefer will be hired. This is a staff position, as he will not work directly to accomplish the program goals but will support the achievement of program goals by monitoring and evaluating the program. This position works with the program director (as shown by the dotted line) but reports to and is responsible to the vice president for clinical services (shown by the solid line). His résumé, showing his qualifications to be the program's evaluator, needs to be included. (If the program has not yet located a program evaluator, this position still needs to be on the organizational chart and needs to have a job description developed and included with the other materials.) You may also be required to have a signed memorandum of understanding indicating that he commits to providing the evaluation services.

Most agencies have an organizational chart already developed for the larger organization. While that is an important piece of "boilerplate" information that should be on the hard drive of every program designer, it is vital to situate the new program within the existing structure. In fact, getting the new program adequately integrated into operations may require changes to the existing reporting structure, so the program designer needs to carefully think through the implications of creating the new program.

Another aspect of the description of the program's staffing is the listing of key staff, what they will do, and the extent of their time devoted to this project. In this case, we can look at the organizational chart for key staff positions and create a list quickly. Other agency documents should provide the details of any current workers' qualifications and background. Starting at the top of the organizational chart (Figure 9.1), we briefly discuss each position.

> VP for clinical services (Rhonda Jones): Provides overall guidance for program and its integration into the larger organization's mission, including evaluation (5% time). Ms. Jones has a MSSW degree from the University of Texas at Arlington, with 10 years of experience.

> Triple A Project program director (to be hired): Supervises all aspects of Triple A Project, including direct supervision of case manager supervisor and client recruitment and follow-up specialist. They must have 3 years of administrative experience. They are responsible for working with the program evaluator to ensure collection of required information (100%).

> Client recruitment and follow-up specialist (to be hired): Works with other organizations and community resources to recruit appropriate potential clients into the program and follows up with them to promote retention during the program. They must have a social work degree from an accredited university. They are the key link in having post-program contact with clients in order to collect evaluation data (100%).

Case manager supervisor (to be hired): Supervises two case managers and provides case management services on an as-needed basis. They report to Triple A Project program director. They must have 5 years of administrative experience. They ensure grant-related reporting and data collection tasks are completed by case managers.

Case managers (two positions; to be hired): Work directly with clients to assess and assist them in achieving their treatment goals. They must have a social work or related degree at the bachelor's level or higher (100%).

Program Evaluator (Dr. Richard Hoefer): Contractor responsible for developing and implementing evaluation plan to meet needs and requirements of organization and funder (10%). Dr. Hoefer has a PhD from the University of Michigan in social work and political science and has been lead evaluator on eight other SAMHSA grants.

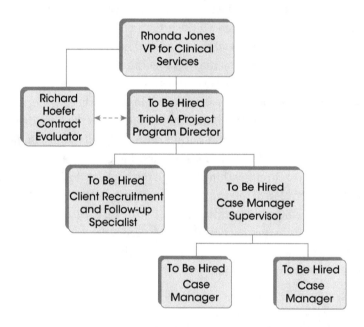

FIGURE 9.1   An organizational chart shows how positions relate to each other regardless of who is filling each position.

Qualifications of Current Staff and Job Descriptions

Getting a grant that creates new positions can be beneficial for organizations that have few other promotion opportunities. Current staff members who could be promoted to work in the new program if it is funded have several advantages over totally new hires. First, they are already on board at the organization and have vital skills in their current position. Thus, they may only need to be assigned the new duties. As an example, someone who is an experienced case manager now may be able to be promoted to case manager supervisor. Someone who works well with clients in a staff position, such as an intake coordinator, might be considered appropriate for the client recruitment and follow-up specialist position.

No matter who is assigned to the positions, it is important that they are qualified. Qualifications can include educational achievement or experience from work or volunteering. The listing of key staff (above) has a one-sentence statement of qualifications for the two known people (Rhonda Jones and Richard Hoefer) who will be involved with the program. These statements should be substantiated with resumes in an appendix.

We have noted several times the need to include job descriptions for proposed positions that are new to the organization. Job descriptions are an important part of running a human services organization. They are particularly important when needed in a proposal to show the potential funder that you clearly understand the tasks and roles of the positions in your program.

A well-written job description is helpful to your organization as well. It ensures that you will have qualified and competent employees implementing the program once the program is fully staffed. Job descriptions attract people with the characteristics and background you want for the job, including education level and previous experience. It assists potential applicants by alerting them to job tasks and expectations before they apply for a position, thus reducing the number of inappropriate applications. You may be able to use currently existing job descriptions from another organization to edit, or create one from the ground floor. As long as what you have is appropriate for your organization and the program you are proposing, you will have an appropriate job description. This section describes the elements needed in an effective job description and shows how they are used (see Box 9.3 for the example job description).

A job description is useful when writing an advertisement or job announcement for the position, but the two are not the same. A job announcement will typically include a salary or salary range (although not all advertisements are specific about salaries for jobs). Advertisements include how to contact the agency and what the requirements are to apply for the job, such as a transcript showing graduation and/or the names and contact information for references. This type of information is not included in a job description. According to the Small Business Administration (SBA, n.d.), the following elements should be included in every job advertisement:

- individual tasks involved
- the methods used to complete the tasks
- the purpose and responsibilities of the job
- the relationship of the job to other jobs
- qualifications needed for the job

The job descriptions for any organization need to be updated every now and then. Positions evolve, and the skills needed to do them well change over time as well.

BOX 9.3	**Example Job Description: Case Manager for Triple A Project Program**

Tasks: Case managers in the Triple A Project program will work with clients directly; coordinate services with other organizations for individual clients; work cooperatively to make and follow-up on client referrals to other organizations; collect information for client services and program evaluation purposes; and maintain the highest levels of client confidentiality and ethical behavior as codified in existing regulations and the NASW Code of Ethics.

Methods used: Case managers will use standard instruments provided by the Triple A Project to assess clients for individual needs. Employing reference materials and personal knowledge of other agency and community resources, case managers match client strengths and needs with available resources and, when necessary, advocate for different or additional resources to be created. Case managers will seek supervision from the case manager supervisor to improve their handling of individual client outcomes as necessary.

Purpose and responsibilities: The purpose of the case manager position is to improve conditions for clients. They interact directly with clients of the Triple A Project to improve their functioning with the goal of attaining self-sufficiency. Case managers are responsible for daily positive interactions with clients and ensuring that clients are given access to programs and resources that lead them to reach self-sufficiency as quickly as possible. Records must be updated frequently and maintained electronically in a secure fashion, as dictated by agency policy. Case managers must be able to work well in a team, taking direction from the case manager supervisor.

Relationship to other jobs: Case managers report directly to the case manager supervisor, who in turn reports to the Triple A Project program director. All case managers are expected to cooperate with each other and other agency personnel in the best interests of the organization and, ultimately, the clients. Working through the program director and case manager supervisor, case managers are also expected to cooperate with requests made by the program evaluator to collect process and outcome evaluation information. Some direct interaction with the program evaluator may take place.

Qualifications: A bachelor's degree in social work is the minimum level of education required. A master's degree in social work is preferred. Licensure at the appropriate level is required within 12 months of being hired. Experience in a case manager position is beneficial.

 SPOTLIGHT ON DIVERSITY

Much of this chapter focuses on the ways that organizational capacity is linked to having strong ties within the agency across diverse categories as well as connections with many different stakeholder groups in the community. It seems that in some organizations any attempt to focus on people from nonmajority racial, ethnic, gender identity, or other groups through a diversity, equity, and inclusion lens is met with resistance, either active or passive. Perhaps the people who are not enthusiastic about DEI initiatives find themselves feeling defensive: "Oh, no! Not another training about this!" We feel that an important aspect of successful implementation of diversity training focuses on what is gained for the agency when everyone and every "type" of person is included and valued. This builds the capacity of the organization and has the potential to increase program productivity and effectiveness, which is the heart of organizational capacity.

It may be that adding diversity is not only a positive situation for an organization, at least in the short run. Different groups will have different ways of seeing the world (in fact, that is the strength of having a diverse staff), and this may lead to more conflict, at least until the culture and processes of the organization learn how to handle this type of conflict. Clearly, however, over time accommodations can be reached, and it is then that the benefits of the diversity can be appreciated.

DIFFICULTIES AND JOYS

One of the difficulties of building organizational capacity is that it is hard to get other people to value it. On the face of it, it is not a very interesting topic to most staff who want to be helping people. Perhaps they figure they will take care of it when it is needed. You can probably hear your colleagues saying, "Are you kidding? There is SO much that needs to be done for our current clients you and the staff you have working with those clients. Creating 'make-believe' disaster scenarios and practicing them certainly sounds like a misuse of limited funds and time. Almost everything that we might plan for is probably not going to happen, so it just doesn't take priority." Just assuming you get approval to make plans, will they ever be practiced? Will anyone know where the plans are when they are needed?

Building organizational capacity, however, is not just preparing for low-frequency, high-impact events. Remember the definition involves equipping your organization with the tools and skills to be both productive and effective. Every organization and all staff members should be interested in that. But let's be realistic—this is one of the difficulties of discussing and doing anything about organizational capacity.

Increased difficulties exist when the organization wishes to include as part of its capacity the relationships that are found between the agency and community members, cultural groups, and the other stakeholders that are mentioned in this chapter. Given how most human service organizations have little in the way of slack personnel resources, it becomes difficult to dedicate time to something as nebulous as "connections with stakeholder groups." Just like people have to schedule time for exercise before it gets done, scheduling time to get out of one's own organizational boundaries has to be scheduled. It should be noted that many people truly look forward to exercising or playing a favorite sport once the habit is begun. Getting out into the community and meeting people with different views and perceptions can be the same way. You may not always enjoy every encounter, but you will be doing yourself and your organization a great service.

Certainly, the joys of being involved with these outside stakeholders and learning more about the community in which you work can be huge. Knowing who you are ultimately planning on providing services for and seeing those services implemented is definitely joyful. The same may be true as you develop deeper relationships with people inside your organization who you may not know well. Relationships smooth difficulties inside the agency and make being at work more pleasant as well.

LESSONS FROM THE PANDEMIC

The massive impact of COVID-19 on all elements of the human services sector is beyond doubt. Disruptions in service delivery came from many angles, simultaneously. Offices were shuttered, staff were told to work from home without adequate technological or personal support, and clients were unable to attend to program elements without technology and other support being offered. Working parents (especially mothers) found that they were doing two jobs because their children were home from school. The situation exacerbated existing inequities in the workforce, with some workers still working at the job site tending to be lower paid.

Off-site work at the scale encountered created a certain amount of chaos because it was unprecedented. In April 2020, it was estimated that more than half of all workers in the United States were working at home. These remote workers comprised over two thirds of U.S. economic activity (Siripurapu, 2020). Managers were not always sure how to manage in this new environment. The first reaction to workers doing their jobs from home for many managers was a desire to keep close tabs on workers to ensure that productivity did not lag. In many organizations across the United States, working from home had both positive and negative impacts. As Siripurapu (2020) states, "Remote work has been shown to increase worker productivity, but it can lead to isolation and stress as the line between work and home blurs" (What's the Economic Impact? section).

The lesson from the pandemic in terms of organizational capacity shows that it is helpful to build resilience and flexibility into work routines. Lloyd-Smith (2020) describes the pandemic as a low-chance, high-impact event. She describes how the best way out of the chaos is not to loosen control (not tighten) and enhance improvisational responses. Three elements are useful in increasing improvisational behavior: "increasing autonomy, maintaining structure, and creating a shared understanding" (Lloyd-Smith, 2020, Abstract).

Organizational capacity is enhanced in some situations by allowing workers to adapt to the quickly changing situation. Still, planning for the unexpected can be "gamed" by organizations. Simulations are not a large part of human services efforts or teaching of human services students, but with the increasing number of large-scale weather events due to climate change, more frequent mass shootings, and other disasters occurring, such trainings may need to become a normal part of organizational life, no matter how difficult (Corbin, 2018; Erfourth, 2020).

CONCLUSION

Many topics were covered that may at first not seem closely related. All of them, however, help a program designer to make the case that the agency proposing the new program can actually get it off the ground and make it happen. This is done by stressing the organization's strengths—the capacity it has and how it has been successful in the past. In some ways, the capacity statement looks both backward to show successes that have occurred and forward, demonstrating how the future can be even better for the agency and the clients to be served. Thus, topics, like job descriptions, that might seem less than exciting are actually part of the gateway to the future of the staff-to-be, the people who will actualize the plans that the program development team put together. Take each component seriously, for you are building the future with your ideas.

 SUMMARY/KEY POINTS

This chapter has covered material to help you communicate the capacities of your agency. Organizational capacity is the potential of an organization to be productive and effective. Given everything that has been written previously in your program proposal, you must demonstrate that you have the ability to make the proposed program a reality, should you be awarded funding. We went into detail regarding the dimensions and subdimensions of organizational capacity set forth by the Child Welfare Capacity Building Collaborative, which has an extensive amount of material to support the importance of its list of five key dimensions of organizational capacity and many subdimensions.

Other aspects of organizational capacity are set forth in federal government grant opportunities. While these are described differently than the Child Welfare Capacity Building Collaborative's dimensions, considerable overlap exists, thus strengthening the importance of these ideas. The federal government's list includes elements to highlight agency experience with similar programs and/or populations; demonstrate that existing and new agency administrative structures and financial capacity are well integrated and set up to accomplish program outcomes; show a history of collaborative efforts (if this is a collaborative project); discuss qualifications of current staff members to implement and run the program; and describe the positions to be funded in enough detail to allow reviewers to ascertain if you grasp what is needed for the program to be successful.

KEY TERMS

Organizational capacity: "The potential of a child welfare system to be productive and effective" (Child Welfare Capacity Building Collaborative, n.d., What Is Organizational Capacity? section).

Organizational culture and climate: One of the five dimensions of organizational capacity described by the Child Welfare Capacity Building Collaborative (n.d.) that relates to factors that impact an organization's culture and climate (e.g., shared values, attitudes, and norms; Child Welfare Capacity Building Collaborative, n.d.).

Organizational engagement and partnership: One of the five dimensions of organizational capacity described by the Child Welfare Capacity Building Collaborative (n.d.) that relates to the development of collaborative relationships between an organization's members and external partners to facilitate effective practices.

Organizational infrastructure: One of the five dimensions of organizational capacity described by the Child Welfare Capacity Building Collaborative (n.d.) that relates to the structural elements (e.g., process and protocols) of an organization that support its functions and practices.

Organizational knowledge and skills: One of the five dimensions of organizational capacity described by the Child Welfare Capacity Building Collaborative (n.d.) that relates to the necessary skills and expertise needed to effectively run an organization.

Organizational resources: One of the five dimensions of organizational capacity described by the Child Welfare Capacity Building Collaborative (n.d.) that relates to the tangible resources needed to support the program.

ADDITIONAL RESOURCES

Organizational Capacity and Assessment

Informing Change. (2017). *A guide to organizational capacity assessment tools.* William & Flora Hewlett Foundation. https://hewlett.org/wp-content/uploads/2017/11/A-Guide-to-Using-OCA-Tools.pdf

Mayer, S. (2021). *Building organizational capacity: A simple useful framework.* Effective Communities Project. https://effectivecommunities.com/building-organizational-capacity/

DISCUSSION QUESTIONS

1. To fully understand an organization's capacity to be productive and effective takes a considerable amount of time and effort. In thinking about the program you are developing, which of the dimensions and subdimensions seem most important to you? Explain your reasoning and decisions.
2. Locate an organizational capacity assessment tool you can foresee using. What makes it good for the organization and situation you are thinking of? How could you improve it?

 YOUR TURN

The exercises for this chapter relate to the program you developed after reading Chapter 5 on program planning (or you may use any program that you are familiar with).

Here is the complete list of elements of organizational capacity from the example RFP:

1. The applicant clearly demonstrates the organizational capacity necessary to oversee federal grants through a description of (a) the organization's fiscal controls or procedures and (b) an explanation of the organization's governing structure.

2. The applicant describes the organization's policies prohibiting harassment based on race, sexual orientation, gender, gender identity (or expression), religion, and national origin.

3. The applicant describes procedures established to monitor harassment claims, address them seriously, and document their corrective action(s) so all participants are assured that programs are safe, inclusive, and nonstigmatizing by design and in operation.

4. The applicant describes policies and procedures that protect the rights of youth with respect to their confidentiality and personal information.

5. The applicant describes the activities or strategies that will be utilized to assess and improve project performance in the areas of safety, well-being, self-sufficiency, and permanent connections, including the methodology and frequency of the data collection and how the methodology and frequency will provide the desired outcomes.

6. The applicant describes policies and procedures for addressing the most likely local and national crises that might pose a risk to the health and safety of staff and youth.

7. Disaster policies and procedures include a plan for how FYSB will be immediately notified in the event of a disaster.

8. The applicant sufficiently demonstrates and substantiates their experience and previous accomplishments in providing shelter and services to runaway, homeless, and street youth.

9. The applicant includes an organizational chart for the BCP that demonstrates the relationship between all positions (including consultants and subcontractors) to be funded through this grant.

10. The applicant provides the name of the person employed in each position on the organizational chart or notes if the position is vacant.

11. The applicant clearly describes the relationship between staff's responsibilities and the educational and professional experience required for staff positions.

12. The applicant provides position descriptions and résumés for all key staff.

13. The applicant includes the agency's policy for conducting criminal history and child abuse registry checks on staff and volunteers who come into contact with children and youth served or proposed to be served by the agency and describes how that policy is in compliance with state, local, or other applicable laws.

14. The applicant describes a plan to train staff on all required training topics listed in "administrative activities" under "program requirements." (See Section IV.2., Project Description.)

15. The applicant describes a supervision plan that ensures the safety of staff both in the shelter facility and nonresidentially, as applicable.

16. The applicant describes a safety protocol that addresses the safety of the youth both in the shelter facility and nonresidentially, including host homes, and meets state and/or local licensing requirements for staff-to-youth ratio.

Below, in Table 9.2, you will see two of the organizational capacity criteria used in reviewing proposals for funding. Immediately after each of the elements is the sample agency's response so you can see how a successful agency handled them.

TABLE 9.2   RFP Elements and Agency Responses

RFP Element 1A	Organizational capacity to oversee federal grants: Fiscal controls
Agency response to RFP Element 1A	***Finance procedures and controls:*** Financial reports are reviewed monthly with the Finance Committee of the Board of Directors, which includes CPAs and other financial professionals familiar with GAAP. A public accounting firm conducts an independent financial audit annually. In addition to all of the above, ACH utilizes professional consulting as needed for new or unusual transactions to be sure they are made according to GAAP. ***Segregation of Duties:*** ACH ensures that assigned responsibilities within the financial management system are clearly delineated and managed only by approved staff. Fiscal duties are separated by task to separate the authorizing, processing, recording, and reconciliation of financial transactions. This procedural distribution limits errors and improves organizational oversight and control of internal accounting activities.
RFP Element 1B	**Organizational capacity to oversee federal grants: Governing structure**
Agency response to RFP Element 1B	The Agency is a 501 (c) (3) private, nonprofit organization governed by a Board of Directors, all of whom are volunteers (uncompensated). The Board directs and manages the affairs of the organization, has control and disposition of its assets, and appoints and directs the chief executive officer (compensated). Members of the Board are elected to 3-year terms and serve a maximum of two successive terms. As per the bylaws, Board membership is capped at no fewer than 15 and no more than 20 directors, and there are three offices: chair, treasurer, and secretary. The bylaws prescribe six standing subcommittees (Advocacy, Board Governance, Executive, Finance, Fund Development and Planning and Evaluation). The Executive Committee conducts an annual formal evaluation of the chief executive officer, involving an electronic survey of the full Board and the CEO's direct reports, in addition to annual objectives. Goals for the following year are identified as well as any areas of performance or professional development.

Your assignment is to select three of the other capacity elements and write out complete responses. You may need to be creative with your answers if you do not have access to an existing agency to gather information from.

REFERENCES

Child Welfare Capacity Building Collaborative. (n.d.). *A guide to five dimensions of organizational capacity.* Children's Bureau, Administration for Children and Families, U.S. Department of Health and Human Services. https://capacity.childwelfare.gov/states/focus-areas/cqi/organizational-capacity-guide/

Corbin, T. (2018). Teaching disaster management using a multi-phase simulation. *International Journal of Mass Emergencies and Disasters, 36*(3), 297–312.

Erfrouth, D. (2020). *Information technology disaster recovery planning by Florida nonprofit organizations* (Publication No. 9133) [Doctoral dissertation, Walden University]. ScholarWorks. https://scholarworks.waldenu.edu/dissertations/9113

Friedman, J., Sutor, C., Warfield, T., Gallant, L., Gettings, R., East, B., Glover, R., Kashen, K., Powers, S., Hollan, J., & Van Lane, B. (2003). *Opportunities for collaboration across human services programs.* American Public Human Services Association. https://web.archive.org/web/20090106000350/http://www.financeproject.org/Publications/EBO_collaborationprograms.pdf

Kennedy, R. (n.d.). Thoughts on the business of life: Robert Kennedy. *Forbes.* https://www.forbes.com/quotes/8031/

Lloyd-Smith, M. (2020). *The COVID-19 pandemic: Resilient organizational response to a low-chance, high-impact event.* BMJ Public Health Emergency Collection. https://www.ncbi.nlm.nih.gov/pmc/articles/PMC7276242/

Office of Justice Programs. (2013). *OVC fiscal year (FY) 2013 services for victims of human trafficking.* U.S. Department of Justice. http://www.ojp.usdoj.gov/ovc/grants/pdftxt/FY13_Human_Trafficking.pdf

Siripurapu, A. (2020). *The economic effects of working from home.* Council on Foreign Relations. https://www.cfr.org/in-brief/economic-effects-working-home

Small Business Administration (n.d.). *Writing effective job descriptions.* http://www.sba.gov/content/writing-effective-job-descriptions

Substance Abuse and Mental Health Services Administration. (2012). *Teen Court Grant, RFA TR-12-004.* U.S. Department of Human Services. http://www.samhsa.gov/grants/2012/TI-12-004.pdf

Figure Credits

IMG 9.1: Source: https://pixabay.com/illustrations/businessman-tablet-concept-4608276/.

IMG 9.2: Source: https://pixabay.com/illustrations/together-earth-human-board-school-2450090/.

IMG 9.3: Source: https://pixabay.com/illustrations/human-resources-icons-network-5033959/.

CHAPTER TEN

Program Implementation Planning

OVERVIEW

This chapter provides you what you need to know to implement your proposed program. A newly emerging field of study called implementation science (IS) is something program planners need to become acquainted with, so we will begin with explaining what that is and how it is useful for planning programs. By the end of the chapter, you will be able to write a comprehensive description of how you will be able to move forward quickly to serve clients as soon as the money starts flowing. This is a challenging aspect of any program proposal because you must have a very specific vision of the program you are asking resources for—who is going to do what, when, how often, and how you (as an agency) are going to move from your current state to having a fully operating new program up and running within a short amount of time.

Once you have discussed the need your community has, chosen or developed a program that has evidence to support its efficacy, drawn a logic model of that program, and created an evaluation plan, you have come quite far in planning your program. You might think that the main work is now done. But in fact, all the work you have put in so far as a program developer is not enough. If your proposal is approved, the funder is going to want to know more before handing you a check for operating expenses. The funder will want to know that you can do what you promise to do. In this part of the proposal, you must show that you have a plan to put your proposal into action quickly. The funder may take a long time to get a decision to you, but once you have been chosen, you must be ready to move.

You need to have this project *shovel ready*, which means that you need to know what type of person to hire, how much to pay, how much activities will cost, and a host of other details that you might think could wait until you know your program idea has been approved. One of the key differences between "almost ready" and "really ready" is that those who are really ready have a plan they can share with their funder at the time the request for resources is submitted, while the almost ready are hoping for more time to "get ready." Another difference is that the really ready get funded and the almost ready do not. A basic understanding of implementation science and techniques to plan starting (and running) your program will help you be in the really ready group.

WHAT IS IMPLEMENTATION SCIENCE?

Earlier in this book we detailed why program planners needed to be able to find evidence-based programs (EBPs) to use in their organizations. We described how to find them and what to do if you cannot find any to fit your population and/or the problem you want to address. What we did not tell you is that, if you follow our advice, you will be among the minority actively finding and implementing EBPs. Some researchers indicate that it takes, on average, 17 years for an EBP to be routinely incorporated into practice—and that is in the field of health care where EBPs have been discussed for longer than in human services (Bauer et al., 2015, p. 1).

Bauer et al. (2015) define **implementation science** as "the scientific study of methods to promote the systematic uptake of research findings and other evidence-based practices into routine practice, and hence to improve the quality and effectiveness of ... services" (p. 3). Means et al. (2020) note that "at the core of IS is the pursuit of effective and equitable collaborations and balancing systematization with system agility" (p. 2).

Implementation science focuses on a few important variables in assessing how well EBPs are being implemented in a field of practice (Means et al., 2020). These are shown in Table 10.1, along with a short definition.

TABLE 10.1 Key Variables in Implementation Science (Means et al., 2020)

Variable	Short definition	Level of operationalization
Acceptability	Perception among implementation stakeholders that a given EBP is agreeable, palatable, or satisfactory	Individual consumer Individual provider
Adoption	Intention, initial decision, or action to try to employ an innovation or EBP	Individual provider Organization or setting
Appropriateness	Perceived fit, relevance, or compatibility of the innovation or EBP for a given practice setting, provider, or consumer and/or perceived fit of the innovation to address a particular issue or problem	Individual consumer Individual provider Organization or setting
Feasibility	Extent to which a new treatment, or an innovation, can be successfully used or carried out within a given agency or setting	Individual provider Organization or setting
Fidelity	Degree to which an intervention was implemented as it was prescribed in the original protocol or as it was intended by the program developers	Individual provider
Implementation cost	The cost impact of an implementation effort	Provider or providing institution
Penetration	Integration of a practice within a service setting and its subsystems	Organization or setting

From Means et al., 2020, pp 3–4.

While this chapter cannot make you a full-fledged implementation scientist, bringing awareness to these seven variables can help you examine your implementation plans in a systematic way. As we point out in the chapter on evaluation, program developers should build in implementation and process measures to be able to assess how well a program (evidence based or not) has been put into practice. This list of variables and their operationalization will help you think ahead to where potential issues can arise. Means et al. (2020) raise two additional issues that may impact human services implementation: **supply chain barriers** and inattention to politics. This is any barrier to full, timely, and accurate implementation caused by being unable to access needed materials and training in the use of those materials. Supply chain problems include the inability to receive training in an EBP in a timely fashion and to expand training opportunities when initial funding is completed. **Politics** can be defined as interference with full, timely, and accurate implementation caused by one or more stakeholders. This can occur at any level, even within your organization. Are some stakeholders likely to undercut the program or be uncooperative due to differing assessments? (An example of this could be that some groups may be against the housing first model that does not require people who are homeless to be "clean" before gaining housing.)

With this theoretical background in mind, let us turn to the practicalities of implementation planning for your program.

WHAT IS PROGRAM IMPLEMENTATION PLANNING?

It has often been said that those who fail to plan, plan to fail. An **implementation plan** for your program is a document that lays out the steps and milestones by which you will start and operate your new program or policy. Thus, implementation planning is the effort that goes into the creation of a **program implementation plan**. Funders often (but not always) allow some time for a start-up period.

By the end of this time period, your staff must be hired and trained, necessary supplies must be on hand, clients must be recruited, protocols for cooperative agreements must be on file, and you must be assisting the population you wrote the program proposal for.

The benefits of an implementation plan are many. Roper et al. (2011) believe that an implementation plan is a useful management tool that acts as a map to illustrate critical steps when beginning a new program or project. A clear plan assists in identifying potential issues early, before receiving the

Having an implementation plan helps you get started to quickly make your program come alive.

Image 10.1

grant. This allows the organization to be proactive rather than reactive. An implementation plan forces you to do a "walk-through" from receiving the go-ahead from the funder to providing services to recipients. As you plan, you are likely to anticipate challenges to successful implementation and operation that you would not have considered beforehand, especially when you take into account the information in Table 10.1.

For example, recruiting and hiring qualified staff members is not always as easy as putting an advertisement in the paper. If you need people with special qualifications, such as fluency in a language other than English, or who live in a certain place (particular neighborhoods in urban centers or rural areas), you may have difficulty in finding appropriate candidates for the amount of money you want to pay. Accordingly, your implementation plan will need to reflect the extra steps you will take in the hiring process. This problem is associated with the variables of feasibility, fidelity, and implementation cost, at least, and might be focused on as an issue at the program's inception.

Recruitment of clients may also need to be planned in more detail than you at first anticipate. If your agency is requesting funding to assist a very particular type of client, you may need to set up additional means to attract such people to your program. An agency I once worked with wanted to expand their program to provide services to people experiencing homelessness, people with mental illnesses, and people who abuse substances, particularly those who were Hispanic. A great deal of thought went into the processes by which they would work with other agencies to receive referrals of potential clients and how the agency would react once a referral was made. Their client recruitment processes were reimagined from the vantage point of attracting that type of client. This plan helped the agency receive a grant worth over $1,000,000 in total from the federal government.

Another benefit of having a clear implementation plan is that it helps staff members share a common idea of how the program will begin and be run. The anticipated activities, outputs, and outcomes of the program are embedded in the plan, and everyone clearly understands how the plan will proceed. Issues can be examined early on, rather than being discovered only once the program commences.

An implementation plan is a guide for *developing* the program as well as for *running* it. It allows you time to pilot procedures, strategies, and techniques to ensure that they are appropriate in your situation and with your clients. These should all be finalized by the end of the start-up period. One way to think of this process is as if you are opening a store: Before the doors open for business, you need to make sure the products are on the shelves, you must have a sales team with training about the products waiting to assist customers, and you should have recruited customers so they are coming in the door to buy as soon as the doors are unlocked. This start-up process is not the same as running the store once it is open, but many of the decisions you make during start-up will have a large impact on the day-to-day operations once your program is operating full-force. The start-up plan just gets you to opening day, but its impact is long lasting.

A final benefit of creating a comprehensive implementation plan before you receive funding is that you can then put the plan into effect immediately instead of having to think through all the details, when time is running, and clients are waiting. Sometimes, before you receive the funds you were awarded, the funder will send a team of people to visit your organization on a site visit. This team is there to ensure that you are able to do everything you have written into your proposal. There is enough pressure during this site visit that you do not want to still be in the development stages of your plan. This is not to say that you will not be able to make modifications as the plan is used. You may find that some program elements were not thought of, despite your best efforts, and so must be developed on the fly. You may also face unanticipated challenges that need to be handled. Some of your initial ideas may not actually work out. But you are much farther along in the implementation process with a well-developed plan than if you did not have a plan at all.

Of course, perhaps the final reason to develop a sound implementation plan is that it is required by the funder to include in the original proposal. While the percentage of points it is worth varies from one funding opportunity to another, it is not uncommon for the implementation plan to be worth 20%–30% of all points awarded.

WHAT SHOULD BE IN THE IMPLEMENTATION PLAN?

While each grant application will be somewhat different (you must always look at what is being requested by *your* potential funder), there are common elements of program implementation plans. Each funding opportunity has both common and unique implementation planning elements. If your potential funder does not provide implementation planning details, however, you may wish to look at examples from a similar federal program. (See Boxes 10.1 and 10.2 for examples of what is required in two different federal agencies' requests for proposals).

Image 10.2

The implementation plan links your program goals to the plan and to achieving success.

BOX 10.1	Grants to Tribes, Tribal Organizations, and Migrant Programs for Community-Based Child Abuse Prevention Programs. HHS-2021-ACF-ACYF-CA-1913 (Due Date 05/20/2021)

Section V.1. Criteria

In reviewing the approach, reviewers will consider the extent to which:

1. The applicant outlines a comprehensive action plan to implement the project and to achieve stated objectives within the scope of the project, reflecting the intent of the legislative requirements of the CBCAP program.
2. The applicant demonstrates a thorough understanding of the challenges that the proposed project would have in planning and implementing the proposed project with tribal and/or migrant communities, to include challenges related to implementing a project during a worldwide health pandemic. The applicant provides a sound plan explaining how the proposed project would successfully overcome these challenges.
3. The applicant outlines comprehensive implementation strategies that are culturally relevant and will effectively address the unique strengths and needs of tribal and/or migrant populations. ...
8. The applicant provides a clear and reasonable timeline (e.g., charts such as a bar chart or other chart that illustrates project schedules) for implementing the proposed project, including the activities to be conducted with milestones and target dates. The applicant describes factors that may speed or hinder the work, as well as how these factors would be managed.

Source: Children's Bureau, Administration on Children, Youth, and Families (2021), p. 39.

BOX 10.2	Social and Economic Development Strategies— SEDS (2021). HHS-2021-ACF-ANA-NA-1906

...

Readiness and Implementation Strategy

17. The application fully describes existing, available, and tangible resources and services that are committed to the project, such as meeting space, equipment, supplies, curriculum, licenses, permits, etc.
18. The application details a plan to obtain resources such as supplies, equipment, curriculum, licenses, permits, and contracted services needed to support successful project implementation.
19. The application's narrative describes how milestone activities and the resulting outputs will be achieved to demonstrate a fully developed implementation plan.

20. The application provides a detailed recruitment, selection, and retention process for project participants.
21. The application addresses project sustainability that should include identification of resources, staff, and/or partners that are necessary to ensure that positive outcomes are achieved by the project will be sustained.
22. The application appropriately cites potential obstacles and challenges to project implementation, such as staffing, partnerships, participant recruitment, or other issues that may impede progress. The application includes specific strategies that will be used to address these challenges.

Objective Work Plan
23. The OWP serves as a stand-alone document for project implementation, consistently states elements from the project narrative, and provides details about the how, when, and by whom activities will be completed.
24. The milestone activities in the OWP are relevant and lead to the achievement of each 55 of 75 objective.
25. Outputs in the OWP demonstrate progression and are logical results of the successful completion of milestone activities within the proposed timeframe. ...

Source: Administration for Native Americans, Administration on Children, Youth, and Families (2021), p. 54.

Clearly, the wording regarding implementation planning is quite different in these two documents, but there is real overlap. Both, for example, want to know what the applicant is going to do, either in an action plan (Children's Bureau, 2021) or in describing existing resources committed to the project, plans to obtain other resources, and use of activities and outputs (Administration for Native Americans, 2021). Both request the identification of challenges/obstacles to implementation and plans/strategies to overcome them. In addition, both sections implicitly want to see how clients are going to be recruited, selected, and retained by using culturally relevant approaches. The Children's Bureau (2021) states it wants to assess a clear and reasonable time line, which is also asked for by the Administration for Native Americans (2021) in the objective work plan set of requirements.

While the language may be different in your proposal (even if just for an internal audience), it is safe to believe that these elements should be addressed in all implementation sections of program proposals.

USING YOUR LOGIC MODEL AS A FRAMEWORK FOR YOUR PROGRAM IMPLEMENTATION PLAN

While the information in the previous section from the federal government is very useful, you may be feeling that you are still not sure exactly what to do in order to be able to write a good implementation plan. Fortunately, the logic model that you created is extremely helpful in providing a framework to write your plan. Let's return to the logic model we used before to demonstrate how to create an implementation plan (see Figure 10.1). As you go through this section, write down each task that you feel needs to take place and how long you believe it will take. At the end of this section, you can use this information to create a chart, as requested in Step 4 of the example RFA.

Inputs (Resources)

The starting place to look in your logic model to help write the implementation plan is the first column: inputs. There are several items listed under resources: funding, staff, and space. Your implementation plan assumes adequate funding, so there is not really much else to think about here. Staff and space, however, need to be included in your implementation plan.

The first thing to consider is what type of staff members you need. If this is a new program, you will have to consider support staff as well as clinical and managerial staff. The staffing plan has enormous implications for both how you implement the program and how you stay inside your budget. The logic model indicates that the activities of the program include both case management and individual counseling. The staff members you hire for this program thus have to be able do these activities. You may hire one person to do both or you may wish to have specialists. This decision will probably hinge on the number of clients you expect in both categories. You do not have to hire people for full-time jobs. The route you go here will of course have implications for your budget, which we cover in a later chapter, but it is vital to realize that there is a back and forth process between your implementation plan, your business model (what you do once the program is up and running), and your budget.

Let's make the assumption that the program we are developing that is depicted in Figure 10.2 will be started in a large school district but with only two high schools involved in a pilot test of the program. If it is successful, the program may be expanded. Let's make the further assumption that case management duties can be handled by a bachelor's level social worker or someone with similar qualifications. The individual counseling duties should be in the hands of someone at a master's level, preferably a social worker who is licensed at that level. Neither one needs to have prior experience in a school setting. It is probably the case that neither high school by itself will require a full-time person, but we believe that there will be a full-time case load when looking at both schools together. We will thus assume that the employees will shuttle between the two schools. One of the job tasks for the MSW person will be to oversee the case manager and coordinate their efforts. This will require additional skills.

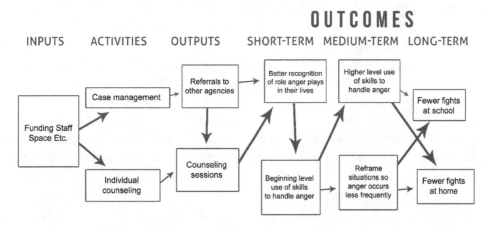

FIGURE 10.1   Logic Model Example

An alternative staffing solution would be to hire one person to do the program at each school. The advantage of this would be savings in transportation and space costs, as well as the one person being in complete charge of the program at their school, easing coordination issues. The disadvantage would be in needing to hire two licensed social workers, which would cost more than a BSW/BA level worker and a MSW level person. The case management tasks would be underemploying the MSW level person.

Either approach is a possibility, but you need to make a choice and plan for it. New hires do not just walk in the door without having been recruited, interviewed, and made an offer. Set aside time in your plan to recruit applicants, interview them, and decide who to hire and then bring them on board.

BOX 10.3	What Is a FTE (Full-Time Equivalent)?

You often hear of jobs being 1.0 FTE or .5 FTE. What exactly does that mean? One FTE is the equivalent of one person working 40 hours per week. Most companies make the assumption that someone working full time for a full year puts in about 2,080 hours (40 hours per week times 52 weeks in a year). Even allowing 1 week for vacation days and another week for sick days, that is 2,000 hours per year. So, when you say that you want to plan on 1 FTE, you need to consider how much work can be accomplished in that amount of time per week/month/year.

An important aspect about FTEs is that you should not assume that 1 FTE is the same as hiring one person. If you hired four people for 10 hours a week, that would still be just 1 FTE. Given that frequently only full-time employees receive benefits, it can be less expensive to hire several part-time staff to make up 40 hours a week altogether than it is to hire one person full time. Having part-time people receive prorated benefits does away with this cost advantage, but you probably get a more dedicated group of staff members if they feel they are treated well, despite being part time.

The funder wants to know who is responsible for the overall project. This will not need to be a full-time position by itself, and the duties will probably be assigned to someone already in place. In our example, this might be the director of student success in the school district's central office. Because this program has activities in two different schools, it is probably not appropriate to assign the oversight duties to one principal. The task of managing this new project may take less than 10% of a person's time, or about 4 hours per week on average. You will also need to think about the possible need for administrative support. Who will do this, and how many hours a week will it take?

Once you have covered all of the staff members needed in your implementation, you will need to turn to the space required to run the program. Do the workers need office space? If so, where will it be located? Do clients need a place to sit while waiting to work with the staff members? Where will any physical files or supplies be located? What furniture will be needed, and when and how will it be procured?

Activities

The second column in the logic model describes the **activities** that will take place. While the implementation plan does not say exactly how the program will be run on a daily basis, it needs to describe for the reader how you will get ready to perform the activities. For example, once you have the qualified staff members hired, what will be necessary for them to be able to implement the program? Will they need additional training, as may be the case for specialized evidence-based programs? Will they need to be oriented to the host organization, such as a program taking place in a school or hospital? What supplies are required to implement the program? Put yourself in the shoes of the newly hired worker as you write this section. What do you imagine will be needed for you to do your work? Be sure to help that future hire, who you probably do not even yet know, to have a good experience by laying the groundwork for success.

Outputs

You may be surprised that you can use the outputs column from your logic model to assist you as you develop the implementation plan. You may have heard it said that if something is not documented, it did not happen. As we write a grant and plan for a program's implementation, we must also plan how we will document both activities and outputs. Without doing so, it may appear that the program staff are spinning their wheels—doing lots of activities (e.g., case management referrals or individual counseling sessions) but with nothing to show for their efforts.

As we have noted, doing activities and even having outputs occur is not the same thing as achieving change with clients. But, according to the program logic (as shown in the logic model), if the resources do not exist, the activities are not done, and the outputs do not occur, we should not expect the client outcomes to be realized. At this stage of the implementation plan, you need to decide how to keep track of the number of activities that take place and how you will document the outputs that result.

The logic model shows that case management activities led to referrals to other agencies. You should already be thinking about how to schedule the case management appointments and how to track completed appointments versus no-shows. Will you try to reschedule missed appointments? How will this be done? How about walk-ins? Will they be permitted? Once referrals are made, who will be responsible for making the appointment for the student? How will you track whether a referral is successfully completed?

Similar issues exist in terms of scheduling, meeting, and tracking students who receive individual counseling sessions. The main difference is that there are no outside actors to involve in terms of follow-up or outreach to outside actors.

The reason to answer these questions in your implementation plan is so that all systems can be put into place at the start of the program, without awkward gaps and realizations that the program has no method to track these matters. Funders will want to know how their money is being spent, and so it is necessary to preplan how to collect the data needed to develop reports of agency activities and outputs.

Outcomes

Columns 4, 5, and 6 relate to the desired and expected outcomes of the program. Measuring these is covered in the program evaluation chapter, as that topic is usually not included in the section on implementation. Program evaluation receives a separate section in the grant proposal. It is worth a considerable number of points in the total score of the proposal.

CREATING A TIME LINE (GANTT CHART)

As noted earlier, requests for proposals often require the inclusion of some type of chart showing the progression of the program's implementation and startup, as does the Children's Bureau (2021) example in Box 10.1. As one older SAMHSA RFA advised, "Provide a chart, graph, and/or table depicting a realistic timeline" (SAMHSA, 2013, p. 24). While not the only way to show the implementation of a program, a Gantt chart is easy to make and can be done in Excel, a software program that most nonprofits already have. From there it can be pasted into the word processing program being used to write the grant proposal.

According to the website (gantt.com), Henry Gantt developed one version of the chart that now bears his name. At its most simple, a **Gantt chart** has a horizontal axis that represents time (the unit of measurement can vary from an hour to a month or longer) and along the vertical axis has the tasks associated with the implementation of the program or other project. The amount of time each task will take is indicated by a bar beginning at the task's start date and ending at the end date.

Image 10.3

Gantt charts help you prepare to implement your program quickly and accurately.

The Gantt chart thus shows all important tasks, how long each will take, when each task begins, when each task ends, which tasks overlap with which other tasks, and when the entire project will begin and end.

TABLE 10.2   List of Tasks, Start Date, Duration, and Finish Date for Example Program

Task	Start date	Duration (in days)	Finish date
Hire two MSW caseworkers	Jan. 1	30	Jan. 30
Select evidence-based program	Jan. 1	15	Jan. 15
Train caseworkers in EBP	Feb. 1	15	Feb. 7
Recruit clients	Feb. 1	135	July 1
First client group begins	Mar. 1	21	Mar. 21
Second client group begins	Apr. 1	21	Apr. 21
Third client group begins	May 1	21	May 21
Follow-up first client group	May 21	15	June 7
Follow-up second client group	June 21	15	July 7
Follow-up third client group	July 21	15	Aug. 7
Analyze data	Aug. 8	15	Aug. 23
Write report	Aug. 24	7	Sep. 1

The chart developer begins by listing all the tasks to be completed and then determining when it will start, when it will end, and the number of days, months, or hours required. One can set this list out in an Excel spreadsheet where it looks similar to Table 10.2.

This information is then transferred to a chart using a process that is not difficult, resulting in a Gantt chart, which is shown as Figure 10.2. The exact process varies somewhat from one version of Excel to another, and a variety of videos exist on YouTube to show the step-by-step processes for different Excel

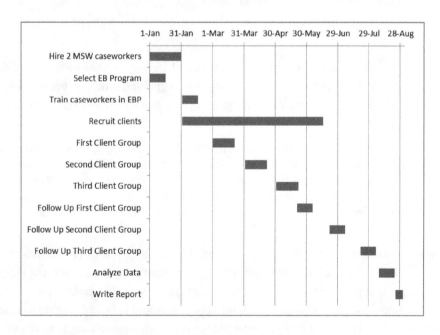

FIGURE 10.2   Excel Generated Gantt Chart Using Tasks List from Table 10.1

versions. (One video that shows how to create a basic Gantt chart in Excel was created by Doug H. and is available online at https://www.youtube.com/watch?v=TjxL_hQn5w0). Specialized project management software can create more detailed Gantt charts that also link tasks, add constraints, include needed resources, and other refinements. For your grant proposal, a basic Excel generated version is enough.

 ## SPOTLIGHT ON DIVERSITY

Implementation planning is predicated on understanding what tasks need to be done, in what order, and how long each will take. It provides a guide to amount and types of resources that are required. One important element in understanding the resources needed to implement a program is staffing. For human services programs, staff costs are often more than 80% of the entire budget. Hiring is a slow process, and hiring people who cannot do the job effectively is a difficult problem to fix. Thus, a clear idea of the skills and characteristics of every position is needed.

At the same time, programs are often looking for special skills among staff members, such as cultural competency with the target population, or non–English language skills to better communicate with clients. When such people also need to have advanced degrees, difficulties may arise in finding and recruiting staff. This needs to be considered in implementation planning, and also in budgeting for positions. It may not be possible to pay everyone in the same job categories the same and still attract specialized skills. At the same time, diversity issues cannot turn into discriminatory practices or even appear to, as this can cause dissension and long-term issues of retention. This is where a skilled human resources department (or consultant) is helpful.

DIFFICULTIES AND JOYS

As is true for many parts of the program planning journey, implementation planning is both difficult and joyful. These two emotions may rapidly alternate as the process begins and continues over weeks and months.

One of the key difficulties of implementation planning was discussed by Pressman and Wildavsky (1974) nearly 50 years ago:

> People now appear to think that implementation should be easy; they are, therefore, upset when expected events do not occur or turn out badly. We would consider our effort a success if more people began with the understanding that implementation, under the best of circumstances, is exceedingly difficult. They would, therefore, be pleasantly surprised when a few good things really happened. (pp. xx–xxi)

Despite the hard-won knowledge of implementation that has happened over the past half century, a significant difficulty in discussing implementation is that most people who are just learning about it still have the sense that it is "no big deal" to implement a program. This makes the job of a program planner more difficult—how do you explain to your supervisor and colleagues that the plan you have all put together is likely to fail? You may be open to recriminations when people have overly hopeful ideas about getting a program going and it is tough going.

If you are the one in charge of always looking out for the bad things that can occur or what the worst-case scenarios are, you may begin to develop a decidedly pessimistic view of life. It is fair to say that few program planners/implementers imagined a worldwide pandemic bringing normal life to a stop in 2020 and beyond. Another event has become distressingly common, and unfortunately, a mass shooting unfolding in your building is probably part of every organization's emergency plans at this point.

Of course, truly bad things do not have to happen for an implementation plan to be derailed. It might be that a supportive official is replaced by voters, falls ills, or retires to enjoy life. In each case, that can have a negative impact on a good program that may never be allowed to flourish. It is useful to have alternative pathways in mind in running programs to go around obstacles. Still, most program planners have other duties than predicting all the ways that plans can fall apart, so no matter how creative a program developer is, it is unusual for a new program to begin with no snags testing everyone's resilience and grit.

At the same time, the process of implementation planning is incredibly interesting. The required skills and competencies are many, yet the end result may be that, despite challenges, one can see people hired, clients recruited, and positive outcomes achieved. People who enjoy this process may be interested in an emerging profession, implementation specialists or implementation support practitioners (Metz et al., 2021). Such people are "capable of integrating implementation research—concepts, models, frameworks, and strategies—into practice to achieve improved population outcomes," according to one description (Metz et al., 2021, p. 1). Other authors state that "implementation support practitioners work with the leadership and staff needed to effectively deliver direct clinical, therapeutic or educational services to individuals, families and communities and support them in implementing evidence-informed practices, policies, programs, and in sustaining and scaling evidence for population impact" (Albers et al., 2020, p. 3).

Currently, leaders in this emerging field are working to refine terminology, identify essential competencies, and to develop programs to certify practitioners (Metz et al., 2021). Even if few job openings call for this job title now, the competencies being suggested will be useful for any program developer and could be the core of continuing education and on-the-job training opportunities. Having such a vista before you can be a joyful way to continue learning and becoming better at having evidence-based programs achieve their full potential.

LESSONS FROM THE PANDEMIC

Means et al. (2020) provide a view of how the COVID-19 pandemic impacted public health programming and implementation science. Among their conclusions are two that are especially pertinent to human services:

- "The COVID-19 pandemic has illuminated gaps in emergency preparedness planning that could be addressed by implementation scientists working in conjunction with … practitioners" (Means et al., 2020, p. 1).
- "To be more responsive to public health emergencies, implementation science as a discipline must evolve to be more rapid, nimble, and policy-oriented in its approaches" (Means et al., 2020, p. 1).

Means et al. (2020) also note that one of the most important lessons in response to the COVID-19 crisis in health settings is that many organizations have ineffective communication channels. This is a problem in all emergencies, but it can be mitigated by careful creation and practicing of plans to ensure they are adequate for most of the likely situations that can be imagined. Redundancy in channels is vital, as is cross-training for the key communication tasks that your organization may encounter.

CONCLUSION

If nothing else, we hope this chapter alerts you to the need to think seriously about how a new program can be brought into the world. Being aware of potential issues can help you and your agency avoid the worst of the negative issues that can emerge. We have no reason to believe that a program will be easy to implement, yet we should know that it is not impossible, either. Knowing the likely places where problems can emerge is helpful—as the old saying goes, "To be forewarned is to be forearmed." It is our hope that with the information in this chapter you are neither naïve nor jaded—but that you are now better prepared to make the program a success from the start.

 ## SUMMARY/KEY POINTS

- Implementation science is a new field of study that seeks to improve the implementation of evidence-based programs. It focuses on seven variables of the implementation process: acceptability, adoption, appropriateness, feasibility, fidelity, implantation cost, and penetration.
- Supply chain and political barriers can also negatively impact implementation efforts.
- **Program implementation planning** is the creation of an implementation plan, which is a document that lays out the steps of getting your new program in place.
- Implementation planning is useful because it prevents some problems from occurring, allows everyone to be on the same page, and speeds the arrival of the program's benefits to clients.
- Not all implementation plans cover the same material, but some elements are common across many funders: having a clear action plan with steps and milestones; identification of possible challenges for implementation and plans to counter those challenges; how clients will be recruited, selected, and retained, and more.
- We recommend using your program's logic model to assist in planning your implementation efforts.
- We explain what a Gantt chart is, what it is used for, and how to create one using Microsoft Excel.

KEY TERMS

Acceptability: One of the important variables examined by implementation science. It is defined as "perception among implementation stakeholders that a given EBP is agreeable, palatable, or satisfactory" (Means et al., 2020, p. 3).

Activities: What is done in the program, intervention, or policy with the inputs allocated. This is also known as "program activities."

Adoption: One of the important variables examined by implementation science. It is defined as "intention, initial decision, or action to try to employ an innovation or EBP" (Means et al., 2020, p. 3).

Appropriateness: One of the important variables examined by implementation science. It is defined as "perceived fit, relevance, or compatibility of the innovation or EBP for a given practice setting, provider or consumer and/or perceived fit of the innovation to address a particular issue or problem" (Means et al., 2020, p. 3).

Feasibility: One of the important variables examined by implementation science. It is defined as the "extent to which a new treatment, or an innovation, can be successfully used or carried out within a given agency or setting" (Means et al., 2020, p. 3).

Fidelity: One of the important variables examined by implementation science. It is defined as "the degree to which an intervention was implemented as it was prescribed in the original protocol or as it was intended by the program developers" (Means et al., 2020, p. 3).

Gantt chart: A planning tool that shows all important tasks, how long each will take, when each task begins, when each task ends, which tasks overlap with which other tasks, and when the entire project will begin and end.

Implementation cost: One of the important variables examined by implementation science. It is defined as "the cost impact of an implementation effort" (Means et al., 2020, p. 3).

Implementation plan: A document that lays out the steps and milestones by which you will start and operate your new program or project.

Implementation science: "The scientific study of methods to promote the systematic uptake of research findings and other evidence-based practices into routine practice, and hence to improve the quality and effectiveness of ... services" (Bauer et al., 2015, p. 3).

Penetration: One of the important variables examined by implementation science. It is defined as the "integration of a practice within a service setting and its subsystems" (Means et al., 2020, p. 3).

Politics (as a barrier to implementation): Any barrier to full, timely, and accurate implementation caused by interference by one or more stakeholders or other actor(s).

Program implementation plan: A document that lays out the steps and milestones by which you will start and operate your new program or policy.

Program implementation planning: The effort that goes into the creation of a program implementation plan.

Supply chain barrier: Any barrier to full, timely, and accurate implementation caused by being unable to access needed materials and training in the use of those materials.

ADDITIONAL RESOURCES

Implementation Science

Fixsen, D., Blasé, K., & Dyke, M. (2019). *Implementation practice and science.* Active Implementation Research Network.

National Implementation Research Network (NIRN) website. Available at https://nirn.fpg.unc.edu/national-implementation-research-network

Nilsen, P., & Birken, S. (Eds.) (2020). *Handbook on implementation science.* Edward Elgar Publishing.

Impact of COVID-19 on Programs

Frontz, A. (2020). *Opioid treatment programs reported challenges encountered during the COVID-19 pandemic and actions taken to address them.* Office of Inspector General, United States Health and Human Services. https://oig.hhs.gov/oas/reports/region9/92001001.pdf

Shantz, K., Hahn, H., Nelson, M., Lyons, M., & Flagg, A. (2020). *Changes in state TANF policies in response to the COVID-19 pandemic.* Urban Institute, Income and Benefits Policy Center. https://www.urban.org/sites/default/files/publication/102684/changes-in-state-tanf-policies-in-response-to-the-covid-19-pandemic.pdf

DISCUSSION QUESTIONS

1. As you think about implementation now after reading the material, what was the biggest misconception you had to start with? What additional information would you like to know about that topic?
2. Do you agree that a need for implementation specialists exists? Can't most human services workers do a "good enough" job of planning and then implementing programs?

 YOUR TURN

So far in this course you have done almost everything needed to have your own program proposal ready. Return to the RFP being used for this course and find the section on implementation planning. Outline this section and create a Gantt chart as an illustration of your time line.

REFERENCES

Administration for Native Americans, Administration for Children and Families (2021). *Social and economic development strategies—SEDS.* Department of Health & Human Services. https://ami.grantsolutions.gov/files/HHS-2021-ACF-ANA-NA-1906_1.pdf

Albers, B., Metz, A., & Burke, K. (2020). Implementation support practitioners: A proposal for consolidating a diverse evidence base. *BMC Health Service Research, 20*(1), 1–10. https://doi.org/10.1186/s12913-020-05145-1

Bauer, M., Damschroder, L., Hagedorn, H., Smith, J., & Kilbourne, A. (2015). An introduction to implementation science for the non-specialist. *BMC Psychology, 3*, article 89. https://doi.org/10.1186/s40359-015-0089-9

Children's Bureau. (2021). *Grants to tribes, tribal organizations, and migrant programs for community-based child abuse prevention programs*. Administration on Children, Youth, and Families. https://ami.grantsolutions.gov/files/HHS-2021-ACF-ACYF-CA-1913_1.pdf

H., D. (2011). *Create a basic Gantt chart* (Video). YouTube. https://www.youtube.com/watch?v=TjxL_hQn5w0

Means, A., Wagner, A., Kern, E., Newman, L., & Weiner, B. (2020). Implementation science to respond to the COVID-19 pandemic. *Frontiers in Public Health, 8*, article 462. https://doi.org/10.3389/fpubh.2020.00462

Metz, A., Albers, B., Burke, K., Bartley, L., Louison, L., Ward, C., & Farley, A. (2021). Implementation practice in human service systems: Understanding the principles and competencies of professionals who support implementation. *Human Service Organizations: Management, Leadership & Governance, 45*(3), 238–259. https://doi.org/10.1080/23303131.2021.1895401

Pressman, J., & Wildavsky, A. (1974). *Implementation: How great expectations in Washington are dashed in Oakland; Or, why it's amazing that federal programs work at all, this being a saga of the Economic Development Administration as told by two sympathetic observers who seek to build morals on a foundation of ruined hopes*. University of California Press.

Roper, A., Hall, T., & White, L. (2011). *Best practices for a strong implementation plan*. Office of Adolescent Health and Administration on Children, Youth and Families/Family and Youth Services Bureau. www.hhs.gov/ash/oah/.../slides_implementationplanwebinar121310.pdf

Substance Abuse and Mental Health Services Administration. (2007). *Targeted capacity expansion program for substance abuse, treatment and HIV/AIDS services* (TI-07-004). http://www.samhsa.gov/Grants/2007/TI_07_004.pdf

Substance Abuse and Mental Health Services Administration. (2013). *Strategic prevention framework: Partnerships for success* (TI-13-004). http://www.samhsa.gov/Grants/2013/sp-13-004.pdf

Figure Credits

CHAPTER ELEVEN

Developing an Information Sharing Plan

OVERVIEW

In this chapter you will learn the skills needed to produce an information sharing plan for your project. To begin, we will review some basic concepts of marketing and then will move on to the more specific topic of reporting on your funded project activity. Program planners who are familiar with this material can lay plans for collecting the right data (see Chapter 7) and then spreading the analyzed information to stakeholders in the organization, community, and beyond. This is a key sustainability strategy—programs that achieve good outcomes for people should be continued but may have funding decreased or eliminated if word does not get out. When planning a program, it is important to also determine how best to spread any good news that emerges because of it.

MARKETING

The American Marketing Association (AMA, 2013) defines **marketing** as "the activity, set of institutions and processes for creating, communicating, delivering and exchanging offerings that have value for customers, clients, partners, and society at large" (Definition of Marketing section). As the definition of marketing has evolved over time, it has become more applicable to the nonprofit and public sectors. In the past, marketing concepts were seen mainly as tools of the business sector, but they now apply equally well to public and nonprofit organizations. Seymour Fine (1992) notes that in 1985 the AMA adopted a definition of marketing that added "the exchange of ideas" to the traditional definition of marketing that had been exclusively focused on goods and services. Fine views the change in definition as a milestone in the evolution of social marketing, as it reflects a new emphasis on the dissemination and exchange of ideas. According to Andreasen and Kotler (2003), "Marketing is ... a means to achieve the organization's goal. It is a tool—really a process and set of tools wrapped in a philosophy—for helping the organization do what it wants to do. Using marketing and being customer-oriented should never be thought of as goals: they are ways to achieve goals" (p. 57).

The conversation in Box 11.1 illustrates the distaste that many human service organization employees have for the concept of marketing human services. The caseworker in the scenario reflects a **product mindset** that assumes if you build a better mousetrap, customers will beat a pathway to your door. The CEO, however, comes from a **sales mindset** that an organization must persuade customers to choose their services rather than those of a competitor (Andreasen & Kotler, 2003). In some ways, both the caseworker and the CEO are wrong in their approach.

BOX 11.1	Isn't It Enough to Provide Excellent Services?

The monthly all-staff meeting included an agenda item called "marketing our services." The CEO talked about the need to increase the number of client referrals to the agency and the need to become better known in the community. She called on everyone to be a marketer for the organization and gave examples of how everyone could play a part in marketing the organization's services.

A hand went up in the back of the room. One of the caseworkers asked, "Isn't it enough that we provide excellent service? People will come to us if we provide excellent services, right?"

"No," answered the CEO. "Sadly, we will go broke providing excellent services if we are unwilling to market our organization."

Providing excellent services is not enough to assure organizational success. Funders must have confidence in the ability and integrity of the organization. They must be confident that the money given to an agency has had a positive impact and has been used as proposed. Persuading potential clients and referral sources to use the organization's services is important but not enough to guarantee success. Both the product mindset and the sales mindset come from an inward-looking focus. More modern approaches to marketing begin by looking at the outside, from the perspective of the **customer mindset**, which "systematically studies customers' needs, wants, perceptions, preferences, and satisfaction, using surveys, focus groups, and other means ... and constantly acts on this information to improve its offerings and to meet its customers' needs better" (Andreasen & Kotler, 2003, p. 42). Of course, a human services administrator must view marketing activities within the context of the mission and goals of the organization. It is important to understand not only the preferences of the clients, funders, and donors but also how these preferences fit within the mission of the organization.

THE 5 PS OF NONPROFIT MARKETING

Marketing has become recognized as an important component of human service agency functioning (Lauffer, 2009; Lewis et al., 2011) and, therefore, an important task for human service administrators. Hardcastle and Powers (2004) review the business literature on marketing and find several sources that refer to the Ps of marketing (Andreasen & Kotler, 2003; Fine, 1992; Winston, 1986). While there are several versions of the **Ps of marketing**, the most common four are products, price, place, and promotion.

Lauffer (2009) adds a fifth P for *publics* to represent the stakeholders in human service organizations.

Products

Products may be tangible goods, such as food, or services, such as counseling or case management. The product may be an idea, such as gun control or social justice. Regardless of the product offered by the organization, the expectation is that there will be an exchange of resources from the consumer (or a third party) to the organization for it to have the capacity to offer the products, services, or ideas (Hardcastle & Powers, 2004). Often, the product that is promised to the funder or to the community is a change in the conditions in the community. For example, if the desired impact is a

The marketing mix.

reduction in childhood obesity or a reduction in teenage pregnancy, then it is an important marketing strategy to be able to demonstrate that the products provided are effective in producing the desired change. This is one reason why program evaluation is a critical component of agency functioning.

Price

Price has to do with the cost of providing the services in comparison to other providers of similar services. The human services administrator must have knowledge of the fees of other organizations providing similar services and of the unit costs. There is also the question of the reasonableness of the price of providing services. As government agencies, foundations and third-party insurance payers seek out contractors or grantees, they seek to find the best services they can find at the lowest cost. Part of a marketing plan is to make the case that the services provided are quality services at a reasonable and competitive price. There are also nonmonetary or intrinsic components when considering "price," sometimes referred to as "social price." These are other things that your stakeholders may pay. For example, there may be a cost in time and emotional energy. The idea of social price is often expressed as "spending time," "paying respect," or "we paid dearly" (Fine, 1992).

Place

What is the geographic location of the agency, and what is the geographic area served? There are several issues related to "place." Government contracts are restricted to the area of their governmental jurisdiction. Similarly, many corporations and foundations are interested in supporting organizations in the area where they have their headquarters or where their consumers are located. For example, think about utility companies that will provide grants in the states where they provide services. In some cases, foundations, donors, or even government agencies will restrict their gifts to an area that they perceive as having the greatest need.

There is also a practical and political dimension to where the human service organization is located (see Box 11.2). Is the agency or branch located in an area that is convenient for the population that it seeks to serve? Is there public transportation available so that the services are accessible? Think about "place" as aligning the needs of the clients served and the resources that can be attracted based on the geographic location of the agency and geographic area served by the agency. Think about the possibilities that exist within that common space.

BOX 11.2	**Location, Location, Location**

The administrator of a human service organization was being interviewed on local TV about the agency's new office location. The reporter made the point that the new office building was located in a very affluent part of town, but that its mission was to serve low-income people. When the reporter asked the administrator why that location was selected, he said, "Because most of our employees live in this area"—not a good marketing strategy.

Promotion

Promotion is the communication between the agency and its various publics. Promotion takes many forms. It is the agency newsletter, the website, the fundraising letters, and the funding proposals. It is public speaking, participation in community activities, special events, and TV interviews. Promotion is about building relationships—with board members, with donors, with funding sources, and with the community. In Chapter 5, we talked about the concept of "friend-raising." It is the same concept in marketing. Promotion is the art and the tools of persuasive communications to interpret the mission of your organization to others and to gain their support of your efforts. Promotion is about motivation and inspiration. As a human services administrator, it is the power of your conviction for the services that you provide and your commitment to those you serve that will inspire others to join you in your life's work.

Publics

Lauffer (2009) adds publics as the fifth P of marketing to recognize the unique character of nonprofit organizations. This characteristic applies equally well to all human service organizations, regardless of their sector. While businesses are concerned with the consumers of their products, human services have other stakeholders that must be considered. Many times, it is not the client who is paying for the services provided; instead, the services are paid for by a third party through a grant or contract, or in the case of nonprofit organizations, the services may be paid for through donated funds. Therefore, it is not only the client (consumer) who must be considered in a marketing plan but other stakeholders as well, such as donors, funders, volunteers, and the community at large.

CONTENT MARKETING

An emphasis on **content marketing** should be an important part of a human service organization's marketing plan. The American Marketing Association (2013) offers the following definition:

> *Content marketing* involves various methods to tell the brand story. More and more marketers are evolving their advertising to content marketing/storytelling to create more stickiness and emotional bonding with the consumer. (Types of Marketing section)

Content marketing is telling the story of your organization in order to strengthen the bond with your organization's stakeholders. In content marketing, the goal is not to solicit an immediate response, such as donating or volunteering, but rather to inform your publics about the organization and build a stronger connection. Of course, you also want to offer these opportunities, but the main focus is to inform and connect. Techniques of storytelling will help you craft your content for this part of your marketing plan. An important part of your story can be presenting the results of your program evaluation. Few things are as powerful as proven results. Elizabeth Chung (n.d.) offers the following takeaways for content marketing:

- Take advantage of your website traffic and use your homepage to capture emails.
- Update your blog consistently to create a steady flow of traffic to your website and landing pages.
- Segment your email lists to create targeted, meaningful messages for different pools of supporters that set your organization apart.
- Include calls to action in your emails to keep readers engaged, whether they lead people to your blog or donation checkout pages.
- Stick to a diligent newsletter schedule to keep your organization, its mission, and its need for support visible throughout the year.
- Use visual storytelling in your email and social media channels to create emotional connections and compel supporters to take further action. (Major Takeaways section)

Content marketing can be a powerful tool for your nonprofit. It plays a huge role in building lasting relationships. Next, we will consider the rapidly changing environment of marketing channels for your message.

MARKETING CHANNELS

An important decision to make is how you will deliver your message (promotion) to your intended target audience. Marketing in the digital age gets more complex every day. The Buzzly Media Blog (Philanthropegie, 2016) shares "The Big Six Channels" for nonprofits:

- Websites: A nonprofit organization must have a website that is easy to navigate and mobile-friendly. If your website is hard to look through, users will get frustrated and leave. And if your site is not mobile-friendly, you could be losing a lot of traffic.
- Email: A survey by Adobe (Naragon, 2015) finds that email is still a key component in personal communications and that even millennials are addicted to email, checking it more frequently than any other age group. Email is a great way to directly reach your followers, but beware of fatiguing them with too much of it.

- Traditional social media: Facebook, Twitter, LinkedIn, Pinterest, and Instagram are valuable tools to an organization seeking to increase its public awareness. These channels will help make your organization more visible and promote engagement with followers.
- In-person events: The best form of communication is telling others about causes you care about. Nonprofits cannot afford to eliminate events from their marketing strategy. Take opportunities to present at civic clubs and be present at community events.
- Print marketing: Printed materials are still an important part of marketing. The response may be skewed toward older stakeholders, but remember from Chapter 5 that the average age of donors is 62 and that board chairs are likely to be over 40. Print is expensive, but used wisely, it can still be an important channel for marketing.
- Media relations and public relations: Media relations is the agency's interactions with editors, reporters, and journalist in the community. Many media outlets have lists of experts as their "go to" people when they need comments or an expert on a topic. As a social work administrator, you have a great deal of expertise and could be a resource. Websites such as Media Helper (www.helpareporter) are good places to make yourself available as a content expert. As an administrator, you will want to have clear policies concerning who on the staff is authorized to contact or respond to the media. There should be designated staff (including yourself) who can talk with the media. It is important to have an emergency communication plan in place in case there is a negative incident in the agency that requires a response to the media.

MARKET SEGMENTATION

To develop an effective marketing plan for an organization, it is first necessary to identify the target markets. Because of the many "publics" of a human service organization, this can be a complex task. Think first about the clients served by your organization. If you serve only one very specific population, then the task of segmenting the client market should not be that difficult, but many organizations provide multiple program services for a variety of populations. The first task, then, is to identify each of the segments of the client market.

Clients are not the only public that requires you to think about **market segmentation**. What are the demographics of your donor population? Do you think it might require a different approach for your donors under 30 years old as opposed to your donors over 60? Is there a difference in your

Image 11.2

To develop a marketing plan, it is necessary to identify the target markets.

donors who have donated to your organization for many years and those who have made their first gift? Will you approach them any differently? Segmentation is required unless you can determine that all the people in the target market are likely to respond in the same way (Hardcastle & Powers, 2004). The first task is to identify each category in your target market and then to further refine these categories into subsets, as appropriate.

COMPONENTS OF NONPROFIT MARKETING PLANS

Marketing plans for nonprofit organizations should specify how the organization plans to reach each target audience group identified in the segmentation exercise. Mary Gormandy White (2013) outlines the typical components of a nonprofit marketing plan to include the following elements for each target population:

- Mission and goal statement: This portion of your marketing plan should express what it is that your organization hopes to accomplish for the clients you serve. Your mission and goal statement should clearly define the overall purpose of your organization. The marketing plan should tie specifically to accomplishing the mission and goal.
- Outcome objectives: Define specific, measurable outcome objectives for each target audience (see Chapter 7). What do you want the results to be of your marketing activities? How many clients do you want to serve in the coming year? What kinds of results do you expect to see with the organization's stakeholders? How much money do you need to raise this year? How many volunteer hours do you hope to log?
- Develop strategies through process objectives: What steps can you take to accomplish your outcome objectives? For example, if you want to increase the number of clients served by 250 next year, what will you need to do to accomplish this result? If you want to attract 50 new major donors, what steps will you take to reach this outcome objective?
- Action plan: How will your organization go about implementing the defined marketing strategies identified in the process objectives? Who is responsible for each component of the plan? What is the time line for each activity to be implemented? The action plan should be written in a manner that makes it easy to determine who is to do what by when.
- Budget: How is the marketing plan built into the organization's budget? What resources will be allocated to the marketing plan?
- Monitoring: How will you evaluate your progress and make any necessary adjustments to the plan? What is the system for evaluation of both outcome and process objectives? Who is responsible to see that reporting and review procedures are followed? How will progress be measured?

MARKETING AND FUND DEVELOPMENT

In many ways, marketing and fund development are inseparable. They both share the responsibility for communicating with constituents and building relationships. Claire Axelrad (2015) states that development and marketing have the same two basic decisions to make: (a) which products to offer and (b) which channels to message in. The right product must be offered in the right way to the right customer. If marketing and development are targeting the same constituents (and in most cases they are) yet each chooses a different product or channel, this may cause confusion. Development and marketing efforts must have coherence. Often, no one has authority, or too many people share authority, for presenting the organization to the community. As the administrator, you will be responsible for assuring that the organizational structure and lines of authority assure that a consistent and appropriate message is being presented in your marketing program.

THE NONPROFIT MARKETING MANIFESTO

Some marketing professionals and scholars believe that traditional definitions of marketing do not capture the reality of the nonprofit sector, and many administrators do not place a high priority on the marketing functions of their organization. Some administrators view marketing as nothing more than a tool for building awareness and raising funds. We join others in calling for a new expanded definition and commitment to marketing in the nonprofit sector.

Conrardy and Mullen (2018), cofounders of Prosper Strategies, contend that "for far too long, the nonprofit sector has thought far too small when it comes to marketing" (para. 1). They propose a new definition of nonprofit marketing: "Nonprofit marketing comprises the activities, touchpoints and messages that motivate stakeholders to take actions that advance a nonprofit's mission and create sustainable social change" (Conrardy & Mullen, 2018, para. 7).

Conrardy and Mullen (2018) contend that marketing is much more than a tool for fundraising and awareness building and that marketing can support every goal a nonprofit sets, from recruiting volunteers to building partnerships to diversifying revenue streams, and when this happens, marketing becomes a tool for advancing the mission and driving social change. In presenting their new definition on nonprofit marketing, they have offered a nonprofit marketing manifesto and ask those who support their concept to make ten commitments in their approach to nonprofit marketing:

- Commitment #1: We will recognize marketing as a tool for driving social change. We will acknowledge that when leveraged properly by nonprofits like ours, marketing is capable of changing the world.
- Commitment #2: We will develop a strong brand image and identity in alignment with our mission and values. We will recognize that our brands are the keys that unlock our mission and values for our stakeholders, and we will treat them accordingly.
- Commitment #3: We will build cohesion internally and communicate with consistency externally. We will recognize that to advance our mission we must build trust, and that to build trust, there must be consistency between how we see ourselves internally, how we act, and how we represent ourselves externally.

- Commitment #4: We will treat all of our stakeholders as brand ambassadors. We will recognize that every person our organizations interact with has the potential to amplify our brands, our missions and our impact.
- Commitment #5: We will develop a marketing plan that aligns with our strategic plan and recognize that marketing can impact every single one of our strategic goals. We will stop developing our marketing and communications plans in a vacuum, and instead make marketing planning an integral part of strategic planning.
- Commitment #6: We will invest properly in marketing and view it as core mission support, not overhead. We will stop short-changing marketing in favor of other "more important" functions at our organizations.
- Commitment #7: We will ensure marketing is overseen at the highest level of our organizations and contributed to by everyone on our teams. We will give marketing and communications a seat at the leadership table and a spot on the board meeting agenda.
- Commitment #8: We will use our brands and marketing to build partnerships and advance the broader causes we're focused on. We realize we're not an island, and we behave accordingly.
- Commitment #9: We will avoid, at all costs, sacrificing the dignity of those we serve for the sake of our marketing and communications goals. We recognize that our marketing efforts are not a success if they marginalize, stereotype, or otherwise disempower the people we serve, no matter how well they perform by other metrics.
- Commitment #10: We will measure the impact of marketing on our missions and continually optimize our efforts to drive more social change. We are unwilling to accept the notion that it is impossible to measure the impact marketing makes on our missions. (Conrardy & Mullen, 2018, Headings)

ETHICAL ISSUES FOR MARKETING HUMAN SERVICES

Murphy and Bloom (1992) outline generic ethical problems for marketers. We borrow heavily from their work to consider ethical issues you may face in marketing human services:

- Is it fair? Are you presenting the story of your agency in a fair and truthful way? Are your proven "results" based on solid research methods, and do you present the true picture or only those findings that support your message? Does the story you tell about your clients reflect the reality of their lives?
- Is your message manipulative? If your childcare institution has millions of dollars in endowments, is it ok to have a fundraising appeal to ask donors to buy a pair of shoes for a child in care? Campaigns that play on pity or guilt are sometimes referred to as *starving baby appeals* (Fine, 1992). Administrators must be careful not to engage in promotions that put their clients in a negative light or present them as the objects of pity.
- Does your marketing play favorites? Is your message directed only toward those who can help your organization financially? Do you put equal emphasis on making your service accessible to those most in need? If your services are fee based, do you target only those with the financial resources to pay your fee?

- Is your marketing seen as wasteful? It is always a balancing act for the administrator to produce marketing materials that are attractive and eye-catching but not to appear wasteful. Those who support your organization do not want to see program money spent on "slick" publications. The move toward social media and electronic marketing will help to alleviate this dilemma, since printed materials are often the target of this criticism. Other marketing strategies may also be criticized as wasteful. For example, you may want to give a parting gift to members rotating off the board, but you do not want these tokens of appreciation to be viewed as a waste of money (even by the recipient).
- Is your approach intrusive? Are you gathering more information on your "publics" than you need? How are you protecting the information you gather? How do you keep your publics informed without becoming annoying and intrusive by having too many contacts with them?

As an administrator, you have an obligation to be fair, truthful, and open in presenting your organization to the public. You are also obligated not to be manipulative, wasteful, or intrusive in your marketing program.

GRANT REPORTING

It is an exciting day when you receive a new grant for your organization. In most cases you have competed with many similar organizations for a government or a foundation grant and receiving the grant is confirmation that you have presented a strong case for your organization and your ability to have major positive impact for the people you serve. In most cases, there will be a requirement that you provide a report on the activities and outcomes of your funded project. The truth is that reporting can be stressful. To compete, you have promised a lot in the volume of activity and in the anticipated outcomes. We suggest that reporting provides two great opportunities for your organization. First, you can view the reporting requirement as a marketing activity. It is probably not the last time you will ask this foundation or government agency for money. Look at the report as a means to strengthen your relationship with the funder and to build confidence in your organization. Secondly, consider the report as means of contributing to the knowledge base of your field. In our opinion, this is one of the great weaknesses in human services. Untold amounts of time, energy, and money are spent on program evaluations, but few reports are shared with anyone other than the funding source. There is a great opportunity for human services to partner with academic researchers to construct meaningful evaluation studies and to publish the results in academic and professional publications. Think of the reporting requirement as being useful not only to the funding source but the other publics identified in your overall marketing plan.

Funders want assurance that their investment in your organization has been a sound investment. In broad terms, they want to know four things (Massachi, 2020):

- what's working and what's not
- what needs are going unmet
- how you can improve in the future
- how you are spending their money

Most funders will require at least one report showing the results of the program they have funded. Generally, reports require a narrative report and a financial report. The terms of the grant will outline the reporting requirements, including what is to be included in the final report and any interim or progress reports required.

Your goal in presenting the program report is to demonstrate the level of activity provided and the outcomes in terms of the difference the program has made in people's lives or improvements in the life of the community. It is also your opportunity to build on your relationship with the funder and the possibility of renewed funding or funding of future projects. Most funders have a required reporting format. Some have detailed requirements or provide grant report templates, and others are more general and give the grantee more leeway in crafting the report.

Massachi (2020) and Reams (2019) provide an excellent overview of a typical report and guidance for each section.

Say "Thank you": Let your funders know that you appreciate them by expressing your gratitude at the beginning of your grant report. A common way of doing this is by adding a cover letter at the beginning of your report.

NARRATIVE REPORTS

Accomplishments and grand activities: Here is your time to take credit for your work. Review each of your proposal's goals and objectives and report on how you met, exceeded, or failed to meet them. Also include any unanticipated accomplishments. Use this section to describe the results of the program, explain the strengths and weaknesses. In this section, you will highlight what your organization proposed to do with the grant money and the activities you implemented.

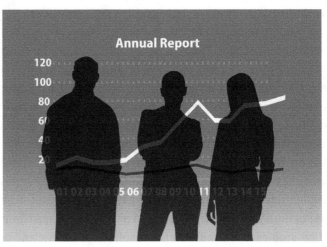

The program report is to demonstrate the level of activity provided and the outcomes achieved.

Outcomes & Impact

The easiest way to write this section is to revisit the goals and objectives you included in your initial grant proposal. Remember, your data do not have to be all numbers. The outcomes and impact section is a great place to share participant quotes, testimonials, or stories of transformation that are a direct result of your project. Tell stories of people who benefited from the grant-funded work. Show how their lives were improved because of your project, using their words as much as possible. Remember the power of storytelling in marketing. This section can make a big impact on your funder. They, too, want to take pride in what has been accomplished.

Challenges and lessons learned: What lessons did you learn during the project? Funders are interested not only in your successes but also in how you modify your work to address any challenges you encountered along the way. Foundations sometimes see themselves as incubators or innovators in providing human services. They can use your experiences to make future funding decisions. Lessons learned is a time to demonstrate your adaptability and commitment to making the program a success.

There will always be unexpected factors that affect your ability to meet proposed goals and objectives. Use the challenges and lessons learned section to share:

- details on the factors that presented a challenge
- how these factors affected your project plans
- the lessons you learned from these experiences
- how you will (or did) incorporate these lessons to improve current and future efforts

This section can be very challenging. It is easy to worry that being honest about challenges and failures will eliminate the chance for future funding. The anxiety is understandable but funders do not expect that projects will run exactly as proposed or hoped for. Sharing your challenges and responses to those challenges can highlight your organization's resilience and creativity.

Your partnership with the funder: Look back at the foundation's goals, objectives, and priorities. Write about how your work addressed and advanced their goals. Demonstrate how your partnership with the funder was a good investment in reaching their goals. Think about the marketing segmentation. Tailor your message to this important stakeholder.

Future plans and sustainability: In this section, describe how you intend to build on this project and show that the funded project was part of a sustained effort. Share emerging trends or shifting contexts impacting your work. Funders want to know the successful projects will be around for a while. In this section share information on your plans for the future of the project and how you will sustain it with other grants, earned income, or fundraising.

Financial reports: In the financial report, you will account for all expenditures you made with the grant funds. The report should compare the actual expenses with the proposed budget expenses. If there were deviations from the proposed budget, you will want to document that these expenditures were approved by the funding source. You will want to have your financial staff involved in this part of the report. Provide an overview of the grant funds received to date, line-item expenses that have been charged to the grant, and the grant funds remaining. For general operating grants, the financial information section will focus on the organization's overall budget, with categories aligned to the budget you submitted with the initial grant proposal.

Deadlines: You should never miss a reporting deadline. Doing so shows disrespect for the funding source and sends the wrong message. The surest way to guarantee you do not receive future funding is to ignore the reporting requirements. If for any reason you are not going to make the deadline, ask for an extension and explain the reason for the delay.

OTHER WAYS TO SHARE INFORMATION

In addition to sharing information with the funding source through the required program reports, there are many other ways to share information about your project. It is important to check with the funding source on their publicity policies. Some may be grateful for the recognition, but others may prohibit you from disclosing their support of your project. Celebrate receiving the grant by including news of your grant in any publications you produce for distribution. This includes press releases, newsletters, brochures, annual reports, board minutes, lists of supporters, blogs, direct mail, and so on. Also, post about your project on Facebook, Twitter, and other social medial platforms. Use your social media presence to highlight the new program and funding.

 ## SPOTLIGHT ON DIVERSITY

Bump (2020) states:

> With successful inclusive marketing campaigns, marketers aim to break advertising norms by highlighting people or groups that might be under- or misrepresented, such as people of color, those who identify as LGBTQ+, those who affiliate with various religions, those who are disabled, or even people of certain ages and genders. But **inclusive marketing** [emphasis added] isn't always easy to do right. An inclusive or thought-provoking campaign takes time, effort, and careful thought to be success-ful. And, it's not just about picking the right stock image and giving yourself a gold star. It's about making a solid effort to include or properly represent diverse people in your campaigns. (Diversity by the Numbers section)

Nonprofit organizations may be particularly interested in communicating with the growing Hispanic population in the United States. Leon (n.d.) lists five insights for nonprofit marketers to heed:

- Hispanic people are changing the face of American society as they increase in numbers and propor-tion of the total population. Now is the time for nonprofits to communicate and collaborate with this population.
- Don't translate. Communicate. Straight translations from English to Spanish may not be in sync culturally. It is important to engage with the culture of your target population, not just use the Spanish language. Remember, many Latin Americans are American citizens and have been born and raised in the United States. They may or may not be fluent in Spanish.
- Digital marketing is a must. This population engages heavily with digital platforms and content. As a population, Latin Americans skew younger than many other groups, and this comparative youthfulness lends itself to online and digital communication.
- Hispanic people are generous. Formerly, much of their generosity was given to religious institutions, but this is changing. The advice given is to engage authentically now to become a trusted partner in achieving mutual goals.

- <u>Collaboration is critical for success</u>. A generalist marketing company or approach may not be as successful in fundraising amongst the Latin American population for your organization as a specialized one.

DIFFICULTIES AND JOYS

Few of the students we have ever taught look forward to the idea of becoming nonprofit marketers. There seems to be a very strong link in our students' minds between "sleazy" and "marketing." Thus, the first difficulty encountered is usually an internal one, an idea that goes against their self-identity. That is one of the reasons we included this chapter.

A second difficulty is that the usual fields that produce human services program developers are not strong in teaching nonprofit marketing and there is little exposure to the concepts. For too many, marketing is marketing and there is little to no difference between selling toothpaste and soliciting donations. Still, it is worth remembering that for-profit marketing usually promotes specific services and products, while nonprofit marketing asks for support for causes. (As with many things, however, for-profits are now connecting themselves with causes, too, linking with charitable organizations through contributions or donations based on sales.) In the Additional Resources section, below, we have listed several non-credit courses that focus on nonprofit marketing.

Marketing your organization and its cause can be a fantastic feeling. Getting a clear message across to potential donors that results in increased funds for your program is life changing—for clients, your organization, and yourself! Writing reports that detail the impact of your agency is another way to benefit your organization. When you combine that skill with advocacy, you are also creating the resources needed to sustain a program in a way that is beyond words to express. It will bring you considerable joy as you explain the good your agency has done using your marketing and reporting skills. As this information gets out to the wider world, you will fill an important niche in your organization's internal environment. You will also be creating important relationships between people in the community, relationships that will be extremely valuable in monetary and nonmonetary ways for your agency.

LESSONS FROM THE PANDEMIC

An important lesson regarding communication, whether at the individual or organizational level, is that you can never not communicate. As an individual, your clothing, body language, facial expression, vocalizations, and other external attributes constantly give away your thoughts, internal status, and many other details about you. Similarly, for an organization, the amount of communication being sent out via mail, email, or on your website is quite telling. Also, if you have social media pages that have not been touched for days, weeks, or even years, you are communicating a great deal.

When organizations were unable to communicate in the ways they were used to, such as through in-person events, what happened next said a great deal. Was the silence deafening? Did it appear that the organization had gone into hibernation, if not suffered an untimely death?

Even in the best of times, donor turnover is around 50%. That is, you may receive a donation from a person one year and nothing in the next year from half of the donors. This churn is hard to reduce, but clear and carefully segmented communications can increase the number of retained volunteers and donors.

The lesson, then, is communicate and report purposefully. If you can reduce donor turnover by just a few percent, year over year and year after year, you will have a gradual but important rise in income from individuals. If possible, your communications will assist in moving your donors up the donor pyramid (refer to Chapter 5 for a reminder of what this means).

CONCLUSION

Human services administrators must be aggressive marketers of their organizations. The organization is in competition for clients, funding, volunteers, staff, and the overall support of the community. Marketing is not advertising or sales. It is understanding the needs of clients and other stakeholders. It is integral to achieving the mission of the organization and, as such, can be a strategy to bring about social change. Like all functions of administration, there is a need to be systematic and to have a well-developed plan for marketing the organization. Understanding the interplay of products, price, place, promotion, and publics are keys to marketing the organization and its services. A clear understanding of the organization's market share and the segmentation of that market guide the administrator toward a well-developed and effective marketing program for the organization.

 SUMMARY/KEY POINTS

- Marketing should be seen and treated as a way to achieve your organization's goals, not a sleazy way to scam the public for donations. Starting from this idea will assist you in seeing great value in "marketing" efforts. Marketing for your organization's good cause allows your staff to do the work they want to do and were hired for.
- Marketing for nonprofits can consist of the several aspects: products (what is your cause, and why is it important?); price (for products that are hardly distinguishable from one provider to another, price is very important); place (where are the services being provided?); and promotion (how well your organization is known to important stakeholder groups and the ways you "get the word out"). The last characteristic is publics, which consist of stakeholders who have influence within the organization due to control of monetary or other resources.
- Content marketing is telling the story of your organization, creating a brand story that tells your publics what the agency believes in and what it can achieve.
- Marketing channels are the avenues you use to deliver your message to your intended target audience. Six are listed: websites, email, traditional social media, in-person events, print marketing, and media relations/public relationships.

- Nonprofit marketing plans make use of the organizational founding principles, such as mission and goals statements, the specific outcomes that are being achieved, the strategic approaches chosen, action plans, budget, and monitoring. The marketing plan can certainly link back to the logic models that have been developed for each program.
- Budgeting is an important part of the marketing plan, as is the monitoring of outcomes and costs.
- Marketing is inextricably connected to fundraising and must truthfully reflect what is going on within the organization, lest the story coming out does not match reality.
- The nonprofit marketing manifesto is worth reading through, as it commits an organization to use only legitimate, legal, and ethical fundraising techniques.
- When reporting to your funder concerning the program, follow the template provided by the funder or ones that are similar to what is provided in this chapter.

KEY TERMS

Content marketing: Involves various methods to tell the brand story. More and more marketers are evolving their advertising to content marketing/storytelling to create more stickiness and emotional bonding with the consumer (Association of National Advertisers, n.d.).

Inclusive marketing: Describes campaigns that embrace diversity by including people from different backgrounds or stories that unique audiences can relate to. While some inclusive campaigns make an effort to break stereotypes, others simply aim to reflect or embrace people in the real world.

Market segmentation: The process of identifying each category of the organization's target market and then further refining the categories into subsets, as appropriate (e.g., the clients and subsets of clients, as well as donors divided into subsets such as age, interest, or motivation).

Marketing: A means to achieve the organization's goal. It is a tool—really a process and set of tools wrapped in a philosophy—for helping the organization do what it wants to do. Using marketing and being customer-oriented should never be thought of as goals: They are ways to achieve goals (Andreasen & Kotler, 2013).

Product mindset: Assumes if you build a better mousetrap, customers will beat a pathway to your door.

Sales mindset: Assumes that an organization must persuade customers to choose their services rather than those of a competitor.

Customer mindset: "Systematically studies customers' needs, wants, perceptions, preferences, and satisfaction, using surveys, focus groups, and other means … and constantly acts on this information to improve its offerings and to meet its customers' needs better" (Andreasen & Kotler, 2013, p. 42).

Ps of marketing: Several authors refer to the Ps of marketing as products, price, place, and promotion. Lauffer (2009) adds a fifth P for "publics" to represent the stakeholders in human service organizations.

ADDITIONAL RESOURCES

Readings

American Marketing Association website (https://www.ama.org)

Common Language Marketing Dictionary (https://marketing-dictionary.org/m/marketing)

Media Helper (www.helpareporter.com)

Miller, K. L. (2016). *Nonprofit communications trends report* [Infographic]. Nonprofit Marketing Guide. http://www.nonprofitmarketingguide.com/blog/2016/01/05/the-2016-nonprofit-communications-trends-report-infographic/

Obrien, A. (2014). Public relations vs. media relations. *Everything-PR.* https://everything-pr.com/public-relations-media-relations/52598/

Pallota, D. (2016). *Advertising & marketing in nonprofit organizations* [Video]. YouTube. https://www.youtube.com/watch?v=6aRUSjGjE9o

Rovner, M. (2015). *Diversity in giving. The changing landscape of American philanthropy.* Blackbaud. http://www.thenonprofittimes.com/wp-content/uploads/2015/03/Diversity-in-Giving-Study-FINAL.pdf

Santo, A. (2019, March 27). 20 books every marketer should read in 2019. *Brafton.* https://www.brafton.com/blog/content-marketing/20-books-every-marketer-should-read-in-2019/

Courses and Certificates in Nonprofit Marketing

At the time of the writing of this book, these sites had opportunities to earn nondegree certificates or noncredit classes. Inclusion here is for information purposes only and does not constitute an endorsement. No benefit accrues to the authors for including these program listings, which charge fees for the courses they offer.

CNM (https://thecnm.org/education/marketing/)

Ed2go (https://www.ed2go.com/courses/business/marketing-and-sales/ilc/marketing-your-nonprofit)

Nonprofit Marketing Academy (https://nonprofitmarketingacademy.com/integrated-nonprofit-marketing-training/)

DISCUSSION QUESTIONS

1. Assume that you are the administrator leading an all-staff meeting for Sheltering Arms and the topic is how to market the organization and its services. If an employee says, "Isn't it enough that we provide excellent service? People will come to us if we provide excellent services, right?" How would you respond? With your small groups, develop a response based on the content of this chapter. You will read your response to the class and ask for their feedback.

2. How would you alter your approach to annual reports or reports to funders if you saw them as strictly informational purposes compared to "marketing" purposes? What makes a product more one or the other?

 YOUR TURN

Find the reporting guidelines for any large foundation or government agency that you might like to receive funding from. Assume you have completed the grant period, and write a report using their guidelines. If there are no guidelines, use the outline provided in this chapter. Be realistic as you create your report.

REFERENCES

American Marketing Association. (2013). *About AMA: definition of marketing*. https://www.ama.org/the-definition-of-marketing/

Andreasen, A. R., & Kotler, P. (2003). *Strategic marketing for nonprofit organizations* (6th ed.). Prentice Hall.

Axelrad, C. (2015, January 14). The shocking truth about marketing and development for nonprofits. *Candid*. https://trust.guidestar.org/blog/2015/01/14/the-shocking-truth-about-marketing-and-development-for-nonprofit/

Bump, P. (2020, February 18). 7 brands that got inclusive marketing right. *Hubspot*. https://blog.hubspot.com/marketing/inclusive-marketing-campaigns

Chung, E. (n.d.). Content marketing 101 for the modern nonprofit. *Classy*. https://www.classy.org/blog/content-marketing-101-modern-nonprofit/

Conrardy, A., & Mullen, L. (2018). *The nonprofit marketing manifesto*. Prosper Strategies. https://prosper-strategies.com/nonprofit-marketing-manifesto/

Fine, S. H. (1992). *Marketing the public sector: Promoting the causes of public and nonprofit agencies.* Transaction.

Hardcastle, D. A., & Powers, P. R. (with Wenocur, S.). (2004). *Community practice: Theories and skills for social workers* (2nd ed.). Oxford University Press.

Lauffer, A. (2009). Confronting fundraising challenges. In R. Patti (Ed.), *The handbook of human services management* (2nd ed., pp. 351–372). Sage.

Leon, I. (n.d.). 5 Hispanic marketing insights for nonprofits. *NextAfter*. https://www.nextafter.com/blog/5-hispanic-marketing-insights-for-nonprofits/

Lewis, J. A., Packard, T., & Lewis, M. D. (2011). *Management of human service programs* (5th ed.). Brooks/Cole.

Massachi, D. (2020, December 7). Managing grant reporting at your nonprofit. *Writing to Make a Difference*. https://www.writingtomakeadifference.com/archives/7501

Murphy, P. E., & Bloom, P. N. (1992). Ethical issues in social marketing. *Marketing, 12*, 68–78.

Naragon, K. (2015, August 26). Subject: Email, we just can't get enough. *Adobe Blog*. https://theblog.adobe.com/email/

Philanthropegie. (2016). *6 essential marketing channels for nonprofits*. https://www.philanthropegie.org/6-essential-marketing-channels-nonprofits/

Reams, M. (2019, July 9). How to write a grant report when your funder has no reporting guidelines. *Upstream Consulting*. https://upstream.consulting/grant-management/how-to-write-a-grant-report

White, M. G. (2013). Nonprofit marketing plans. *LoveToKnow*. https://charity.lovetoknow.com/charitable-organizations/nonprofit-marketing-plans

Winston, W. J. (1986). Basic marketing principles for mental health professionals. *Journal of Marketing for Mental Health, 1*(1), 9–20.

Worth, M. J. (2009). *Nonprofit management: Principles and practice.* Sage.

Figure Credits

CHAPTER TWELVE

The Joy of Grantwriting, Program Development, and Implementation

The often-overlooked element of training in the area of program development and design is that professionals in the field need more than technical skills. Much of your success and your longevity in the job will depend on having good relationships with others and in finding joy in working with others. This chapter provides information on what joy in the workplace means and how you can realize it for yourself.

In the previous chapters, we have looked at many aspects of grantwriting, program development, and implementation. As you look back across the topics covered, you will find that a common denominator in almost all the functions is the ability to form and maintain relationships. The functions related to understanding the context of the community are highly dependent on forming and nurturing relationships. To go into a community and gather personal information requires a great deal of trust and level of comfort with the program developer. To truly understand a community requires the formation of personal relationships within the community. Likewise, seeking funding for a project requires that the program developer gain the respect and trust of potential funding sources. The old fundraising slogan "People don't give money to organizations, they give money to people" is true in all aspects of fund development for a new program. Fund development from grants, contracts, and private sources all require a solid relationship base. During the implementation phase, it is critical to maintain and develop new relationships as the program is integrated into the larger community of service providers. New projects most often require new staff, and the success of the project will depend on the relationships developed with those new to the organization. Sustaining the program depends on success demonstrated through program evaluation and the reporting of results to the community and the funding sources. Finally, ongoing support for the project will depend on the strength of the relationships built in the community and with the funding sources.

BUILDING RELATIONSHIPS

Program development is about forming relationships at all levels. Relationships are vital for dealing with funding sources, regulatory agencies, the general public, boards and commissions, referral sources, staff, clients, and all other stakeholder groups related to the organization. **Relationship** is a term of great historical significance in the social work literature (Johnson & Yanca, 2010) and in other disciplines as well. While it is often used in relation to the direct service worker–client dyad, it is of equal importance in administrative practice and program development. Perlman (1979) describes a relationship as "a catalyst, an enabling dynamism in the support, nurture and freeing of people's energies and motivation toward problem solving" (p. 2). This definition describes the tasks of program developers well.

The importance of administrative relationships is documented in a study of 37 companies from 11 parts of the world in which Kanter (1994) found that relationships between companies grow or fail much like the relationships between people. Kanter reported that when relationships between organizations were built on creating new values together, rather than on a mere exchange arrangement, both partners considered their alliance a success. True partners valued the skills that each brought to the relationship.

Program development is about forming relationships.

The same can be said for all levels of program development. Human service administrators understand intuitively the importance of relationships. Relationships are key to our professional identity. Skinner (2018) incorporated the rise of internet-powered communication into this conclusion, adding further power to the idea that relationships are keys to success.

Hoefer (2009) refined the ratings of 37 skills, attitudes, and knowledge areas needed for human service administration into four categories: people skills, attitudes and experiences, substantive knowledge, and management skills. Of these four, people skills are the most important set of skills for the nonprofit administrator. Management competencies are not a substitute for core social values and interpersonal skills. Denhardt (2015) advises public administrators not to define their role or gauge their actions based solely on business values and market-based approaches but rather on democratic ideals such as citizenship, community, and participation in decision making. These are all ideals strongly rooted in relationship building.

THE JOY OF ADMINISTRATION

Edward Deming, the father of total quality management, often promoted the idea that every employee should be able to achieve joy at work and that joy would lead to improved quality and a high-performance organization. "Management's overall aim should be to create a system in which everybody may take joy in his work" (Neave, 1990, p. 36). Deming's instruction at the time was not research based, but it has been echoed in the past few years as those in the field of positive psychology have explored psychological wellness rather than illness. The subfield of positive organizational behavior (POB) is attempting to apply the concepts of positive psychology to the workplace (Youssef & Luthans, 2007).

Image 12.2

We should aim to create an environment where everyone may take joy in their work.

A roadblock to the study of joy is the lack of an operationalized definition of the concept. It is not a clearly definable emotion and is expressed in a variety of ways by different individuals (Hoskote, 2009). Joy is not the same thing as happiness. Happiness often requires a series of events to occur, and when those events end, happiness may disappear. In contrast, joy is long-lasting and can be recalled at will by the person who has experienced it (Lazarus, 1991). After an extensive literature review, and based on the findings of her interviews with health care professionals, Manion (2003) defined **joy** as "an intensely positive, vivid, and expansive emotion that arises from an internal state or results from an external event or situation. It may include a physiologic reaction, an expressive component, and conscious volition. It is a transcendent state of heightened energy and excitement" (p. 653).

Manion's approach is comprehensive but not easily operationalized. Watson and Hoefer (2016) adopted a definition of joy provided by William Schutz (1967):

> Joy is the feeling that comes from the fulfillment of one's potential. Fulfillment brings to an individual the feeling that he can cope with his environment; the sense of confidence in himself as a significant, competent, lovable person who is capable of handling situations as they arise, able to use fully his own capacities, and free to express his feelings. (p. 15)

Watson and Hoefer (2016) used this description of joy because it focuses on administrative tasks: coping with a difficult environment, building a sense of self-confidence through competence, handling situations by using one's own capacities, and expressing feelings appropriately. Social work and other human services have a rich history of seeking to build on strengths rather than building on weaknesses. Saleebey (2008) argued that for macro practitioners to focus only on deficits would further marginalize oppressed communities and groups. Likewise, in human service administration, we need more focus on the positive aspects of leadership and administrative practice. In teaching administration, we should follow the lead of positive psychology in embracing the idea that "what is good about life is as genuine as what is bad and therefore deserves equal attention" (Peterson, 2006, p. 4).

Fredrickson's (2002) work in positive organizational psychology found that negative emotions are undone by positive emotions, such as joy and amusement. Positive emotions were found to promote resilient coping in the midst of adversity. Positive emotions, such as joy, broaden people's mindsets and promote unique and creative lines of thought or action. Being more creative allows one to push the limits for bringing innovative ideas to fruition (Fredrickson, 2002).

Little research has been conducted in the area of the joy of administrative practice or program development. In fact, there is little research on the topic in any related discipline. The most extensive work has been in the area of POB, which attempts to apply the concepts of positive psychology to the workplace (Youssef & Luthans, 2007). Kim et al. (2019) note that their research results indicate that having meaningful work leads to higher levels of job satisfaction and well-being in sports organizations. Currently, the literature relating POB to administration in human services as a field and program development particularly is scant. Even the latest texts on POB include no work on human service organizations in particular (Pina e Cunha et al., 2020). We believe it is vitally important to create more of it.

You may have noticed that every chapter of this book has information on the difficulties and joys of being a program developer and human services leader. This is because we believe joy is an important aspect of the profession but is seldom mentioned or studied. We came to this conclusion in our role as professors.

One of the assignments that we give to the students in our advanced classes is for them to go into the community and interview an agency executive director or other leader, depending on the class. During a class discussion of the students' interview experiences, one of the students made a very interesting comment. She said that she was fascinated when the administrator she was interviewing began to talk about the joys of being a human services administrator. During the next class after the interview, the student said, "You teach us about the challenges and the tasks of administration, but we don't hear about the joys of being an administrator." This comment led to a modification of the assignment and the beginning of a research project to explore the joys of human services administration. The early results of this exploration, with 20 executive director interviews, have revealed several themes. We will review here the joyful aspects of being a human service leader that current administrators mentioned in their interviews (seen in Box 12.1). These components of joy in administrative practice are most evident in the area of program development.

BOX 12.1	**Six Ways Human Service Leaders Find Joy in Their Work**

- making a difference in people's lives
- mentoring staff
- finding meaning in work
- being an advocate
- giving and receiving recognition
- seeing it in their (your) eyes

Making a Difference in People's Lives

Without exception, the human services administrators said that the greatest joy of their job was knowing that their agency was making a difference in people's lives. If administrators or program developers have true passion and a heart for the people served by the organization or program, they will find joy in the work. As you consider where you will expend your time and energies in your career, be sure that you have passion for the people served and a belief in the mission of the organization. This is one of the true joys of program development. To see a need and then bring together the resources to make a positive impact in people's lives is an amazing experience.

Mentoring Staff

The second most common source of joy identified by the human services administrators was helping their staff to grow and to advance in their careers. Several talked about people who had been mentors in their lives, and they now found joy in helping others to reach their career and professional goals. As you advance in your career, remember those who have served as your role models and mentors. Remember your responsibility to be a mentor and to help others to meet their professional goals. When program development is successful in creating new program services, it can provide wonderful opportunities for young professionals and give experienced professionals the opportunity to advance their career and move to more advanced positions within the agency.

Finding Meaning in Work

Some of the administrators had come to the human services field by way of the business world. In their interviews, they talked about the difference in the setting and what that difference meant to them. One said, "At my other job, we were concerned about money. Here, we are concerned about helping autistic children learn to speak." To identify a need, develop a program to address that need, and then see the positive impact that a program has on people's lives is a powerful experience. The deep sense of purpose and meaning fosters joy for the program developer.

Being an Advocate

Other administrators said they found joy in advocating for their clients who could not advocate for themselves. In most cases, they spoke of being an advocate at the community level and seeing that services were available for their client populations. Many who had come from direct services spoke of feeling they could help more people as an administrator than they could as a direct service provider. Many saw their work in the community of human services as a function of advocating for the people served by their organizations. This is the heart of program development. To be an advocate in the community for a population in need is powerful. Program development is advocacy in action. It is making something happen by creatively bringing together all of the resources needed to have a positive impact.

Giving and Receiving Recognition

Moments of joy come when respondents see staff and volunteers get the recognition they so richly deserve. Joy is found when everyone comes together to provide needed assistance to agency clients. Joy also comes about when receiving compliments from others about one's department. It is important for funders, staff, and clients to be recognized. The program developer can assure this recognition by building in periodic reporting to funders and to the community at large. It is important to say "thank you" to funders, staff, and other stakeholders who are invested in the success of the newly developed program.

Seeing It in Their (Your) Eyes

Several students commented that when they asked the question, "What brings you the most joy in your work?" they could see a physical change in the administrator's facial expression. "Their face lit up" and "I could see the passion in their eyes" were common observations made by the students. Find a position that will be so important and meaningful to you that others can see it in your face when you talk about your work and the programs you develop.

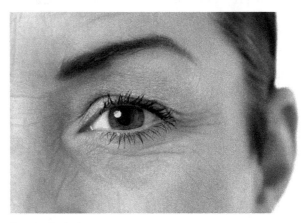

Image 12.3

Passion in their eyes

Much literature exists regarding burnout among human services workers. No matter which academic field you choose, you can find studies about the extent and problems when workers and administrators are burdened by the opposite of joy, burnout (see Additional Resources below for a few very recent resources). We hope the exposure to how to find joy in your work as a program developer or other human services leader will help you avoid this problem.

SPOTLIGHT ON DIVERSITY

It is undoubtedly true that most of the scholarship and writing about "joy at work" takes as its unstated starting point being White and working in a (prepandemic) office position (Johnson, 2020).

Meadows (2014) found that joy can be experienced mostly (70%) in an affiliated way (shared with others) rather than as an individual experience (30%). This leads to questions regarding how joy can be felt or expressed differently within cultures that are more individualistic or more collectivist in nature (Johnson, 2020). Johnson (2020) describes results of studies about emotions in different countries along several dimensions: where the emotion is felt in the body (Lee et al., 2015) and how open to strangers people in the culture are (Kahneman & Riis, 2005). Johnson (2020) also speculates on the role of language on experiencing joy, asking whether "cultures that have more words for different types of joy experience a broader range of types of joyful experience" (language and cross-cultural considerations).

As with all other explorations of the topic of diversity in this book, we believe that social workers, public administrators, public health workers, and all others who develop human service programs need to broaden their horizons to seek out and incorporate the different information and viewpoints of everyone in the situation—funders; staff; community leaders; potential, current, or past clients; and other stakeholders. Building such relationships is not always easy or quick, but it is essential.

DIFFICULTIES AND JOYS

We have so far extolled the virtues of relationships and joy in this concluding chapter. Nonetheless, difficulties exist. All of us who develop programs are humans. This leads to negative emotions as well as positive ones, and these emotions may lead to conflict. Conflict at work has an enormous amount of literature, thus attesting to its universality. Still, in many situations the best approach to reducing workplace conflict is the usual: Communicate more, not less. When, for example, different ideas for program details emerge, a fact-based discussion of pros and cons is better than tension-filled shouting or disengagement from the tasks. While every program development team needs to have a final decider (as noted in Chapter 2), people whose ideas are not fully accepted should still be acknowledged and kept in the loop. Often, when a person stops talking or interacting on a project, they are feeling disempowered or unappreciated. To retain (or regain) their interest, the team leader should act to solicit the person's ideas on other topics.

It may seem redundant at this point to speak of the importance of joy for program designers and other human service leaders. Still, the following quote is inspirational, so we share it with you: "Properly situated joy leads us to stand up to injustice, as a vision of a better world encourages us to work to inaugurate it in the present" (Johnson, 2020, "Acedia" section).

LESSONS FROM THE PANDEMIC

One of the clearest lessons of the COVID-19 pandemic is that, despite difficulties and strains, the important work of program designers to create solutions for social ills goes on. Bebes and Ray (2021) report from their survey of nonprofit leaders that one of the top five goals they stated for 2021 was to "start new programs or expand current programs" (p. 2). Despite predictions at the start of the pandemic in the United States, total giving to charities in 2020 did not collapse across the sector. In fact, it increased by 5.1% compared to 2019 as a whole, and donations to human services increased by 9.7% to a total of $65.14 billion (Giving USA, 2021). The pandemic forced changes in the way program development work was done, and will be done in the future, but we learned the work is still needed, valued, and funded. It is up to us, as students, educators, and practitioners, to keep going. We hope you find the material in this book helpful in learning important skills and in knowing why you are willing to make this part of your life's work.

CONCLUSION

As we bring this book to a close, we want to emphasize the positive aspects of human service leadership, administration, and program development. Educators must take it upon themselves to balance descriptions of the difficulties of human services administrative tasks with the joys of the work as well. The contradiction between only describing how awful being a program developer or administrator is and exhorting students to become leaders needs to end. Education on the positive elements of leading a human service organization should be included in all course work touching on leadership and organizational development topics. Doing so helps students thinking about getting their education in management to see that leaders help people in many ways, even if not in the same ways that their direct practice colleagues hope to.

Focusing on joy is also a way to keep qualified administrators and program developers in the field and to attract new and talented people to the work. Human service organizations can help their leaders and program developers find and focus on these elements to delay or prevent ongoing high levels of stress, burnout, and early retirement from the field.

As a human service leader, you will want to master each of the program development areas discussed in this book. While the tasks and skills are important to making a difference with your work, much of your success will be related to your ability to form and maintain relationships with the stakeholders of the organization. You will be the face of the organization in the community you serve. Serving as a leader will no doubt bring great challenges, but it can also be a fascinating and rewarding career that will bring you great joy.

 SUMMARY/KEY POINTS

- Program development is about forming positive relationships at all levels and with all stakeholders.
- Administrative practitioners report that they are able to find joy in their work through at least six ways:

  o making a difference in people's lives
  o mentoring staff
  o finding meaning in work
  o being an advocate
  o giving and receiving recognition
  o seeing it in their (your) eyes

- Joy has a positive impact on how organizations function.
- Joy and other emotions can be expressed differently by different populations and cultures.
- Program developers and human service leaders should work to prioritize the mental health of themselves and other stakeholders as they continue learning about and performing their essential work.

KEY TERMS

Joy: "An intensely positive, vivid, and expansive emotion that arises from an internal state or results from an external event or situation. It may include a physiologic reaction, an expressive component, and conscious volition. It is a transcendent state of heightened energy and excitement" (Manion, 2003, p. 653).

Relationship: "A catalyst, an enabling dynamism in the support, nurture and freeing of people's energies and motivation toward problem solving" (Perlman, 1979, p. 62).

ADDITIONAL RESOURCES

Addressing Mental Health and Burnout Among Human Services Workers

Edwins, M. (2021). Developing a model of empathy for public administration. *Administrative Theory and Praxis*, *43*(1), 22–41. https://doi.org/10.1080/10841806.2019.1700459

Fernando, R. (2018). I love the profession, but hate where I work: Remembering the value of organizations in social work practice. *Reflections, 24*(1), 45–55. https://reflectionsnarrativesofprofessionalhelping.org/index.php/Reflections/article/view/1509/1522

Sovold, L., Naslund, J., Kousoulis, Saxena, D., Qoronfleh, Grobler, C., & Münter, L. (2021). Prioritizing the mental health and well-being of healthcare workers: An urgent global public health priority. *Frontiers of Public Health, 9*. https://doi.org/10.3389/fpubh.2021.679397

Wilson, F. (2016). Identifying, preventing, and addressing job burnout and vicarious burnout for social work professionals. *Journal of Evidence-Informed Social Work, 13*(5), 479–483.

DISCUSSION QUESTIONS

1. What is your view of the importance of striving for a joyful workplace (whether you are working in an office, remotely, or some form of hybrid situation)? What might you be able to do regardless of your level of formal authority?
2. In your work or schooling, how have you seen similar emotions be expressed differently by members of different cultures or communities? How did this impact the ability of the people involved in working together?
3. Where will you be able to find your own joy at work? Why will this be so impactful to you?

 YOUR TURN

We believe it is always a good learning experience to interview working professionals when you are studying what is entailed in a certain profession. This course has led down many related paths—advocate, grantwriter, program planner, budgeting/financial expert, and so on. Choose to contact someone currently in one of these jobs (they may be doing more than one role, so you may want to explore several ideas at once!). Ask to speak to that person for about 30 minutes to ask about the work they do and their feelings toward it. Be sure to find out what brings them joy in their job. How well do their answers reflect the material you have learned from this book? Share with others what you have learned to get a more well-rounded look at the role. How does this impact your desire to go into the field in that capacity?

REFERENCES

Bedes, J., & Ray, K. (2021). *2021 Plante Moran nonprofit outlook survey report*. https://www.plantemoran.com/explore-our-thinking/info/industries/nonprofit/2021-nfp-outlook-survey

Denhardt, R. B., & Catlaw, T. J. (2015). *Theories of public organization* (7th ed.). Cengage.

Fredrickson, B. L. (2002). Positive emotions. In C. R. Snyder & S. J. Lopez (Eds.), *Handbook of positive psychology* (pp. 120–134). Oxford University Press.

Giving USA. (2021). *$471.44 billion* [Infographic]. https://store.givingusa.org/products/2021-infographic?variant=39324695068751

Hoefer, R. (2009). Preparing managers for the human services. In R. J. Patti (Ed.), *The handbook of human services management* (pp. 483–501). Sage.

Hoskote, R. T. (2009). *The dynamics of joy in work* (Publication No. 3401322) [Doctoral dissertation, Benedictine University]. ProQuest Dissertations and Theses Global.

Johnson, L. C., & Yanca, S. J. (2010). *Social work practice: A generalist approach* (10th ed.). Allyn & Bacon.

Johnson, M. (2020). Joy: A review of the literature and suggestions for future directions. *The Journal of Positive Psychology, 15*(1), 5–24. https://doi.org/10.1080/17439760.2019.1685581

Kahneman, D., & Riis, J. (2005). Living, and thinking about it: Two perspectives on life. In F. A. Huppert, N. Baylis, & B. Keverne (Eds.), *The science of well-being* (pp. 285–304). University Press.

Kanter, R. M. (1994). Collaborative advantage: The art of alliances. *Harvard Business Review, 27*, 96–109.

Kim, M., Kim, A., Newman, J., Ferris, G., & Perrewe, P. (2019). The antecedents and consequences of positive organizational behavior for promoting employee well-being in sport organizations. *Sport Management Review, 22*(1), 108–125. https://doi.org/10.1016/j.smr.2018.04.003

Lazarus, R. S. (1991). *Emotion and adaptation.* Oxford University Press.

Lee, S. W. S., Tang, H., Wan, J., Mai, X., & Liu, C. (2015). A cultural look at moral purity: Wiping the face clean. *Frontiers in Psychology, 6*, 577.

Manion, J. (2003). Joy at work!: Creating a positive workplace. *The Journal of Nursing Administration, 33*(12), 652–659. https://doi.org/10.1097/00005110-200312000-00008

Meadows, C. M. (2014). *A psychological perspective on joy and emotional fulfillment.* Routledge.

Neave, H. R. (1990). Deming '88. Part 1: Win-win, joy in work, and innovation. *Total Quality Management, 1*(1), 33–48. https://doi.org/10.1080/09544129000000004

Perlman, H. H. (1979). *Relationship: The heart of helping people.* University of Chicago Press.

Peterson, C. (2006). *A primer in positive psychology.* Oxford University Press.

Pina e Cunha, M., Rego, A., Volkmann Simpson, A., & Clegg, S. (2020). *Positive organizational behavior: A reflective approach.* Routledge.

Saleebey, D. (2008). *Human behavior and social environments: A biopsychosocial approach.* Columbia University Press.

Schutz, W. C. (1967). *Joy: Expanding human awareness.* Grove Press.

Skinner, P. (2018). *Collaborative advantage: How collaboration beats competition as a strategy for success.* Robinson.

Watson, L. D., & Hoefer, R. A. (2016). The joy of social work administration: An exploratory qualitative study of human service administrators' positive perceptions of their work. *Journal of Social Work Education, 52*(2), 178–185.

Youssef, C., & Luthans, F. (2007). Positive organizational behavior in the workplace: The impact of hope, optimism, and resilience. *Management Department Faculty Publications, 36*, 774–800.

Figure Credits

Index

Printed in the USA
CPSIA information can be obtained
at www.ICGtesting.com
LVHW072325201223
767039LV00003B/13